The UNIX™ Shell
Programming Language

The UNIX™ Shell
Programming   Language

Rod Manis
Marc H. Meyer

Howard W. Sams & Co.
A Division of Macmillan, Inc.
4300 West 62nd Street, Indianapolis, IN 46268 USA

International Standard Book Number: 0672-22497-6
Library of Congress Catalog Card Number: 86-60029

Edited by: *Welborn Associates, Inc.*
Designed by: *T. R. Emrick*
Cover art by: *Gregg Butler*

Printed in the United States of America

Contents

PART IV   UNIX SHELLS

Foreword

To many people hearing about it for the first time, the UNIX operating system sounds like a good idea, but one that might be too complex for them to use. After all, most operating systems found on personal computers have less than a dozen built-in commands, and people find it reasonably simple to use these computers. UNIX has literally hundreds of commands, so it's easy to assume that it must be somehow harder to use UNIX.

Nothing could be further from the truth. In fact, when taught correctly, people tend to learn and understand faster on UNIX than on "simpler" operating systems such as CP/M and PC-DOS.

Why? Because UNIX programs tend to work together, and they work in the same way. Even application programs written for UNIX take advantage of this cooperation, so once you've learned a few simple conventions on UNIX, you can enjoy greater productivity with any program. Many end-user application programs available for personal computer operating systems are "self-contained," and aren't set up to work with other programs. On these systems, you could very well find yourself working for weeks typing data into a program and then having to re-enter some or all of it to use in another program. That's not what using computers should be all about.

UNIX works in a natural way, especially when passing data from one program to another. The best part is that programs don't have to be written in tricky ways to take advantage of these features. This, in turn, means that the programs this book teaches you to write will work just like standard UNIX commands—and work with them too. *The UNIX Shell Programming Language* is all about using the *shell,* which is the standard user interface on every UNIX system. No additional, sometimes expensive, computer languages are required. You will be typing your programs right at your terminal, watching them run, and gaining confidence with every program. I can only hint about how exciting and useful this is; this book will show it to you and get you excited too.

That brings us to this book and the people behind it. Rod Manis and Marc Meyer live their philosophy, not just write it. Rod, who has been using UNIX for a long, *long* time, believes strongly in making the power of UNIX available to as many people as possible. He authored the */rdb* database system, which takes the concepts presented here to their logical conclusion: a fast, easy way of working with almost any type of data and completely compatible with UNIX commands.

Together, Rod and Marc bring the true flavor of UNIX to this book. You'll use common sense—not computerese—in learning how UNIX programs work with each other, and how to create your own UNIX programs without studying to be a programmer. In fact, the shell programs you learn to write are treated so naturally that they seem more like *fun,* rather than the stodgy discipline people usually think of when the word "programming" comes to mind. Before you realize it, you will be caught up in the excitement, and you'll know how to make your UNIX system do just what you want it to do. Then you will understand why UNIX has spread from research labs and universities to machines as diverse as personal computers and mainframes—not as the result of some marketing campaign, but because of a groundswell of people finding their work was simply, almost magically, a great deal easier using UNIX and their very own shell program.

DAVID FIEDLER

David Fiedler is the Editor of UNIQUE, *the premier newsletter for serious users of the UNIX system. Mr. Fiedler acts as a high-level UNIX marketing and technical consultant for the top companies in the field, and is often quoted in major magazine articles. He is also the President of InfoPro Systems (Denville, NJ), which publishes* UNIQUE *and* The C Journal, *a magazine for C programmers.*

Preface

The shell is the command interpreter for the UNIX operating system. It is also a powerful programming language for quickly building software applications. This book teaches UNIX shell or shell programming through examples. While the standard UNIX documentation is excellent for looking up details, it is as difficult to learn from, as trying to learn French from a dictionary.

The authors had to figure out shell programming the hard way. We tried things on the computer and worked with others who could answer some of our questions. It was a slow process. So many times we would read a terse, cryptic statement in the UNIX Manual and wish we could just see one example of what that statement meant. Therefore, we have written a book full of examples. It is going to save you a lot of time.

In the first part of this book we cover all of the features of the language with examples of each. The first few chapters discuss the power of UNIX, integrated software, and fast prototyping. Then, starting with basics, each of the features of the UNIX shell is described. There are chapters that survey several ways to do input/output, string processing, etc.

In the second and third parts, we show a number of very useful shell programs to do menus, report writing, relational database commands, mailing labels, form letters, cash flow, file update locking, screen handling, system utilities, language translation, etc. These examples are in UNIX manual format style, which tells what each program does, shows examples of its use, shows the shell source code, and discusses the code.

Finally, in Part 4, we discuss the UNIX System V, Release 2 shell, the Korn shell, and the C shell. There is also a formal grammar of the shell language and a table of which UNIX programs are in which UNIX systems.

A NOTE ON OUR READERS

We welcome everyone to the power of UNIX, so this book is written for readers from a variety of backgrounds.

If you have no computer experience at all, we have a chapter on getting started that aims to bring you up from zero. There is a common misunderstanding that UNIX is hard to learn and to use. In fact, UNIX is not only easy to learn and use, it is like a fascinating story that keeps unfolding. Learning the basics can be fast, simple, and fun. The trouble is, if you start learning computers with UNIX, you might never really appreciate UNIX. You will not understand the pain and suffering people endure on other systems.

Users with other computer experience come in two flavors. One group is happy to be on UNIX and sees each new powerful feature as a relief from the drudgery of the systems that they were accustomed to. This is how the authors felt about UNIX when we started many years ago.

Another group believes that their other system has it all and that UNIX is (pick one) not as good, not worth the bother to learn, missing cherished features, just a fad, or simply nothing new. This group has the hardest job of all, because they must keep an open mind for the time it takes to learn why UNIX is so powerful. The power of UNIX comes from the accumulation of hundreds of features that can be flexibly combined to make it easy to accomplish what you want.

The *aha!* will probably not come for several chapters. These people will have to radically change the way they look at programming. We have been through this experience with some like them in our consulting and our classes, and we hope that we can take others through it in this book. They should remember we are not their enemies. We are simply trying to share with them a tool that we think will make their lives much easier.

Experienced UNIX users want all the tricks and techniques and understanding they can get and know that too little has as yet been written. Here we will not just cover the basics but will get into the heaviest stuff we know.

HOW TO USE THIS BOOK

Most of the examples in this book should be tried out on a terminal connected to a computer running UNIX. We find that there are three ways to learn computers:

- *Read First*—Some people like to read a lot, then try things out on a computer. There are plenty of examples here that look like what you would see on the terminal.

- *Read, Then Try Out*—Others like to jump right on the terminal and try things as they go along. These people can work each example as they read, and they can spin off other possibilities from each example.

- *Read Last*—Some like to work on the computer and read only when they have questions. This last group will find this book divided into many small chapters with a detailed table of contents. They can quickly find the part that discusses what interests them.

We appreciate correspondence from our readers. Your comments and suggestions are welcome. You may contact us at either of the following addresses:

Multinational Software, Inc.
40 Bigelow St., Suite 1
Cambridge, MA 02139
617-497-9422

Robinson Schaffer Wright
711 California Street
Santa Cruz, CA 95060
408-429-6229

ROD MANIS
MARC H. MEYER

To Michele Manis,
Mary Anna Montgomery,
Durk Pearson,
Sandy Shaw, and
Shawn Steel

—ROD MANIS

To my parents, Irv and Charlotte Meyer,
to my joy, Karen, and
to my fun, the UNIX community.

—MARC H. MEYER

PART

I

THE POWER OF UNIX

- Introduction
- The Power of UNIX
- Integrated Software and Fast Prototyping
- Getting Started
- UNIX Documentation
- The **vi** Editor

Button often seen at UNIX conventions.

1

Introduction

A speaker at a UNIX conference once observed: *UNIX people say that UNIX is the greatest thing in the world. But if you asked them in private, they would admit that UNIX is much more important than that.*

Why the devotion? Because of the power of UNIX—the ability to do so much with so little effort. It is the UNIX shell that gives you the access to that power. It is the language with which you express your desires to the omnipotent and obedient UNIX operating system. This UNIX not only guards the harem but does countless other tasks for you.

According to *Fortune*[1] magazine, "Astrophysicist Arno Penzias, Nobel Prize winner, and AT&T's Vice President for Research, ranks UNIX second in importance to the transistor among Bell Labs inventions."

Another brilliant scientist, Durk Pearson,[2] says that working with UNIX is like Christmas every day. He is constantly finding new features and powers to help him with his advanced scientific work. By using UNIX programs and the UNIX shell programming language, he has done much of his work without having to write C, or other language programs.

An estimated 80 computer companies in the US produce about 150 computers that run UNIX. The six major European computer manufacturers, and in Japan, the powerful government Ministry of Trade and Industry have adopted UNIX:[3] "MITI also hopes to get approval of a five-year software development project that would soak up $122 million of government and industry money. One of the project's apparent goals is to break Big Blue's stranglehold by getting Japanese computer companies to standardize on Unix."

The authors have witnessed the "Christmas every day" phenomenon time and time again as we introduced groups of people to UNIX, its

---

1. Gene Bylinsky, "The Holes in AT&T's Computer Strategy," *Fortune,* 17 September 1984, p. 50.

2. While at MIT, Durk Pearson got the highest score on the Graduate Record Exam the year he took it. He wrote the safety manual for the Space Shuttle and, with biochemist Sandy Shaw, the best selling book *Life Extension: a Scientific Approach.*

3. Bro Uttal, "Japan's Persistent Software Gap," *Fortune,* 15 October 1984, p 112.

diverse utility set, and the UNIX shell language. It has been a delight to see personal computer users, who have known only DOS, realize that with UNIX they can quickly build their own personal applications, share mail with other users, and send information to other computers.

A similar enthusiasm is shown by groups of COBOL and FORTRAN programmers, who learn how easy it is to build complex applications, and also, to modify them later on. Experienced UNIX users, while using the UNIX shell to execute single commands, have most often built their programs in the compiled C language and have never used the UNIX shell to quickly prototype their work and deliver solutions. Our teaching experience with this group is one of rediscovery.

We are convinced that UNIX is a watershed development in computer software and is central to the future of computing. There is hardly a field of human effort that is not leaping ahead with the use of computer power. As UNIX spreads, computer power will be much more accessible to many more people.

WHAT IS UNIX?

UNIX is both an operating system and hundreds of programs. An operating system is a program that controls the computer. It lives in the memory of the computer and fetches programs from the disk to do the real computer work. It is the coordinator and chief executive of the system. It decides which programs to run and when. It takes its orders from the user and handles myriad details so that the user doesn't have to worry about them.

WHAT IS THE SHELL?

UNIX uses a program named **sh,** which we call the *shell,* to talk to users. That's us. We humans can get the computer to do what we want by giving commands to the shell. The shell, in turn, calls upon the operating system to actually perform the functions required. It is called the shell, because, like the shell of a nut or an egg, it is the part that we see from the outside. The inside part is called the *kernel.* The shell talks to us and to the kernel.

WHAT IS SHELL PROGRAMMING?

We give our commands to UNIX by typing command lines on our terminals. But we can also write our command lines into files and cause them to be executed simply by typing the names of the files. These files, then, are programs, and the process of developing them is *shell programming.* This is what this book will teach you how to do.

UNIX Power

There are many reasons why UNIX is becoming the standard operating system. But there is one main reason why we love it so much POWER!

UNIX is far more powerful than any other operating system and its software. By power we mean the ratio between how much effort a human has to do and how much the computer does. You can do a great deal on UNIX with a few keystrokes or a few lines. You can do in minutes and hours what takes weeks and months to do on other systems.

Some people think of computer power as what the computer can do. But most computers, from the tiny and cheap to the big and expensive, can do the same things with enough human programming effort. More money generally buys you more speed. Power to us is doing a lot with just a little human effort. We are lazy, and we want a lot. UNIX spoils and indulges us.

It is hard to explain in a few words what makes UNIX so powerful. We have to show you what it can do, and how easy it is to get UNIX to do it. At some point while you are reading this book, the understanding will hit you—you'll reach the point where you say, "Aha, I've got it!"

The next few chapters discuss UNIX power, and the rest of the book fills in the details. But before we get down to cases, here is a partial list of the reasons most people give for liking UNIX.

Portability—Portability means that UNIX can be made to run on any computer easily. UNIX now runs on most of the hundreds of computers in the world today. It also means software portability in that you can develop a program on one computer and move it to another as long as they both have UNIX. This is great if you write software to sell, because you don't have to worry about whether a potential customer has the same machine as you do.

It is also great if you have several computers or want the freedom to get the newer faster computers. You can develop software and run it on all of your computers if they are running UNIX. If a new computer comes along that you want, you can get it and move your software onto it. It keeps you from being locked into any one manufacturer. This is why old established computer manufacturers with big client bases, especially IBM, resist UNIX.

Price—UNIX is inexpensive if you consider all the capability you get with it. In the 1970s it cost $20,000 unsupported and $40,000 supported. Now you can get it for about a thousand dollars, depending upon your computer and the number of users.

Software—UNIX includes several hundred programs. Some studies estimate that the software that comes with UNIX would cost $100,000 if you tried to buy it separately. And you probably couldn't find a lot of it. In addition, an evergrowing library of applications software exists for UNIX. This software is, in general, of higher quality and more powerful than software that runs on other systems. In the long run almost all software will run on UNIX, because UNIX will have the largest hardware base and because it is a better environment for developing software.

THE SHELL IS A PROGRAM

Most operating systems have the shell, or command line interpreters, built into them. This makes them very inflexible. The UNIX shell is much like any other program on UNIX. In fact, sharp programmers can, and have, written their own versions of the shell to give it different functional capabilities. The UNIX shell is being improved all of the time. The UNIX *System V, Release 2 shell* is several times faster than the older shell and has new features.

The current UNIX shell, which we will call the *Bell shell,* was first written by Steven R. Bourne at Bell Labs in the mid 1970s. It is often called the *Bourne shell.* Bill Joy wrote the **csh,** pronounced *sea* shell and also written as C shell, at Berkeley in the late 1970s. His shell is a big improvement in many ways, but also has some disadvantages.

BELL SHELL OR C SHELL

We have enormous respect for both Bill, the C shell, and his other work, but have decided to concentrate on the Bell shell in this book for the following reasons:

1. The Bell shell is on all UNIX computers, while the C shell is on many, but not all.

2. Even on UNIX computers that have the C shell, there is always the Bell shell.

3. The Bell shell has always been faster than the C shell, and now is much faster.

4. The C shell takes more memory.

5. The Bell shell is constantly being improved with the vast resources of AT&T Bell Laboratories. The C shell depends upon a hardy little group of sharp people at Berkeley, but with fewer resources.

6. There are so many annoying little differences between the two shells that switching between them is difficult and error prone. It is much better to get good at using one of them.

7. The next Bell shell, the *Korn shell,* named after David Korn at AT&T Bell Labs, Murray Hill, New Jersey, has all of the important features of the C shell, plus many more lip-smacking goodies. The Korn shell is completely compatible with the current and past Bell shells, so that all of our programs will continue to run on it.

So the future is clearly in the direction of the ever more-powerful Bell shells.

2

The Power of UNIX

One source of confusion about UNIX is referring to it as an operating system. That makes people equate it with the other operating systems they are familiar with. The operating system part of UNIX is its least interesting part and, in fact, probably its weakest feature.

To think of UNIX as an operating system is like thinking of a Porsche as a gas cap and forgetting that there is a precision automobile screwed onto it. Most comparisons of UNIX to the other operating systems in the literature are like comparing auto gas caps. Imagine how silly such a discussion would sound. Many people are trying to decide whether to go with UNIX on its operating system features.

UNIX is much more. It is a collection of several hundred programs. With their options, at least a thousand "functions" can be performed. One study compared the software that comes with UNIX to that in the Digital Equipment Corp. software catalog and the Perkin Elmer catalog. The researchers found that they could buy only about 30 percent of the software that is in UNIX in the other catalogs, and that software alone would cost about $30,000! So one could say that there is about $100,000 worth of software included with UNIX.[1]

OTHER APPROACHES

If UNIX programs were like programs on most systems, a person would have to run them one at a time. They would each have different user interfaces and different data formats. Each would have its own documentation, features, and environment. The user would have to relearn all of this and live in a different world in each program. If the user were doing word pro-

---

1. Gene Amdahl has been saying for years that there is $200 billion worth of software written for the IBM computer. Of course he means development costs. The real value is probably substantially less. It will usually cost 10 times as much *per month* to lease this software than to buy software of similar function for microcomputers.

cessing, and needed to do a database function or a spreadsheet calculation, he or she would have to get out of the word processor and get into a database program or a spreadsheet program. But it gets worse. The user left all of his or her data behind. Usually there is no way to transmit the data to the new program. It must be re-entered!

The hottest idea in the microcomputer market today is the idea of integration. There are a few products out there that "integrate" word processing, database, and spreadsheet, such as Lotus 1-2-3®. The literature is full of articles about them, the software dealers and public are snapping them up, Wall Street and venture capitalists are throwing money at their producers. What is not so well publicized is that UNIX has hundreds of integrated programs, not just three or four!

MANY DATA FORMATS

As awkward as most microcomputer programs are, they are a big improvement over the old batch programs of mainframe computing. In that world, many programs each have their own data structures hard-coded. In COBOL you define, in the DATA DEFINITION section, your data as fixed-length records and fixed-length fields. This was a hangover from the old punch card formats.[2] Enormous effort goes into modifying these programs. It was recognized two decades ago that having fixed data structures around with dedicated programs was very expensive. One of the big reasons for database management systems was to have one data structure and access routines that the programs could use to get at them. This was a big help, but now a lot of time is spent restructuring the databases to meet changes in the environment of the organization.

UNIX FLAT ASCII FILES

UNIX has a very simple solution to all of this. It uses *flat* ASCII files. They are flat in the sense that there is no structure such as fixed-length records and fixed-length fields. They are ASCII in the sense that they are not binary numbers that only a program knowing the structure can interpret. Rather they can all be sent to a video terminal and will display on the screen as text. There is a small extra computation required to convert string numbers to binary numbers for calculations, but this is found to be insignificant. What takes, by far, the most time in accessing data is disk reads and writes. A few extra CPU cycles are seldom noticed. Having UNIX tools to look at the data is a big advantage. Being able to send the file to any UNIX program is great.

If a record/field structure is needed in a data file, the **newline** character is

---

2. Brian Boyle calls this the ghost of Herman Hollerith, the inventor of the punch card code.

used to delimit lines (records). A **tab** or other character can be used to delimit columns (fields). Many UNIX programs such as **sort, awk, cut,** and **paste,** use this convention. One of the big advantages is that it makes all the files of variable length. Therefore, they take about one-third of the file space that would normally be taken by fixed length record files. This not only saves disk space, but reduces the amount of data that must be transferred to and from the disk and processed by the programs. It is often thought that fixed-length records are necessary for fast access. But this is not true. You can use all of the fast-access methods (**hash, index, binary, b-tree,** are the standard test access methods in the database world) on variable-length files just as easily. Another advantage is that data in a variable-length field can be increased without any change of the program. The new 9-digit zip codes are no problem for UNIX flat files, but a crisis for the COBOL world!

UNIX COMMANDS, PIPES, AND FILTERS

UNIX programs can do their I/O with terminals, other files, and even other programs. With pipes, the output of any program can be the input of another. This allows data to flow through the programs, being transformed in some way by each one. The flat ASCII files are seen as a stream of characters.

In UNIX you can input data from a file into a program by simply typing:

```
$ command < file
```

You can send the output of the command to another command with a pipe symbol (|).

```
$ command1 < file.in | command2 > file.out
```

In this way, you can build up new programs simply by transforming or filtering data through several commands and save the result in a new title. This makes possible an entirely new software design philosophy. Instead of the traditional structure chart or tree approach, in which the main program is the root and each called subroutine a branch or leaf, UNIX makes possible a pipeline or filter linear structure. The data enters the program on the left, which transforms it in some way, and pipes it on to the next program, which transforms it in another way. Most of the programs to do these transformations already exist in UNIX.

```
$ firstfilter < inputdata | nextfilter | anotherfilter > realgoodstuff
```

A study, at Bell Labs, showed that when using UNIX, 80 percent of the functions in the programs studied were handled using existing UNIX commands and shell scripts. Only 20 percent had to be coded. This means that,

9

when using UNIX, you only have to do one-fifth of the programming work that you would do in a normal write-it-all project.

This makes possible a radically different and enormously more powerful way of programming. We can process the data in one way with one command and pass it on to another command to do another kind of processing. By linking or piping together programs in this way we can solve most of our computer problems. When we need a function that none of the UNIX commands provide, we can program it in C or some other language, and fit it into the pipe.

ASTRONOMICAL POSSIBILITIES

When we pipe together UNIX commands and others that we write, we have new programs. There are several hundred UNIX commands, from 250 to 500 depending on which UNIX you have. With their options, there are over 1000 different functions. If you pipe two UNIX commands together to form a new program, you have 1000 times 1000 possibilities, or 1 million possible programs that you can create. Three commands, linked with two pipes, give you a billion possible programs. Four commands make a trillion programs, and so on, all on one or a few lines. This is the astronomical power of UNIX!

Of course some of these programs make no sense when combined together. But many do, so you start thinking what processing steps are needed to do your computer work, instead of writing a whole program from scratch.

SUPERHIGH-LEVEL PROGRAMMING

We can see this power in another comparison with traditional programming (Table 1). Assembler language programs have one line of code for each machine instruction. High-level languages like Fortran, COBOL, Pascal, C, and Basic produce about 10 machine instructions per line of code. But shell programs invoke one or more programs per line of code. Since a program invokes thousands, or tens of thousands, of machine instructions, shell programming is about a thousand times more powerful than what we call high-level programming.

Table 1. Levels of Programming

Line of Code	Machine Instructions	Language
1	1	Assembler
1	10	High-Level Languages
1	10,000	UNIX Shell Programs

NONPROCEDURAL PROGRAMMING

Almost all programming is procedural, in that the programmer must write down the exact procedure or steps for the computer to follow. Nonprocedural programming means simply telling the computer the result desired, without having to specify the steps. It means telling the computer to sort a file, without having to tell it how to sort a file. This is largely realized with UNIX shell programming.

There is an analogy with chemical systems in which a chemical is filtered with one filter, then piped to another filter for further processing, then piped to a third filter, and so on. In other systems we have to write all of the programs or use limited purpose programs that do not transmit their data easily to other programs. On UNIX we just think of the basic transformations we need to get our data from the way it is to the way we want it to be. By piping together commands we can often do what we want quickly and easily.

Modern computers are put together from chips and other devices, each of which does a part of the whole job. This is the way we want to do software. Hardware would be in as big a mess as software is today, if hardware developers started from scratch and tried to build every part of an electronic device. Hardware designers have large books on their desks in which are listed the specifications of thousands of chips. They think about the processes they need, look up the chips, and design them together.

The UNIX manual is like their chip books. It has hundreds of programs that perform different functions on data. UNIX shell programmers can think about what they need, look up what they want to know, and put together the programs that will do the job.

Of course you can always write whole programs from scratch, using compiled languages, in the traditional way if you wish. UNIX is noted as an excellent programming environment. In the early days of UNIX at AT&T Bell Labs, programmers often chose to do their programming work on UNIX and transmitted their programs to mainframes for execution in a batch environment.

It is common to mix your own programs with existing UNIX programs. The rule is, use what you can, write only what you have to.

SAME RESISTANCE

Back in the 1960s, the computer profession went through a similar revolution. We went from programming mostly in assembler to programming in the compiled languages. The resistance to that change is the same as the resistance to shell programming today. Many programmers had become fairly good at practicing the old art. They thought in the old ways. Programmers are as resistant to change as any other profession, even though you may think they are modern and progressive. Their arguments against the compiled languages then were the same as the arguments you hear today against shell programming with UNIX.

SPEED

The main argument is that the higher-level interpreted-language programs, such as the shell, are slower. Many programmers spent their careers squeezing a little more speed out of very expensive, very slow computers. Large computer staffs tried to get their mainframe computers to do the work of large corporations, institutions, and governmental organizations. Those computers cost millions of dollars, yet only had the power of today's microcomputers. Today, it is much cheaper to buy computers than programmers' time. We must change our thinking—speed is important because the user is waiting.

The answer to this argument is that almost all speed improvements in programs are in the innermost loop, usually only in a few lines of code. These few lines can be recoded in the lower-level language for speed. Then you get the best of both worlds: the programs can be developed and tested fast in the high-level language, and they can readily be speeded up. This is true of shell programming with respect to compiled language programming, as it is true of compiled language programming with respect to assembler programming.

MEMORY

The other major concern was memory usage. Memory was very expensive, and squeezing programs into small memories was the second biggest job programmers had. Today memory is cheap and plentiful, but UNIX shell programming still has a big advantage over traditional programming. Other large programs must all sit in memory, even when most of the code is not used. Shell programs, however, call many small programs which swap in and out of memory as needed. The total memory needed is much smaller. And this all comes with no extra effort on the part of the programmer.

3

Integrated Software and Fast Prototyping

The importance of integrated software is starting to be understood. Many software packages for small computers keep data in their own special format. Furthermore, each package requires that its users learn a whole new system of commands and procedures. These packages make computerizing a whole business very difficult. Data entered into the order entry system cannot be easily used in the accounting system. Information entered in word processing is difficult to extract for a spreadsheet. Data collected from an instrument is difficult to graph.

As users become familiar with their new computers and software, they are running into this problem. A few software companies have started to integrate a few functions. Lotus 1-2-3 has integrated word processing, spreadsheet and graphics. Other companies are working on integration, but UNIX already has several hundred integrated programs which solve the problem in an elegant way.

INTEGRATED SOFTWARE

Integrated software has two features: each program uses the same data format for both input and output, and each program uses the same conventions for interfacing with its user. Historically, integration was very difficult. Most programs (60–80 percent) were written in COBOL for mainframe computers. COBOL requires that the structure of data be defined early in the program (in the DATA DEFINITION section). It saw the world of data as fixed-length records and fields. So the programmer had to decide exactly how many characters to allocate to each field and what type of data was to be found in that field. Then the data had to be carefully prepared and maintained to fit those exact specifications. If you wished to change that data structure, say to add more characters for the new 9-digit zip code, you would have to get a programmer to modify and recompile the source code. You would also need programs to convert the old data into the new format.

Data Base Management Systems (DBMS) helped some. They kept all of a company's data, or at least a lot of it, in one structure and maintained a data dictionary or schema that told programmers what that structure was. Programs would ask the DBMS for data and give data to the DBMS to store. But this still required a lot of programming and was not much help to the end user.

With microcomputers and supermicrocomputers have come many software packages. Unfortunately, running on primitive operating systems like CP/M and MS and PC-DOS, these microsoftware programs had to create a whole environment for the user. A floppy disk is inserted and the program takes over the computer for each function, i.e., word processing or spreadsheet. Some nice interfaces have been developed and some new ideas have come forth, but these systems are inadequate for complex computing.

Users need to be able to run many different programs without having to spend weeks learning how to run each one. Users also need multiuser (several users at one time) and multitasking (each user running one or more programs) software. Data must flow from program to program. The geniuses at AT&T Bell Labs understood all of this in the 1960s. They built a well thought out system of integrated software.

UNIX SOFTWARE

It is the amount of excellent integrated software that makes UNIX powerful. The operating system that comes with UNIX is nice, but not as important as the software. In fact some of the UNIX software has been ported to other operating systems and is made available by such groups as the *Software Tools User Group*. To get anywhere close to UNIX, other operating systems would have to offer about 400 programs in addition to basic operating system functions. At $100 per program, that would be $40,000 worth of software. Even so those other systems would lose to UNIX, because all of that software is not integrated. Can you imagine reading 400 manuals? UNIX has such an easy standard user interface that its manual has about one page per program.

USING FLAT ASCII FILES

Further, UNIX programs can both read and write the same data files. They can also pass data to each other. The data files are very simple. As we said earlier, they are called *flat ASCII* files, that is, they have no structure like fixed-length records or fields. Instead they use the carriage return or line feed ASCII character to mark the end of a line or record and any character can be used to separate fields, such as tab, colon, or comma. Therefore, all UNIX programs can find the structure of the data embedded in the data. The programs do not have to be hard-wired with the lengths of records and fields. They also do not have to be modified for different data and recompiled.

Incidentally, variable-length records and fields significantly compress the files because there is not a lot of wasted blank space. Our tests indicate that a variable-length UNIX file is, on average, one-third the size of a fixed-length file. It not only uses a third less disk space, but disk-bound programs will run three times faster because they only have to read a third as much data off of the disk.

As was mentioned briefly before, every UNIX command can use the same data. Whether data comes from a terminal, a disk file, a tape drive, an instrument, or another program, the data is simply a stream of characters to UNIX programs. Each program can pass its output data to another program. Commonly, in UNIX, one program modifies data in one way and passes it on to the next program which makes another modification and passes it on. Instead of having to have a program for everything, UNIX has hundreds of basic programs which perform most of the operations that one needs to do to data. By *piping* these programs together, data is transformed. A single pipe character (|) typed at the terminal will take the output of one program and pass it on to another.

OPEN VERSUS CLOSED INTEGRATION

Integration must be open. Open integration means that any program can be added or inserted into the system. You cannot add another program to most of the so-called integrated software packages or replace their spreadsheet with a better spreadsheet package. On UNIX you can use any editor, spreadsheet, sort program, or whatever that you want.

Unfortunately, many software packages that currently run on top of UNIX have not been integrated with UNIX in either data or user compatibility, or both. Many packages and programmers have come over from other systems. The availability of UNIX to software developers is rather recent. The power of UNIX dawns slowly to both new programmers and programmers who have learned other systems.

Fortunately some software developers have recognized the importance of open integration. MultiNational Software's /rdb™ relational database management system, Schmidt Associates' menu shell™, Robinson Schaffer Wright's ve™ form editor, Urban Software's Leverage™ form and list manager, and others are excellent examples. All use flat ASCII files and have friendly user interfaces. Each has its own strengths and weaknesses, but they share an open integration philosophy.

FAST PROTOTYPING

We have, with UNIX, a set of facilities that allows us to quickly and easily put together software applications. Not by the automation of programming, but by being able to avoid a lot of programming. Each line of a shell program invokes one or more whole programs. Now we can think about how our data is, how we want it to be, and assemble UNIX commands to transform it step by step. We do not need giant single-purpose programs. We can put together what we need from the parts we have.

Tools for Prototyping

With these UNIX tools we can now put together a model or prototype of a new application in a few days or weeks. We can show it to the user early. They can see the menus, screens, reports, etc., of the system. They can point out what they like and don't like. We can modify the system quickly and show it to them again. This process can be repeated until the user is happy with the system.

After prototyping, there is still much work to do. All of the real data of the system must be loaded in, because the prototype just uses a few sample records. The user manuals and other documentation of the system must be written. And the user personnel must be trained to operate, modify and fix the system. Some functions may need to be sped up with C programs.

This fast prototyping approach replaces or complements the current structured design and analysis methodology. Fast prototyping can be the requirements and, perhaps, the early design phase. In other cases, fast prototyping can replace the whole formal specification and development process.

HARDWARE ANALOGY

It is useful to compare software tools with hardware. Hardware electronics is done spectacularly well, while software is in trouble. Hardware has seen enormous increases in productivity and decreases in price, while software is unreliable and getting more expensive. Hardware has mastered its tools and technology and levels of integration, while software is still mostly custom made, individually crafted, labor intensive, unautomated. Software projects often reinvent and rebuild **all** of the software components. To extend the analogy, Table 2 relates the levels of hardware and software.

Table 2. Hardware and Software Levels of Integration

Level	Hardware	Software
Tools	scopes, testbeds. . .	editors, debuggers. . .
Parts	transistors, wire. . .	lines of source code
Chips	memory, usart. . .	UNIX commands. . .
Board	CPU, I/O, memory. . .	ADT, state tables. . .
Box	computer, modem, disk. . .	database systems. . .
System	computer, hifi, switch. . .	application packages

No hardware designer would waste time and money starting from discrete parts or even building all of the chips used in a product. Hardware designers look up chips, that perform needed functions, in large data books. They put these chips together on a breadboard and quickly have a prototype. They buy printed-circuit boards that are cheaper and better than those which they could design in their available time.

It would be outrageous for a hardware designer to propose that all the hardware chips should be designed, developed, tested, and manufactured on the project for the project. It would involve getting a lot of equipment and people, which means a lot of money. They would probably fail to get all of the chips working. The ratio of development costs, to units produced, would be terrible. Yet this is standard procedure in software development.

Programmers write the *whole program*. If sorting is needed, they write another sort routine. If database facilities are needed, they develop a new one from scratch. If a menu system is needed they reinvent one. The problem with "reinventing the wheel" is that it usually comes out flat on one side.

The user has to learn a new system, because the interface has been reinvented. The data interface is also reinvented so that data cannot be easily shared with other programs.

THE UNIX APPROACH

UNIX offers us a great escape from this situation. UNIX commands, system calls and library functions can be put together to perform many of the functions of a new program. What is missing can be handled in several ways.

1. More commands and library functions can be developed that are general purpose and "man" documented. They can be exported to other parts of your company or institution, and sold outside.
2. Table-driven code can be developed that can be modified simply by editing tables (with or without recompilation).
3. As a last resort, on pain of death, and as an admission of failure, programs can be written, line by line, from scratch. But only to fill in gaps that were not covered above.

It is critical that the designers and programmers on a project understand the *UNIX idea*. The idea is the realization of how powerful UNIX is and that we can design and implement software in a new way. UNIX changes the way we develop programs, from writing everything from scratch in one large program, to piping together *filters* and writing only a few new ones. The realization of how powerful a tool UNIX is does not come immediately.

INTEGRATABLE VERSUS INTEGRATED SOFTWARE: MORE UNIX POWER

So, our argument is that there is a fundamental difference between "Integrated" software and Integratable software. The dominant phenomenon in computer software for the office environment today is "Integrated Software," the primary example being Lotus 1-2-3. This is true even for computer users that show an active interest in UNIX. In a seminar on, "Integrated Software for the Officeplace" at a recent UNIX Expo in New York City over half of the several hundred seminar attendees indicated that instead of using UNIX applications for their office work, they opted for DOS and Lotus. UNIX had won their hearts, but not their minds.

However, integrated software packages, which often offer advanced spreadsheet capabilities, moderate text editing, and limited database management, present a "closed" environment to the user. In other words, the user must live within the confines of the functionality provided by the package. The design of integrated software is "monolithic." It tends to be a single large program that requires substantial amounts of memory. Many integrated packages ignore the benefits of using fast winchester disks to store information while the program is running. With Lotus for example, if users want to build large spreadsheets, even with a winchester, on their personal computer they have to go to a computer store to buy more memory so that the spreadsheet can "fit" into memory. Further, the user cannot combine the integrated package with other programs that may be on the computer. Rather, integrated software enforces the rule that it must be used separately.

Integrated software makes life terribly difficult for systems integrators who need to build office systems. Users' recognition of what can be done with computers has grown exponentially in the past few years, and requests for office systems have become highly and deservedly complex. Since it is difficult and time-consuming to combine Lotus, for example, with dBASE II, the integrator trying to put an office system together must search the marketplace for the single package that meets the most requirements, then explain why other requirements cannot be satisfied. The problem with this approach is that no single software vendor can satisfy all the requirements of today's office place. There is no monolithic, single package that can offer the advanced text editing, the database, spreadsheet, graphics, and communications that users want, need, and should get, with all the hundreds of software companies making products today.

UNIX provides an approach to using computers in the office that is the antithesis of the "closed environment." It teaches us that the most important features of applications software are small, modular programs that can be combined with each other in many different ways. It also teaches us that programs should have a common data format, simple ASCII text and that data can be read into a program from "standard input" and written to "standard output." In this way, programs can be easily combined from the shell through "pipes." UNIX also teaches us that users should be allowed access to their computing environment. If something goes wrong, users can easily look at their files and correct bad data, fix file access permissions, or clear out a line printing spooler. Further, if users want to try something new, they can explore the different commands on the computer and experiment with linking these programs to their current programs to get new results. This flexibility means that applications software can be easily customized and extended in the future. This may be the most important lesson in UNIX: a users software package and all the data that they build under it should never have to be thrown away. An "open environment" guarantees longevity and the protection of the users "software assets."

As opposed to integrated software, UNIX espouses "integratable" software. Software developers of different companies can write applications that can be easily combined by adhering to the underlying principles of UNIX. In consequence, the combination of different programs can offer a synergy that is orders of magnitude more powerful than anything on the market today. With UNIX, the users can run their applications on many different computers, ranging from deskstop microcomputers, to SUN or MicroVAX workstations, to VAXes, Ahmdal, and even the Cray super computers.

UNIX also teaches us that the isolation that microcomputer users in offices now face with their DOS packages is totally unnecessary. Already, UNIX users on different machines can easily send messages and reports to one another. The "distributed file systems" that are now being developed for UNIX implementations will mean that users on different computers can share data with a high degree of transparency and simplicity.

Now, we want to show you that working with UNIX is not only the best way to build applications, but also fun.

CHAPTER

4

Getting Started

If you already know how to sign on to UNIX, skip to the next chapter. If you have already worked with UNIX, you can skim, and probably skip several chapters. If you have a lot of UNIX experience, you may find the chapter on standard I/O the first one of interest. Of course, the further you go in this book, the thicker and deeper it gets. In this chapter we will step through the very basic things you will need to know, assuming you know nothing about UNIX and very little about computers.

LOGGING IN

When you turn on a terminal connected to a computer running UNIX and hit the *Return* key, you should get:

    login: __

The underscore (__) represents the cursor. Type in your account name. If you don't know your account name, ask someone who knows your computer. If you have just bought your own UNIX computer, your account name is *root*.

You may then be asked for your password:

    passwd: __

Type in your password. The letters you type will not echo back to the screen for security reasons. If you don't know the password, ask the person who set up your account.

If all is well you will get the UNIX prompt, which is usually:

    $ __

This prompt comes from the shell which is now waiting for you to type commands at it.

LOGGING OUT

To logout, type **CNTL-*d***. That means hold down the control key, **CNTL**, like a shift key, and press the letter *d* key. Then you will get the *login:* again.

TERMINAL KEYBOARD

Your terminal keyboard is like a typewriter keyboard, with a few extra keys. When you press them they send an 8-bit message, called a byte, to the computer. The character you type is encoded in this 8 bits. There is a number for every character. This coding is the *ASCII* standard, which stands for *American Standard Code for Information Interchange.*

UNIX is *full* duplex, which means every time you press a key, a byte is sent to the computer and the computer echoes the character back to your terminal screen. It seems instantaneous to you, but the characters on the screen have made a round trip to the computer and back.

Note that there are lots of special character keys like |, ', ~, etc. These are used a lot in UNIX and the shell. You might want to look around your keyboard and find them.

A control character is sent to the computer by holding down the **CNTL** key while pressing another character. We write control-d as ∧*d* or **CNTL-*d***. **CNTL-*d*** is used to log off of UNIX or to end a file. **CNTL-*s*** will stop the data from rolling past you on your screen. **CNTL-*q*** will start the data coming to your screen after you stopped it with **CNTL-*s***.

COMMANDS

On UNIX you execute a command simply by typing its name. For example **date** is a program that outputs the date and time.

```
$ date
Sat Aug 10 12:58:57 EDT 1985
```

UNIX executes the command by finding an executable file with that name, bringing it into memory from disk, and telling the computer to execute the code.

In UNIX there is no distinction between a program, a command, a utility, or a filter. These are just different names for the same thing; we will use them interchangeably in this book. Also, it does not matter to UNIX whether a program it executes was part of the original UNIX system or one that you or another user wrote. One size fits all—one simple system.

In contrast, on many other operating systems these different kinds of programs are treated differently and cannot be mixed together. Often a system command will produce the data your program needs, but you cannot catch it. It displays on the screen and that is that. Throughout shell programming, we catch UNIX command output, transform it, and pass it on to other UNIX commands and programs that we write.

OPTIONS

Many UNIX commands can be told to act in special ways. The user specifies *options,* or *flags,* on the command line. In most cases these options are single letters preceded by a minus sign.

```
$ cmd -o
```

This says run the **cmd** command and give it an option of *-o.* There is no UNIX program named **cmd.** We use it to stand for any command. Inside the command, whether a shell command or a program written in a language like C, the program can see the option on the command line and modify its own behavior. You will learn how to do this in shell programs.

The **ls** command has many options. Just by itself, it prints a list of the files and directories in our current directory. But with the *-l* (for long list) it gives a whole line of information on each command.

```
$ ls
Macros
Makefile
$ ls -l
-rw-rw-r--   1 root   super   250 Aug 10 05:37 Macros
-rw-rw-r--   1 root   super   355 Aug 10 05:23 Makefile
```

5

UNIX Documentation

It is important that you know your way around UNIX documentation. It is an excellent reference, but a poor tutorial. The people at Bell Labs who developed UNIX are brilliant programmers, engineers, mathematicians, and physicists. They like to program, not write. They seldom show examples. They seem to think that an abstract definition or mathematical equation is easy to learn from. But very few people can look at Maxwell's equations on electromagnetism and immediately deduce computers, television, and communications. Most of us need examples. This is why we wrote this book. We want to give examples of the different UNIX shell programming facilities. Once you understand something, you can go to the UNIX documentation for a terse exact definition of its syntax and use.

As a reference, the UNIX documentation is excellent. There is an enormous amount of information, and it is organized in such a way that you can quickly find exactly what you want. We urge you to get your UNIX documentation, keep it near you, and look up things you want to know. As we discuss features in this book, turn to the manual for answers to detailed questions.

The UNIX documentation comes in two parts: a manual and a tutorial, which may be broken into several different books. They each take different approaches. The manual is for reference and the tutorial is for learning. Read the tutorial first for examples and understanding of the principles, then use the manual to look up specific questions.

UNIX USER'S MANUAL

The manual, called *UNIX Systems User's Manual* in System V, is like a dictionary. It lists each of the UNIX programs, system calls, and so on, in alphabetical order.

In the front of the manual is a table of contents and a permuted index. (Sometimes the permuted index is at the end of the manual.) This index takes every word in the one-line descriptions of the commands and sorts it into keyword-in-context listing. When you are looking for a command that will do something, this is the place to start. Just think of one or more words that describe what you want and look them up. You will see many commands that might be helpful.

Sections

Commands—There are eight sections to the manual. In the first section (the largest) are the commands that you can type at your terminal and use in shell programs. It has the **sh,** shell program. See if you can find it. It will be helpful to have it nearby as you read this book. The programs are in alphabetical order.

System Calls—System calls are invoked from programs in C or other programming languages. These are all of the procedures that the UNIX kernel will respond to. The shell does its work by calling these programs. Some of the UNIX commands and many of the facilities of the shell are implemented as these system calls.

You can open, close, read and write files, fork and execute processes, get clock time, and much more. If you are going to write C, or other language programs, you will need to know the material in this and the next section. Also, if you want a deeper understanding of what the shell and the UNIX kernel are doing and how they work, get to know these functions.

Subroutine Library—These functions are also called from C, and other language programs. They allow you to do character-at-a-time (stream) input and output with files. These functions handle the standard in and standard out that is used so much in UNIX. There are functions for math, character and string handling, and much more.

File Formats—There are many files and tables in UNIX. In this section you can see the C language **struct** (record) formats for them. From a C program you can access these structures. Many details of UNIX are revealed here.

Miscellaneous Facilities—Leftovers are thrown in here. The *termcap* file codes are defined here. There is a nice ASCII table and the word processing macros for **mm, man,** etc.

Games—Some nice little games like blackjack and fortune are documented here. If you are lucky, there will be the greatest UNIX computer games of all: Adventure and Rogue.

Devices—Devices are terminals, disks, printers, and such. This section discusses the software handlers which are called *device drivers* in UNIX. Here are the details of how UNIX talks to hardware.

Administration Commands—In the older UNIX manuals, the last section contained more commands that can be typed at the terminal or used in shell programming as in section one of the manual. But these commands are for system administrators. They are more dangerous to the system and usually can only be run by the super user. The super user on UNIX can sign on as *root* and has permission to do anything.

In the recent System V, Release 2 UNIX manuals, the system administrator commands have been moved to Section 1, of a new System Administrator Manual, along with Sections 7 and 8. The new Section 8 contains programs that are called by the kernel or other programs.

We strongly recommend that about every month or so of your UNIX career, you take the manual and turn all the pages. Don't read the whole manual—that is overwhelming. Just look at the one-line descriptions of each command. If something catches your interest, read more about it.

You will find commands that you wish you had known about in the previous month and ones that will solve current problems. You will find commands that didn't make sense last month but are now understandable. You will find options to commands you already know that are very useful. You will suddenly understand something that has eluded you in the past. You will often have fingers in several different places as one piece of information leads you to look up something else.

It is also good to do this near a terminal, so you can quickly test out a new command. Create tight feedback loops for yourself. It speeds up your learning process and makes it fun.

TUTORIAL

UNIX tutorials are writeups on various facilities of UNIX. They were originally written by the authors of the software as technical papers at Bell Labs. Their quality varies widely. In recent years the tutorials have been worked over by professional technical writers which has brought some modest improvements. The tutorials document the larger systems of UNIX: word processing, **awk, make, vi, lex and yacc,** C programming, etc.

We recommend that you first look through the tutorials and see what is there. When you want to use a program, or facility, you start with the tutorials. After you have learned the basics from the tutorial, you can look up details in the manual. For many small programs, however, the only available information is in manual reference pages.

6

The vi Editor

WHY vi TEXT EDITOR

In order to write shell programs you will need a text editor. If you already know a text editor and know how to use it, then you can skip this chapter. There are many that are available and you can use any one you want in shell programming.

We are going to show you how to use **vi** because only **vi** comes with UNIX for free and is on almost all computers that run UNIX. Less than a fraction of a percent do not have **vi** today because they have very old UNIX versions. But even they will have **ed,** an early, line oriented (painful) predecessor of **vi.**

Also, **vi** is very good. Everyone has their own preferences for editors, but **vi** is very powerful. You can do a lot with it. We cannot begin to cover all of the features of **vi.** Almost every key on your keyboard is a command to **vi,** including shift (uppercase) and control keys. It takes a whole book to cover **vi.** Fortunately, that book has been written, and is excellent; see, Mohamed el Lozy, "Editing in a UNIX Environment: The vi/ex Editor" in the Bibliography.

GETTING IN

To get into **vi** simply type:

    $ vi filename

where *filename* is the name of a file you want to edit. In shell programming it is the name of the text file you want to create or modify. It is ok if the file does not exist yet. You can create it in **vi.**

Once you are in, **vi** will clear your screen and display the top of the file on it. If the file does not yet have anything in it, you will have an almost blank screen. Notice though that your cursor (the blinking underscore or block on your screen) is in the first column of the first row of your terminal. Down the side are tildes (~) indicating: *no lines yet*. At the bottom of the screen is a message that says something like:

"filename" [New File]

or

"filename" 86 lines, 2315 characters

If your screen does not look like this, if it seems all garbled, you will have to get out of **vi** and change the setup so that **vi** will know what terminal you are on. If you can get help from someone who knows this procedure, do. Otherwise, get out of **vi** and change the setup. Both steps are explained in the next two Sections.

GETTING OUT

One of the authors remembers studying the **vi** manual for a long time when he was just starting to use **vi**. He could not find out how to get out of **vi** once he had entered it. His terminal would lock up (meaning it would not do anything) never mind what he did. Finally, his office partner came in and he asked him how to get out of **vi**. The other fellow laughed and said, "Oh, that is an undocumented feature . . . and a secret!" After threats to his life, he divulged the secret.

Here is the secret. There are two ways out of **vi**. One is:

:q

where *q* stands for *quit*. If you want to write out the text, that you have been editing, to the disk, type:

:wq

for *write* and *quit*.

The second way to get out is:

ZZ

That is two capital *Z's*. (Use the shift key to get capital letters, just like on a typewriter.)

When you are out of **vi** you will know, because the shell will write the standard prompt to the screen:

$ __

SETTING UP FOR vi

If **vi** came up just fine, you can skip this section. Here we try to set up correctly for **vi**. Here is the problem. **vi** is a screen oriented editor, meaning that it takes control of the screen and lets you move around your text to edit it. **vi** refreshes your screen to show you how your text currently looks. This is all wonderful. Unfortunately, there are hundreds of different terminals. So, **vi** has a */etc/termcap* file or */usr/lib/terminfo* directory that keeps information on hundreds of terminals. But you must tell **vi** which terminal you are on. To tell **vi** you must know the name of your terminal as it is listed in **vi's** terminal file.

First, let's assume you know. We will show you how to find out a little later. Suppose you are on an IBM PC or XT or AT or one of their many compatible clones. And suppose the UNIX you have is **Venix** from Ventur-Com. Then the terminal will be named *pc*. So type the following two lines:

```
$ TERM = pc
$ export TERM
```

This sets a shell variable called **TERM** to be *pc* and then exports it to the environment. This may all be magic to you now, but you will understand it by the time you finish reading this book.

Now how do you find **vi's** name for your terminal. Here is some more magic. Type:

```
$ grep pc /etc/termcap
```

You'll get a lot of stuff that looks like garbage.

```
cpc|pc|PC|ansi standard pc console: \
cpo|pco|PCo|old VENIX 2.0 standard pc console: \
    :ma = ∧K∧P:pc = \ 177:
```

Don't panic. You do not have to understand this. Just look for a line that starts on the left and that has a lot of pipe characters (|) in it. It is a list of names for a terminal.

In the example above, the line:

```
cpc|pc|PC|standard pc console: \
```

is the one we are interested in. It gives three different names separated by the pipe symbol for the same terminal: *cpc, pc,* and *PC.* You may use any one, but the first is slightly preferred.

Now that you know the **vi** name for your terminal, set the *TERM* variable as described above and rerun **vi,** like this:

```
$ TERM = cpc
$ export TERM
$ vi filename
```

MODES

The only really difficult thing about **vi** is that it has three modes. The keys on your keyboard mean different things, depending upon which mode you are in. In the *command* mode, every key is a command to **vi** to do something like move the cursor or delete a character or a line. In the *input* or *text* mode, every key will be typed into the text file you are editing until you type the escape key (ESC). In the *colon* mode, you can issue many commands from the old text editor. To help you keep track of where you are, look at the map in Figure 1.

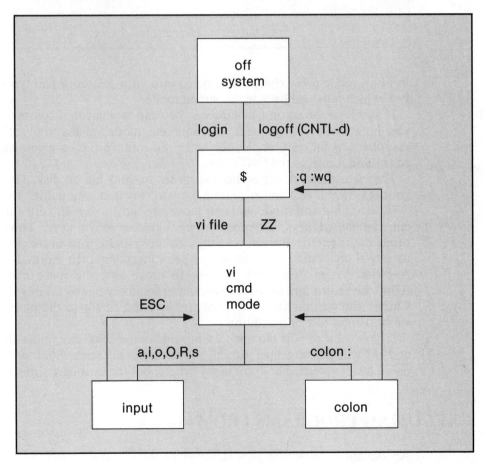

Figure 1. *vi* Modes

You start at the top where you are off the computer. You log in and are talking to the UNIX shell which gives you the dollar prompt. You type **vi** *file* and you are in **vi** in command mode. There you issue commands.

ENTERING, EDITING, AND SAVING TEXT

You enter input mode by typing one of the characters shown in Table 3.

Table 3. *vi* Input Characters

a	append after current character
i	insert before current character
o	open line after current line
O	open line before current line
R	replace/write over characters to right
s	substitute for specified characters

In input mode every character is typed into your text until you type the **ESC** key, which puts you back in command mode.

If you type the colon (:) character, you can type a colon command. When you hit return, you go back to command mode, unless your colon command was *:q* for quit, or *:wq* for write and quit. In this case you leave the **vi** editor and return to the UNIX shell.

The *:w* command writes the text buffer to your file on disk. Only then is your text saved. Remember to do it, or you may lose your editing work.

In the command mode you can move around the screen with three different systems of keys. Beginners often like the arrow keys. Touch typists often use the letter *h* to move left, *l* to move right, *j* to move down and *k* to move up. This lets them keep their fingers in their normal positions. Another system uses the backspace to move left, the space bar to move right, the return key to move down and the minus or the *k* key to move up. Choose the set you like. You need to move the cursor to the place that you want to enter text or do editing.

If you want to edit the text, *x* will remove the character under the cursor, and *dd* will delete a line. ∧*d* will move up a half screen and ∧*u* will move down a half screen. There are many others, but these will get you started.

EXECUTING PROGRAMS FROM vi

An advanced trick you should know about for shell programming is that you can execute programs from **vi**. This means that you can stay in the editor, write your programs, save them, execute them, look at the output, and, if necessary, go back and edit the programs again. It helps you do fast editing and debugging.

Type your program and hit ESC to get back to command mode. Then type :w to write your program to the disk. To execute it you must first make it executable. From then on, as you edit it, it stays executable. Type:

    :!chmod +x %

The colon (:) gets you to colon mode. The exclamation mark (!) tells **vi** that the rest of the line is a command to be run at the shell level. The *chmod* + *x* command makes the file executable, and the percent sign (%) is a short way of typing the name of the current text file. From now on, you can execute the text file by typing:

    :!%

The results will come to the bottom of the screen. When you are through looking at them, press the return key and you will return to the **vi** editor screen ready to modify your program.

vi AS A FULL SCREEN COMMAND EDITOR

Another advanced feature of **vi** gives us the ability to use it as a full screen command editor. We can type a command in the text file and cause the command to be executed and replaced with the output of the command. With one key we can bring back the original command, edit it, and re-execute it.

Type a command while in **vi.** Then, while your cursor is still on that command line, type *!!sh* and hit the return key. This causes the current line to be submitted to the shell, which executes and writes the results into the text in place of the command line.

Type the letter *u* which undoes the last command and your original command line will reappear and the old output will go away. Re-edit the line and hit *!!sh* again. Now your new command line will be executed.

You can submit any number of lines to be executed. The instructions

    :1,20!sh

will send lines 1 through 20 to the shell and replace them with the output. You can send the lines to any command, not just the shell. Send them to the **sort** command and they will be sorted and replaced with the sorted lines. In short, you can use the computer to help you write your text and programs. This is how we wrote this book. We typed in the examples and then had the shell execute them to give us the output that appears after them.

PART

II

OPERATIONAL SHELL COMMANDS

- Shell Programming and Debugging
- UNIX Files
- Standard I/O and Redirection
- Pipes and Filters
- UNIX Commands
- The Shell Monster
- Shell Variables
- Control Flow
- Shell Built-In Commands
- More Shell Meta Characters
- Shell Options, Inputing Data, and Parsing

7

Shell Programming and Debugging

Here we show you how to write a shell program. It is much easier than writing a program in a normal programming language. Anything you can type at the shell on your terminal you can also type into a file, and it will be a shell program.

Shell programming is simple.

1. Just type the shell commands into the text of a file using any text editor. Any command you can type on your terminal to UNIX, you can also type into a program file.
2. Then save the text file on the disk, giving it the name you want to call your new program.
3. Make the file executable.
4. Then simply type the shell program's filename, and it will execute.

We will go over these steps in more detail below.

INPUT A PROGRAM

You can use a text editor such as **vi** to create a shell program. We recommend that you use whichever editor you like. Shell programming doesn't care. If you only have **vi**, use it. If you don't have **vi** or can't get it to work, use **ed.** If you don't even have **ed**, do cat editing with the **cat** command.

vi EDITING

vi is described in more detail in another section, including instructions on what to do if it doesn't work. Here we will give you the simple sequence of keystrokes to create and execute a program file:

```
$ vi cmd
adateESC:wq
$
```

The *vi cmd* fires up **vi.** The letter *a* tells **vi** you want to add or append text. The *date* is the line you are entering. The *ESC* stands for the escape key on your keyboard. It tells **vi** that you are through inputing. And the *:wq* says to write out the file and quit.

OLD ed EDITING

You could also use the old **ed** editor:

```
$ ed cmd
?cmd
a
date
.
w
5
q
$
```

ed is painful to use for large programs but is easy for a few lines like we will be doing at first. After you type: *ed cmd,* **ed** fires up and displays the *?cmd* to mean it can't find a file named **cmd.** That is because we have not created it yet. The *a* is a command to **ed** telling it you want to append some text, and *date* is your program. The dot alone on a line tells **ed** that you are finished appending. The *w* tells **ed** that you want the text you have entered written out to the disk file named *cmd.* **ed** responds with the number five, which means it wrote five characters to the disk—the four letters in *date* and the unseen newline character. Finally, the *q* tells **ed** to quit.

cat EDITING

In case you have problems with these text editors, the most primitive way to create a shell program is with the **cat** command. It is called **cat** editing. For example, let us create a command that we will call *cmd.*

```
$ cat > cmd
date
Ctrl-d
```

Here we tell **cat** to write into a file called *cmd.* On the next line we type the commands that we want to put into the *cmd* file. Here we are just going to put the *date* command into the program. After all of the lines are typed in, we end our input by typing CNTL-d.

CHECK THE PROGRAM FILE

Let us check to see if our new *cmd* program has the right stuff in it. Use cat again to see what is in *cmd*. Type:

```
$ cat cmd
date
```

If you did it right, **cat** should show you that **date** is in the *cmd* program file.

MAKE IT EXECUTABLE

When the text editor creates a file, it assumes that it is a regular file, not a program. So, since you want this shell program to be executed, you have to change the permissions to make it executable. There is a simple command to do the job.

```
$ chmod +x cmd
```

The *chmod* is an abbreviation of change mode. It changes the permissions on a file. It has many uses, but here we just want to make our file executable. That is what the +*x* option does.

RUN THE COMMAND

Now that we have written our program and made it executable, we can run it by simply typing its name.

```
$ cmd
Sat Jul 27 02:24:41 MST 1985
```

It worked! Of course, all it does is duplicate the **date** command. But the point is that we have a working program. Now you can start playing around with your own programs.

DEBUGGING SHELL PROGRAMS

Debugging shell programs is easy because of a couple of options to the shell. If you run the shell with a −*x* or −*v* option it will trace the execution of the program.

−x Option

For example, suppose our *cmd* program looked like this:

```
$ cat cmd
echo Hi, it is now:
date
```

When you type

```
$ sh −x cmd
+ echo Hi, it is now:
Hi, it is now:
+ date
Fri Jul 26 11:21:20 MST 1985
```

the shell will list each command line, with a plus (+) in front, before the shell executes the line. This lets you see what is going on as the shell program runs.

But it is even better. The command line the shell displays, after the plus sign, is not the one you typed. Rather it shows you the line *after* the shell has applied all of its rewrite rules. Therefore, it shows you what the shell did to your command line as a result of all of the file, variable, and command substitutions. This is extremely useful to check to see if you got what you wanted.

Let's see this by changing our *cmd* shell program to:

```
$ cat cmd
echo Hi, it is now:
echo `date`
```

Note that this time command substitution is used. Command substitution is explained in a later chapter. Briefly, the single backquotes tell the shell to execute the enclosed command and write the results on the line in place of the command. Let's see what happens:

```
$ sh −x cmd
+ echo Hi, it is now:
Hi, it is now:
+ date
+ echo Fri Jul 26 11:33:40 MST 1985
Fri Jul 26 11:33:40 MST 1985
```

Look at the second *echo* command. Note that it has the output of the *date* command written on its command line. Then it displays its command line. Note also the + *date* line. That tells us that the shell executed the date command along the way. It had to get the output for the echo command line.

−*v* Option

−*v* stands for verbose. It will cause each line to be displayed *before* shell rewriting.

Use These Trace Options

We strongly urge you to get in the habit of using these trace options for several reasons. First, of course, it will enormously simplify debugging. If you are used to assembled or compiled languages, this is a great luxury, but you may forget to use it. Use this feature and you won't forget so easily. We have been with new shell programmers who sat and thought about what might be going on with a program that was not working right. We would say, "Well, let's look at it with **sh −x.**" And they would say, "Oh, yeah, I forgot." As we watched the program scroll by, they would quickly see the bug.

Secondly, the trace options are an important learning device. This is especially important while you are reading this book and hopefully trying out the sample programs. Running them with **sh −x** gives you even more insight into what is going on. You are less likely to develop superstitions in which you invent an explanation to fit a particular experience. Superstitions are common in programming because you cannot see what is going on, and they interfere with your learning and your work. We have seen many people make typing errors and convince themselves that a program does not work.

Finally, you may find that using **sh −x** shows bugs that you were not even looking for. Our experience is that, for every bug we were chasing with **sh −x,** we would find another bug along the way as we watched the programs scroll by.

EXPERIMENT

Throughout this book, as we show you little experiments, we hope that you learn an important technique. Whenever you are learning a new feature, think up and try experiments. They are usually quick and easy. Test things before you put them into programs. They are much easier to check out in little programs than in a big program. The results are easier to see. If they don't seem to work, try different approaches. When you are sure of a feature, then you can put it into your programs correctly.

8

UNIX Files

A filename in UNIX can be up to 14 characters long. (On the Berkeley 4.2BSD UNIX, the names can be longer.) In general it can be almost any ASCII character. However, it is very unwise to use special characters in filenames because the shell may see them as meta characters instructing the shell to do various rewrite substitutions.

You are safe with uppercase and lowercase letters, numbers, the dot (.) and the underscore (_). Be sure to avoid the star or asterisk (*), the question mark (?), and the square brackets ([ ]), for these are filename substitution meta characters to the shell. A leading minus (−) is the way many UNIX commands distinguish between options and files. So don't give a filename a leading minus sign. There are many other characters that will cause confusion and sometimes disaster. If you really have to use a special character in a filename then you must put single quotes around it when you use it.

```
$ ls '*bad$filename?'
```

DIRECTORIES

Files are kept in directories, and directories can have other directories under them. You can list the files in your directory with the **ls** command.

```
$ ls
file1
file2
dir1
dir2
```

ls has many options you should know about. Look them up in Section 1 of your UNIX manual.

A directory is really another file that lists the names of the files and directories in it, and pointers (called inodes) to data blocks with information about the file. You can see your directory with the **od,** octal dump, command. See Chapter 11 on UNIX commands.

HIERARCHY

UNIX has a file system that is called hierarchical. It looks like a corporate or governmental organization chart (Figure 2).

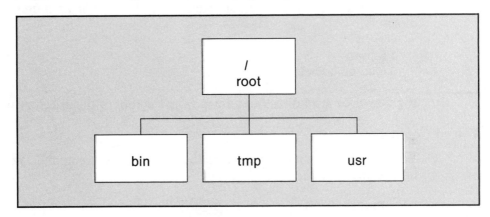

Figure 2. Directory and File Hierarchy

On a simple system like CP/M the **DIR** command lists all of the files in the form of a small table. Since there are only a few files, there is no problem. But with UNIX there are over a thousand files to begin with. Then the users add many more. They cannot all be listed on a screen. So, on UNIX, files are grouped together under directories. Each directory can contain files and more directories which are, therefore, subdirectories. When you log in to UNIX you are in a special directory called your *HOME* directory. You can also move around to other directories.

PATH NAMES

Every file has a base name like *file1, payroll, phonebook,* etc. But it also has a path name that lists the directories, starting from the root, which must be traversed to get to the file. The **vi** text editor is a file in the *bin* directory under the root. So its complete path name is */bin/vi.*

Every file can also have many relative path names. For example, if you were in the */bin* directory, you could refer to the *vi* file as just **vi.** If you were in the */tmp* directory, you could give a relative address (relative to directory */tmp*) of *../bin/vi.* This means go up one directory (the two dots

(..) are the parent directory), then down to the *bin* directory and there find a file named *vi*. In fact, the path gives directions to the shell to find the file.

The pwd Command

To do relative paths, the shell must have some idea of where you are. It keeps a path to your current directory in its internal buffers. So that any time you refer to a file without the leading slash (/), the shell knows you mean relative to the directory you are in.

You can ask the shell where you are with the **pwd** command. The only way we can remember this command is to think of it as *present working directory*.

```
$ pwd
/usr/rod/book/sh/tut
```

Right now we are 5 directories down from the root of the directory tree.

The cd Command

You can change your current directory with the **cd** command. You can go up one directory like this:

```
$ cd ..
$ pwd
/usr/rod/book/sh
```

Now you are in the *sh* directory above the *tut* directory. You can return to *tut* with:

```
$ cd tut
$ pwd
/usr/rod/book/sh/tut
```

Back. There is another *bin* directory below this directory which we can visit with:

```
$ cd bin
$ pwd
/usr/rod/book/sh/tut/bin
```

You can go to your home directory with a simple:

```
$ cd
$ pwd
/usr/rod
```

Home again, home again . . . Remember, **cd** go home.

DEVICES ARE FILES

We have been talking as if files lived only on disks. UNIX, however, thinks of line printers and terminals, modems and instrument communication ports, robots and satellites, and space ships and laser cannons, etc., as files. It talks to them all in the same way, with streams of characters. We can also send data to any device in the same way we send data to a disk file.

```
$ echo Hi, there > /dev/lp
```

If your computer calls the line printer */dev/lp,* then this command will send its output to your printer.

Actually, */dev/lp* is not a real UNIX file. What is there is a program, called a driver, that takes every character sent to it and sends it on to the device it knows about. Drivers can also read from devices.

When you get a new floppy with data on it, you might read it like this: **WARNING:** do not try this command until you know what you are doing! You might write over important files.

```
$ cpio -icvdB < /dev/f0
```

Here we are inputing the floppy on drive f0 to the **cpio** command which will break out the separate directories and files and write them on the hard disk.

9

Standard I/O and Redirection

There is a concept in UNIX called *standard I/O*. The idea is that a program should take data from standard-input and send data to standard-output. From inside the program, it should not matter where the data is actually coming from, whether keyboard, hard disk, tape, floppy, satellite link, or whatever. The code simply reads characters from input, processes them, and sends them on to output.

On the command line, or shell program level, the data can be directed to and from anywhere. So we can decide at a higher level where to get the input data and where to send the output. This makes the program much more flexible, and is a key element in UNIX power.

STREAM OF CHARACTERS

To make this work, UNIX considers all data as a stream of bytes or characters. There is no structure to the data, just bytes. The programs can insert structure into the data by putting in characters like newlines to separate records and tabs or other characters to separate fields. But these characters are embedded in the data, not hard-wired into the program.

Therefore, the records and fields can have variable lengths. This saves a lot of disk space over fixed-length records and fields. It also makes the programs run faster since there are less characters to move around. Our experience is that variable-length files are about one-third the size of fixed length-files, and three times faster to process. More importantly it keeps programs from being hard-wired to their data.

FILE REDIRECTION

Also to make this work, we have some file redirection characters. With these characters we can tell a program to take its data from different sources and send them to different destinations. The default standard-in for a program is the terminal keyboard and the default standard-out is the terminal screen. For example, when we type:

```
$ date
Mon Aug 12 20:17:42 EDT 1985
```

The standard-output of the **date** command is the terminal screen where the date line appears.

> File Redirection

Now suppose we want to send that output to a file on the hard disk, instead of to our screen. We can redirect the output of the **date** command, or any command, with a single character and the name of the file:

```
$ date > datefile
$
```

The *right arrow* (>), also called *greater-than* character, is the single character needed to send our output somewhere else. Note that nothing came to the screen. The output of **date** was written into the datefile. Let's look in the datefile and see if it got there:

```
$ cat datefile
Mon Aug 12 20:22:12 EDT 1985
```

Sure enough, there it is. This was one of the revolutionary ideas of UNIX, to make data redirection so simple. The idea has been adopted more and more by other operating systems in recent years.

We can just as easily send a file to the line printer:

```
$ cat file > /dev/lp
```

Here is another example:

```
$ pr *.c > /dev/lp
```

This command sends all of the files ending in .c, the C language source files, to the line printer. **pr** puts nice headers on each file with page numbers, etc.

< File Redirection

We can also get data from sources other than the keyboard with the left-arrow character (<). We can type:

```
$ cat < datefile
Mon Aug 12 20:22:12 EDT 1985
```

In this case, the **cat** command took data from standard-in. This differs from the earlier example where we typed

```
$ cat datefile
Mon Aug 12 20:22:12 EDT 1985
```

We get the same output, but the input was set up differently. In this last example, the shell handed the word *datefile* to the **cat** command in a special array of pointers which its C code could handle. The **cat** command then made system calls to open a file by that name and connect it to the standard-in of the **cat** program. It then read characters from the standard-in.

In the earlier example, with the left arrow, the **cat** command also read from its standard-in, but the shell opened the file. In that example the shell saw the redirect character, the left arrow (<), and opened the file and connected it to the **cat** command's standard-in. The **cat** command did not have to open the file itself; the shell did all the work.

To prove this to yourself, try the following experiment. Let's use the **echo** command to see what the shell does in each case.

```
$ echo datefile
datefile
$
```

In this first case, *datefile* is just an argument to the **echo** command, which is faithfully sent to standard-out, which is our terminal screen.

```
$ echo < datefile
$
```

Hey, what happened? Nothing printed out. What happened to < *datefile?*

What happened was that the shell saw the < *datefile* and knew to open the file for standard-in. So the shell did the work, *AND* removed the string < *datefile* from the command line. This left no arguments for the **echo** command to echo. The line was empty after the shell got through.

echo does not read from its standard-in, only from its command line. Its standard-in was set up, but it did not use it. That is ok. UNIX generally does not display error messages when unusual things happen.

>> file

Sometimes we want to append data to the end of a file rather than creating a new file or writing over an old file. A common example is a log file that is periodically written to like this:

```
$ date >> logfile
$ who >> logfile
```

These commands write out a date stamp and a table of who is on the system. With the **sleep** command it could be run every hour for a usage log.

```
$ cat logfile
Mon Aug 12 21:01:15 EDT 1985
rod            console        Aug 11 17:38
```

Note the **date** command opened the logfile which had not existed before. The **who** command appended its output to the logfile rather than clobbering the old dateline as a single right arrow would have done:

```
$ who > logfile
$ cat logfile
rod            console        Aug 11 17:38
```

<< file

Sometimes you want to write the input data into the shell program with the command. The double left arrows are called a *here* file, meaning that the data is right here.

```
$ mail rod <<EOF
The cmd program has just been run.
EOF
```

EOF means *end of file* and must be on a line by itself to signify the end of the *here* file. Between the command line and the *EOF* line is the file to be input to the standard-in of the **mail** program. This might be used to send yourself mail whenever a program is run.

We chose the string *EOF* arbitrarily. Any word and many characters will do. Some use the exclamation mark (!). Pick something you like. Be careful that no line in your text matches your end-of-file word.

To make the *here* file look better in your program, put a minus in front of the *EOF* word and use tabs to move the data over to line up under the command it is going into. The minus tells the shell to strip the leading tabs from the here file to the final end of file.

If you quote the end-of-file word, it is like quoting the whole document.

```
$ cat edhere
: edhere—show a here file for the ed editor.

ed $1 > /dev/null <<-\!
    1,2d
    1,$s/ /,/g
    1,$s/.*/Define(&)/
    w
    q
    !
```

The minus sign (−) lets us put tabs in front of the here file so that it looks better. The backslash (\) quotes the exclamation mark (!), which quotes the entire here file and all of its special characters, which are often special to the shell also.

What will this program do? It is similar to a program that uses **sed.** Except **ed** edits the file in place. This program changes a table-formatted file into an **m4** define macro list.

```
$ cat inventory
Item        Amount      Cost      Value      Description
1              3          50        150      rubber gloves
2            100           5        500      test tubes
3              5          80        400      clamps
4             23          19        437      plates
5             99          24       2376      cleaning cloths
6             89         147      13083      bunsen burners
7              5         175        875      scales
$ edhere inventory
$ cat inventory
Define(  1,      3,    50,    150,rubber gloves)
Define(  2,    100,     5,    500,test tubes)
Define(  3,      5,    80,    400,clamps)
Define(  4,     23,    19,    437,plates)
Define(  5,     99,    24,   2376,cleaning cloth)
Define(  6,     89,   147,  13083,bunsen burners)
Define(  7,      5,   175,    875,scales)
```

digit< file and digit> file

So far the left- and right-arrow characters have been used by themselves. You may not have realized that they were both opening files and assigning file descriptor numbers. When one types:

```
$ cmd   < file
$ cmd 0< file
```

the two command lines are synonymous. A left-arrow character, by itself, means file descriptor zero (0). Likewise, these two lines have the same meaning:

```
$ cmd   > file
$ cmd 1> file
```

We are showing this to you to make the next idea easier. You can now open many files for input or output. Not just the standard-input (file descriptor 0), output (file descriptor 1) and error (file descriptor 2).

First, let's look at standard error. Ordinarily it is directed the same as standard-out. But you can change its direction. You can save the error messages in a log file or throw them away, for example.

```
$ cmd   < file1  > file2 2>> logcmderrors
$ cmd 0< file1 1> file2 2>> logcmderrors
```

These two command lines have identical effects. The second just makes the file descriptors explicit. All of **cmd**'s error messages, which go to file descriptor 2, are appended to the log file.

<&digit

Ordinarily a program on UNIX can open 20 files. The first three (0,1,2) are opened automatically by the shell. So you have 17 more you can open (3–19).

Once we have opened a file and assigned it a file descriptor number we can then read or write the file using that number.

```
$ cat openfile
: openfile—show how to open other files
exec 3> file3
exec 4< file3

echo 'This is file3' >&3
cat <&4
: which is the same as
echo 'This is file3' 1>&3
cat 0<&4
$ openfile

This is file3
This is file3
```

We opened *file3* for output and assigned file descriptor 3 using the **exec** command which does this job for us if we give it no other arguments. Then we opened it again for input with file descriptor 4. We echoed a line out to file descriptor 3 *(>&3)*. Then read from file descriptor 4 *(<&4)*. The second part of the program was explicit about the fact that the commands write to standard-out and read from standard-in and we are redirecting their file descriptors to other file descriptors.

To make this a little clearer, let's do it another way. The **read** command is built into the shell so it cannot be redirected. But we can take another file and make its file descriptor the same as the standard-in. Then when we use the **read** command it reads from the file we want.

```
$ cat trickread
: trickread—make read read from another file.
exec 3< file3
exec 0<&3
```

```
      read LINE
      echo $LINE
      $ trickread
      This is file3
```

First we open *file3* and assign it to file descriptor 3. Then we make file descriptor 0 read from file descriptor 3, i.e., we make file descriptor 0 a duplicate of 3. Then when **read** inputs a line from 0, it is getting 3's file. The *echo* proves that we got what we wanted.

<&- and >&-

You can close standard-input with <&- and standard-out with >&-. Why close files? When the programs exit, all of the files are closed automatically. If you only open a few files, you don't need to bother with closing them. However, sometimes you may open many files, perhaps in a loop. You can only have twenty open at one time. Since you may run out of file descriptors, it is good practice to close each file, after use, whenever you are not sure of how many will be opened.

10

Pipes and Filters

In addition to being able to redirect standard-I/O from and to different files, the shell will also allow you to send the output of one program to the input of another.

```
$ ls /bin /usr/bin | wc −l
    217
```

Here we send the output of the **ls** command to the input of the **wc** command. **ls** will list all of the files in a directory, in this case two directories. The **wc** word count command counts lines, words, and characters. But with the −*l* option, only the number of lines is printed. So the first command gives us a list of files in the UNIX *bin* directories, and the second command counts them. Thus by putting together two UNIX programs, we now have a new program that tells us how many UNIX programs there are on our system. This little pipe could be put into a shell program and given a name like **howmany** and we could have a UNIX command counter.

There are a couple of glitches in this program. The **ls** command throws out a blank line and a little */bin:* or */usr/bin:* header line for each list.

```
$ ls /bin /usr/bin

/bin:
adb
ar
as
basename
cat
(. . .)
write

/usr/bin:
admin
```

```
asa
at
awk
(. . .)
yacc
```

The ellipses (. . .) stand for a long list that has been truncated here.

We can take care of the first problem by counting words instead of lines with the − w option to **wc.**

```
$ ls /bin /usr/bin | wc −w
   215
```

We can remove the pesky */bin:* lines with the **sed** command. But it will take a longer pipe.

LONG PIPES

```
$ ls /bin /usr/bin | sed '/:$/d' | wc −w
   213
```

Here we insert the **sed** command and another pipe. The **sed** command will delete all lines ending with a colon. We use that test, because it is true for the head lines, and false for the UNIX commands. However, let's check to be sure that there is no command with a colon in it. Think about how you would do it before we show you one way.

```
$ ls /bin /usr/bin | grep ':'
/bin:
/usr/bin:
```

Sure enough, the test worked. Note that we use **grep** to find all of the lines with a colon in them. We don't give **grep** the name of a file, because it gets its input from the pipe to the **ls** command.

PIPES DOWN THE PAGE

Pipes can get very long. We recommend that when a pipe starts getting long and hard to read, that you start listing it down the page. When the shell sees a pipe-symbol (|) at the end of a line, it knows that there is more to come. It prompts with the secondary prompt, *PS2=>*.

```
$ ls /bin /usr/bin |
> sed '/:/d' |
> wc − w
   213
```

When you put this in a shell script, it is much easier to read and easier to modify. You can add or delete commands to the pipe by adding or deleting lines.

THE freq COMMAND

Now let's write a program that uses a long pipe. First we will give you the problem, ask you to estimate how long it would take to write a program to solve the problem, how long that program would be, in lines, based on your experience, and then give you a UNIX pipe program.

We want a program that will read in a text file and print out a table showing the 10 most frequently used words, sorted with the most frequent on top. Think about how you would write such a program in a language you are familiar with. How many lines would it take? How long? We have heard estimates from 20 lines to 10,000 lines. What a business programming is. Imagine if house builders, when asked how long it would take to build a house, would say "Oh, between a few minutes and a few centuries."

Here is one way you can do it with pipes. We have written a little shell program called **freq.**

```
$ cat freq
: freq produces table of most frequent words in input text
USAGE = 'usage: freq < textfile'

tr '[A-Z]' '[a-z]' |
tr -cs '[a-z]' '[012*]'|
sort |
uniq  - c |
sort  - nr |
sed 10q

$ freq < pipe.mm
   40 the
   38 a
   20 to
   20 bin
   15 we
   15 of
   14 and
   13 command
   13 b
   12 you
```

Our **freq** program uses the **tr** command twice. The first time it converts all uppercase letters to lowercase. The second time it converts all characters that are not letters to newlines, which makes a long list of words. Can you visualize this? There is a string of letters, a word, followed by a newline so that the next word is on the next line. The −s option of **tr** suppresses all repeated newlines so that we will not have a lot of blank lines. Then **sort** sorts the list for **uniq. uniq** will give only one copy of each word in the list, and with the −c option it will count and give us the number of times each word appeared. Then **freq** sorts the new double-column list again. This time the first column, the count, is sorted on. The options −nr mean numeric and reverse sort. Numeric is different than string sort. Reverse puts the highest numbers on top. The last command, **(sed)** cuts off only the top 10 lines. *10q* means print 10 lines and quit. When we run the command we get the list we want.

The UNIX **spell** program is a lot like this **freq** program. Originally it was a simple pipe. Then it got to be a bigger shell script. Now on UNIX 5.2, **spell** is a C program. The **spell** program gets the sorted and uniqued list of words as above, then compares the words with an online dictionary which had been entered for another reason. Only words that do not appear in the dictionary are listed out by **spell.**

The pipe could be done with *tmp* files.

```
$ ls /bin /usr/bin > tmp1
$ sed '/:/d' < tmp1 > tmp2
$ wc −w < tmp2
   213
```

This will do the same as the pipe in our first example. There are two big advantages to pipes over the temporary files. One is that pipes are easier to type; a single keystroke instead of several. Pipes are also much faster. Reading to and from the disk is very slow compared to processing in the memory of the computer.

HOW PIPES WORK

When the shell sees a pipe, it sets up internal buffers of usually 10 blocks (5120 bytes) to store the data from the left command until the right command takes it. The shell executes the commands which are now called processes. Each process reads and writes from and to its own standard-io, ignorant of the pipes. Even though UNIX is multitasking, only one task or process can be executing at a time. While it is executing, it writes its output into the pipe buffer. If it fills the buffer, then the process must suspend and give other processes a chance to run. The UNIX kernel detects the suspension and checks its process table for the next highest priority process. Eventually the process that reads the buffer fires up and starts taking bytes out of the pipe buffer. If it empties the buffer, it must suspend.

Of course, either process may write only a few characters into the buffer or read from the buffer before it suspends. But the shell and the kernel manage all of this correctly. There are UNIX system calls that allow a C, or other language, program to get at the same functions that the shell uses.

SYSTEM CALLS

It is important to know that a C, or other language, program can execute other programs and pipes with the system call: **system** *(string)*. The string can be a UNIX command, pipe, or other strings.

If you have this function call in your C program you will send the date-line to *standard-out*.

```
system ("date");
Fri Aug 16 12:34:36 EDT 1985
```

And, of course, a shell program is able to call any program. Therefore you can mix programs, having a shell program call a C program, which in turn executes a shell pipeline, which in turn executes another shell program, which in turn executes a C program, and so on. The limits are the number of processes that a user can have. This is normally 20, but the system administrator can increase that number with the *config* files and relink the UNIX operating system.

AUTOMATION

These facilities make possible the automation of your work. You write some shell programs; then you can write a shell program which invokes the others from a higher level. Later, with more programs on each level, you can write a shell program that executes the top level programs. You can imagine having several programs to run every Monday. Write a shell program, called **monday,** which executes all of your programs for you (perhaps with prompting for needed names, etc.). Then on Monday, you type **monday** and all the day's work is done. Then you can write one for each day of the week. Then you can set up their execution with the **at** command to be run on their respective days of the week. Then you can write a payroll program to put your paycheck into your bank. Then you will not have to go to work at all. You can lie on the beach and sigh, "Ahhhhh, UNIX."

11

UNIX Commands

UNIX comes with hundreds of commands, but about twenty or thirty are used most frequently in shell programming. These are the real work horses that you will see many times in this book. Their complete description is in your UNIX *User Manual*. See the chapter on the UNIX documentation (Chapter 6). Here we will mention only some of the important basics of each of these handy commands.

THE awk COMMAND

The **awk** command has a wide range of functions. It is a batch spreadsheet, a programming language, a calculator, a string matcher and replacer, and much more. In the section on relational database management, **awk** is shown performing most of the basic relational database functions. **awk** can take a file and process it many ways. When the simpler UNIX programs cannot do a job, **awk** often can.

We can only touch on a few of the **awk** powers here. A whole book could, should and probably will be written on this program. It is a sleeper in UNIX software. Many UNIX people do not appreciate its power. In fact, for years there has been a bug in Berkeley **awk.** It was fixed recently, but many computers with older Berkeley UNIX distributions still have the bug. It must not be used much to go so long without fixing.

Here is a simple **awk** program in which we get the account number from the password file.

```
$ awk − F: '$1 == "guest" { print $3 }'
/etc/passwd
100
```

awk knows about files that are in table form. It expects rows or records containing columns or fields. Ordinarily it uses a space character as the field separator. Here we have used the − *F* option to change the field separator to the colon (:), because that is the field separator of the password file */etc/passwd.*

The characters between the single quotes are an **awk** program. You can also write the program in a file and simply tell **awk** its name with the $-f$ option.

```
$ awk  - f awkprog filename
```

The input file in our example is */etc/passwd.* The program tells **awk** to look for the string *guest* in the first column *($1)*. When a record or a row of the file matches, then **awk** should do the action inside the curly braces. In this case, print the third column *($3)*.

As **awk** reads each line of the input file, it divides the line into fields, calling the first $1, the next $2, etc. The whole line can be referred to by $0. The double equals ($= =$) means logically equal. The string *guest* is delimited by double quotes (") to tell **awk** that it is a literal string, not a variable. In this example we see many of the basic features of **awk**.

Pattern and Action

awk expects its command to be in the form:

```
pattern { action }
pattern { action }
(. . .)
```

This means that for each record or row read in, **awk** will try to match a pattern to that row. There are many kinds of patterns that **awk** knows how to match. When there is a match, the action part in the curly braces ({}) will be performed upon the record. In the example above, *$1 = = "guest"* was the pattern and { *print $3* } was the action.

If there are several pattern-action commands in **awk's** program, then **awk** will apply each in turn to the current line. If a *pattern* is missing, then the *action* will be applied to every line. If an *action* is missing, then the whole line will be printed whenever the *pattern* matches.

Patterns—Patterns can be either numeric or string comparisons. Here are some examples (Table 4):

Table 4. *Awk* Patterns

$2 = = 45	Column Two is Equal to 45
$0 = = ''''	The Whole Row Is Empty
$4 + $8 < $3	Columns 4 and 8 Added Together Is Less Than Column 3
$10 ~ /file/	Column 10 Has the String *file* Somewhere in it
NR ! = $1	Record Number (NR) Is Not-Equal (! =) to Column 1
NF > 8	The Number of Fields (NF) Is More Than 8

Actions—**awk** actions are a programming language similar to C. In fact there are University computer courses that teach introductory programming with **awk.** Table 5 will give you just a flavor of some of the possibilities.

Table 5. *awk* **Actions**

print $4 $2	Print Column 4 and 2 Jammed Together
print $10,$1	Print Column 10, The Field Separator, Then Column 1
printf ("%7.2f", $2)	Print Column 2 with Two Decimal Points
$5 = $2 + $4	Column 5 is Assigned The Sum of Columns 2 and 4
sum += $1	Add The Value in Column 1 to The Variable *sum*

There are several examples of **awk** later on in this book.

THE bc COMMAND

bc is a powerful and handy basic calculator. It is always available to you while you are at the terminal. But it is also good for doing math in shell programs. There is another program, **expr,** that we also use, but **bc** can do floating-point math and other things that **expr** cannot do.

To use **bc** in interactive mode just type:

```
$ bc
2 + 3
5
quit
$
```

In this mode it is a quick calculator for you to use when you need it. It takes its instructions from standard-in, so you can type at it interactively or redirect or pipe instructions to it. In this case we typed bc and 2 + 3 and **bc** responded with the 5. Note that **bc** does not give any extra messages, just the answer. The answer is going to standard-out so it can also be redirected, or piped to another program, or grabbed in a shell variable.

```
$ echo 'scale = 2; 134.73 * .05' | bc
6.73
```

Here we are using **echo** to send instructions to **bc** through a pipe with the single answer coming to standard-out. Note we used the *scale* instruction to tell **bc** how many digits we wanted to the right of the decimal place. Note also that we did not use a *quit* command. **bc** quietly quits when it gets to the *end of file,* which in this case is the end of the **echo** string.

THE cat COMMAND

cat is the UNIX command for sending a file to the screen. It stands for concatenate, which means to put together. **cat** was originally written to put several files together, one after another. But if you only mention one file, you will get that file. When you are sitting at the terminal and want to see what is in a file, you just type:

```
$ cat file
Hi, I am inside this file.
Nice to come out and say hi.
Bye.
$
$ cat file1 file2 | wc
            2       6      26
$
```

First we **cat** out the contents of a file named *file*. The second **cat** program sends *file1* and then *file2* through the pipe to **wc** (word count) command which will count all of the characters, words, and lines in the two files together.

THE date COMMAND

date prints both the date and time from the computer's clock, or timekeeping function.

```
$ date
Sat Aug 10 21:16:25 EDT 1985
```

This standard line can be used as is for date stamps, etc. The newer **date** commands have options for controlling the formatting of the date and time. You can also use the string parsing powers of the **set** command to chop up the date line and reformat it. See Part 2, Chapter 17 on parsing.

THE dd (DATA DUMP) COMMAND

dd is not really used much in shell programming, but it is so important to your computer work and so few UNIX people appreciate it that we want to mention it. **dd,** abbreviation for data dump, is a powerful command for pulling data off tapes, floppies, and other media. It can ignore format or look for one. It can change from ASCII to IBM formats, swap bytes, change from uppercase to lowercase or vice versa, plus other operations. When other commands fail to get data off a tape, use **dd.** If **dd** cannot get the data, forget it.

```
$ dd if = /dev/f0 of = floppy
60 + 0 blocks out
60 + 0 blocks in
```

The entry *if* means *input file* which is assigned to the floppy driver *(/dev/f0)* and *of* means output file which is assigned to a disk file we are calling *floppy*. Here we got 60 blocks off the floppy disk. Once you have gotten data off into a disk file, you have many tools to transform it into what you want.

THE diff COMMAND

Every line that differs between two files is output by **diff.**

```
$ diff file1 file2
$
```

No output tells you that the two files are identical.

```
$ diff file1 file2
1c1
< Line 1 file1
-
> Line 1 file2
```

Here the *1c1* says that the difference is in line 1. The < means the first file and > means the second file. The lines that differ from the two files are displayed.

The **diff** command also has an option that will cause it to produce a file of commands that the editor, **ed,** can use to transform the first file into the second file.

THE echo COMMAND

The **echo** command simply sends its arguments to its standard-out. It has several important uses.

Display

echo is like the Basic Language *print* statement. You can use **echo** to send some string of characters to the computer terminal.

```
$ echo Hello, world.
Hello, world.
```

You can use it for prompts along with the **read** command which will be discussed later.

```
$ echo Enter Your First Name
Enter Your First Name
$ __
```

If you want the cursor to sit at the end of the line, you can suppress the newline that **echo** normally prints. Unfortunately, the option for doing this has changed from old to new UNIX. The old way was:

```
$ echo − n "Enter Your First Name "
Enter Your First Name __
```

The underscore (__) above shows where the cursor sits. Note that we had to use quotes around the *Enter* . . . message to preserve the space at the end. Otherwise, the shell would strip it off and put the cursor right after the *e*.

The new way is:

```
$ echo "Enter Your First Name " \\c
Enter Your First Name __
```

That funny \\c means suppress carriage return. The UNIX manual says \c, but the first backslash (\) is needed to protect the next backslash from the shell.

Start Pipe

Some commands only take their input from standard-in. There are three ways to input data to these commands. One is with file redirection and another is a *here* file. These are discussed in the chapter on inputing data (Chapter 17). Another way to send data to such programs is with **echo** and a pipe.

```
$ echo perminent permanent | spell
perminent
$
```

The **spell** command will look up words in a dictionary file that is on the UNIX system. If the word is spelled correctly, nothing comes out. But a word **spell** cannot find is sent to standard-out. In this case *permanent* must be spelled right since we did not get it back.

We sent **spell** the word through the pipe. This method is good when you have only a small amount of data to send, a few words or a line or two.

Debugging

A very important use of **echo** for shell programmers is to show you what the shell is doing with your command line. In Chapter 12 on the shell monster, we explain that the shell takes your input line and rewrites it if there are any special meta characters. **echo** lets you see what the shell has done.

```
$ echo $HOME
/usr/rod
```

Here the dollar sign *($)* told the shell that the following word was a shell variable. The shell took the *$HOME* and rewrote it with the value the shell has for it. In this case */usr/rod*. The **echo** command was innocent of any changing. **echo** only saw its command line after the shell had rewritten it.

```
$ echo HOME
HOME
```

Here there is no dollar sign, so the shell leaves the line alone and echo displays it. Therefore, **echo** is an important tool to let you see what the shell is doing to your command lines.

THE grep COMMAND

grep is the strange name of a very useful program. It will look for a string of characters in a file and display every line that has that string in it.

```
$ grep guest /etc/passwd
guest::100:100::/usr/guest:
```

Here we look for the string *guest* in the password file. Only one line was found and it was displayed. The command **grep** can be used as a search tool to find a line in a database, a misspelled word in text, or a variable name in program source files.

THE od (OCTAL DUMP) COMMAND

The command **od,** short for octal dump, lets you inspect all of the characters in a file including the special nonprinting characters. To see what your directory file really looks like, type:

```
$ od −c .
0000000    M 005  . \0 \0 \0 \0 \0 \0 \0 \0 \0 \0 \0 \0 \0
0000020    @ 004  .   . \0 \0 \0 \0 \0 \0 \0 \0 \0 \0 \0 \0
0000040  214 007  f  i  l  e  1 \0 \0 \0 \0 \0 \0 \0 \0 \0
0000060  215 007  f  i  l  e  2 \0 \0 \0 \0 \0 \0 \0 \0 \0
0000080
$
```

The $-c$ option tells **od** to show the character representation for each byte, rather than the octal or hex number. The dot (.) means the current directory.

The first column of the output is the address in octal of the first of the 16 characters displayed. The first two bytes are a binary number that is the UNIX inode pointer. The next 14 characters are the letters of the filenames. The $\setminus 0$ stands for null. The dot (.) is the current directory. The two dots is the parent directory. Then you can see the two filenames, *file1* and *file2*. Any file that has special characters you want to see can be displayed in this way.

THE pr COMMAND

The **pr** command does not *print* on a printer, rather it prepares a file for printing. It breaks the file into page-size chunks and puts a one-line header on each page. The headline has the date, name of the file and the page number. The name of the file can be replaced with a header of your choice. **pr** does a few other tricks like printing multicolumn, which is useful for mailing labels.

```
$ pr *.c | print
```

This is a nice way to print all of your C program listings. This assumes your system has a **print** command that knows how to send its standard-in to the line printer.

THE rm COMMAND

To get rid of a file you use **rm**. With the $-f$ option, it will not complain if the file you ask it to remove does not exist. With the *-r* flag it will remove a directory and all of its subdirectories. **WARNING:** The $-r$ option is very dangerous—be careful. Once you have removed a file you can *NEVER* get it back in UNIX.

```
$ rm  −rf olddirectory
```

Say goodby to *olddirectory*. We hope you didn't want it any more. It is gone forever.

THE sed (STREAM EDITOR) COMMAND

The stream editor is **sed**. It takes a file in from standard-in, edits it, and sends it to standard-out. It uses most of the same commands as the old **ed** text editor and the colon commands in **vi**. Occasionally you may need to edit a file with the **ed** editor, when you need to edit the file in place, or use some of the commands that only **ed** knows. But usually, **sed** will be the best in shell programming.

You can do so many things with **sed**. In the chapter on string processing (Chapter 17) we show how **sed** can find a string pattern and rewrite it.

```
$ sed 's/Rod/Marc/g' < textin > textout
```

The argument in single quotes (') tells **sed** to substitute every string of *Rod* with a new string of *Marc*. The *g* means to do the substitution globally on the line, not just the first occurrence of the first string. **sed** can delete all blank lines with:

```
$ cat textin
This is line 1
This is line 2
This is line 3

This is line 5
$ sed '/^$/d' < textin
This is line 1
This is line 2
This is line 3
This is line 5
```

The up-arrow character (∧) means the beginning of a line and the dollar sign *($)* means the end of a line. So this says that every line that has nothing between the beginning and the end, i.e., a blank line is to be deleted. Note that we need the single quotes to protect the special meta characters. We want those characters to go to **sed** and not to the shell.

We can display only the first two lines with:

```
$ sed 2q textin
This is line 1
This is line 2
```

Note that we have no special characters that would get the shell excited, so we don't need to quote the instruction. Also, **sed,** like several commands, will accept the input filename on its command line and open the file itself.

We can remove the first two lines with:

```
$ sed 1,2d textin
This is line 3

This is line 5
```

This says, from line one to line two delete. **sed** has many other tricks. It is important to know it well.

THE sort COMMAND

As you might have guessed, **sort,** sorts a file. It thinks of a file as a sequence of lines ending in newline characters. It also knows about fields within the line and can sort on the fields you choose.

```
$ ls −l ..
total 1268
−rw−rw−r−−   1 root    super    237255 Aug 21 22:48 Book
−rw−rw−r−−   1 root    super       245 Aug 21 21:31 Makefile
drwxrwxr−x   2 root    super       768 Aug 20 10:35 bin
drwxrwxr−x   6 root    super      1456 Aug 21 10:01 man
drwxrwxr−x   4 root    super      1104 Aug 22 08:34 tut
$ ls −l .. | sed 1d | sort −nr +4
−rw−rw−r−−   1 root    super    237255 Aug 21 22:48 Book
drwxrwxr−x   6 root    super      1456 Aug 21 10:01 man
drwxrwxr−x   4 root    super      1104 Aug 22 08:34 tut
drwxrwxr−x   2 root    super       768 Aug 20 10:35 bin
−rw−rw−r−−   1 root    super       245 Aug 21 21:31 Makefile
```

The first **ls** command shows us a long listing *(−l)* of the parent directory (..), which is the directory above the directory we are in. Then we pipe the output through **sed** to delete the *total* line. The **sort** command is told to do a numeric sort *(−n)* in reverse *(−r)* on the fourth column *(+4),* counting the first column as 0. The fourth column is the number of bytes in the file. So we have sorted the listing with the largest files on top. (There is an option to **ls** to do this.)

A string sort is different than a numeric sort. In this case it would not matter, because the numbers are right-justified. But if they were left-justified, there would be a difference. Let's look at a simple example.

```
$ cat numberfile
1
2
10
20
$ sort numberfile
1
10
2
20
```

sort seems to have unsorted the file. The *numberfile* is already in numeric sequence. 2 comes before 10, numerically. But the string 10 comes before the string 2, because the first character of each string is compared first. The 1 in 10 comes before the 2 in 2. The $-n$ option tells **sort** to see a field as a number instead of a string.

Normally **sort** uses blank and tab to delimit fields. But you can have it use other characters with the $-c$ option. With the $-m$ option **sort** will merge sorted files into one sorted file. If you have a file that is too large to sort, break it up (see the **split** command) and sort each smaller file and finally merge them all together.

You will use **sort** a lot. Several commands need a sorted file to do their thing correctly. We usually sort a file before sending it to **uniq.** A lot of clever algorithms and tricks need **sort.**

WARNING: *do not try to sort a file in place.* What is wrong with this?

```
$ sort < file > file
```

This is a very natural thing to do. You want to sort a file where it sits so that when you are through it will be sorted. *DO NOT DO IT!* It will not work, but much worse it will zero-out the file! Whatever was in the file will be lost.

```
$ ls  −l file
−rw−rw−r−−    1 root    super        0 Aug 22 09:25 file
```

The **ls** command with the $-l$ option shows us a lot about a file. The *0* right before the date *Aug* means that there are zero characters left in the file. Whatever was there before, has gone poof.

We want to explain what happened, because it helps you understand how the shell works. The $<$ *file* told the shell to open the file *file* for input. No problem so far. The $>$ *file* told the shell to open the same file for output. To do this the shell calls the **open(2)** UNIX system call with a write mode. This causes the system to zero-out the file, i.e., to set the byte count to zero in preparation for writing. Then the shell fires up the **sort** command which reads from standard-in and writes to standard-out. But the standard-in is now zero. So the first read statement gets an *end-of-file*. The **sort** command thinks, "Gee, that was easy. No characters." It quits without any complaint. You will not know that your file has been clobbered until you look at it or try to use it.

Here is the right way to do it:

```
$ sort < file > tmp
$ mv tmp file
```

Write the output to a temporary file and move the temporary file to the original filename.

Question: would this be ok?

```
$ sort < file | cmd1 | cmd2 | cmd3 > file
```

In other words, does passing a file through a pipe solve our problem? Can we then write the results back into the original file?

NO! It is essentially the same thing. The shell scans the entire line and opens the file twice in the same way described above.

THE tail COMMAND

The **tail** command throws away the beginning lines of a file and displays the rest. You can tell **tail** to start counting lines from the top of the file or from the bottom. **tail** *−3* shows the last three lines of a file and **tail** *+3* shows the third line to the end of the file.

The opposite of **tail** is **head,** a command that was implemented in the Berkeley enhancements. But the head function can be performed by **sed,** so it is not on any Bell UNIX Systems.

THE tee COMMAND

The **tee** command allows you to split your pipe stream, send characters from standard-in to standard-out and also to a file.

```
$ wc file | tee file.wc
    800    3548   18017 file
$ cat file.wc
    800    3548   18017 file
```

tee wrote its input to two directions. It wrote into the file named on its command line *file.wc,* and it also sent it to the standard-out which was displayed on our screen.

You can see what is going on in a pipe with the **tee** command. This is useful for debugging. When the output from a pipe is bad, the question is, what went wrong?

```
$ ls −l | grep total | wc −l
    2
```

We are counting the number of files that have the string *total* in them. But we think there should only be one. Where did the other come from? Let's use **tee** to peek into the pipe after the **grep** command.

```
$ ls −l | grep total | tee /dev/tty | wc −l
total 468
−rw−rw−r−−    1 root    super          38 Aug 20 10:21 total
    2
```

The file *dev/tty* is our terminal. This tells **tee** to copy the input to our terminal and to the pipe on the right. So we get to see what is in the pipe before it gets to **wc**. Now that we can see what is going on, we can see that we had forgotten about that silly little total line at the beginning of the **ls** output. It is being counted by the **wc** command. One fix is to put a **sed** command before the **grep** to delete the first line of the **ls** output.

THE wc (WORD COUNT) COMMAND

The word count program is **wc.** It counts lines, words and characters in a file. It can be used to test to see if a file is as big as it should be. Many programs in which we need the number of something can use **wc.**

With the −*l* command it will only give us a line count.

```
$ ls | wc −l
    66
```

Here is a quick way to find out how many files there are in the current directory. **ls** sends a list of all of the filenames on separate lines. **wc** counts the lines and displays them.

You can count the number of files that have a certain pattern in them like this:

```
$ grep −l UNIX *.mm | wc −l
    28
```

The −*l* option tells **grep** to only list the names of the files that match, not the whole lines. The **.mm* stands for all of the files ending with *.mm* which are our **nroff** −*mm* text files. We pipe this list of files to **wc** which only counts the lines. This tells us how many files have the word *UNIX* in them.

12

The Shell Monster

FILENAME SUBSTITUTION

The shell has a way of letting you type only one or a few characters to represent many files. You can use the star (*), or asterisk, character to represent any number of characters.

```
$ ls /bin/a*
/bin/adb
/bin/ar
/bin/as
. . .
```

The star after the letter *a* means that we want all files that start with the letter a, regardless of what follows. The star character can represent zero to many characters. It would match with a file named *a* and a file named *antidisestablishmentarianism*.

The shell sees the star special character and knows what it must do. It looks in the current directory for all filenames that match the pattern you have requested. In this case, filenames starting with the letter a. The shell then replaces the filename, including the star, that you wrote, with a list of the matching files. It then executes the command and hands it an argument list as if you had typed in all of the filenames.

Let us see what the shell does by using the **echo** command. **echo** shows us the result of the shell's work.

```
$ echo *.c
prog1.c main.c func.c
$
```

In this case *.c matches all files ending with a *.c.* These are usually C language source files. **echo** shows us that the shell replaced the string *.c with the string *prog1.c main.c func.c.* If **echo** had been another command, it would see the files in its argument list just as if you had typed them. Table 6 shows some more examples of the star meta character.

Table 6. File Substitution

Pattern	Will Match	Description
*	a file1 dir	All Files and Subdirectories
*.s	prog.s .s	All Files Ending With *.s (Assembler Files)
a*b	ab aabb axb	All Files That Start With a and End With b
.	. a.c .profile	All Files with a Dot in The Name
/bin/*	/bin/vi	All Files in The /bin Directory

? ANY ONE CHARACTER

If you only want to match a single character, use the question mark.

```
$ ls ?
A
f
```

Above, only filenames that have a single character are matched. Below all files ending with a dot and a single character are matched.

```
$ ls *.?
anova.f
main.c
prog.o
prog.s
```

[ ] LIST OF CHARACTERS

Instead of just any character, you may want to match only certain characters.

```
$ ls *.[cs]
main.c
prog.s
```

In this case we only want *C* and assembler programs which end in *.c* or *.s* respectively.

[−] RANGE OF CHARACTERS

If you have a long list of characters, it is easier to type a range.

```
$ ls [A-Z]*
A
Makefile
Words
```

Here we ask for all files that start with a capital letter.

These file substitution characters help save us typing and are used in other programs to match strings. This is called regular expression or pattern matching. You will see a lot of it in this book and in shell programming.

QUOTING AND REWRITING

So far we have seen several characters that make the shell do work for us. The greater-than character (>) got the shell to redirect our output. The pipe character (|) got the shell to set up a pipe for us. These characters with special meaning are called *meta* characters. We have seen < > | * ? [−] and so forth. And we are going to see more in this book. They are used throughout UNIX. The price we must pay for the power of these meta characters is that, when we want to use them as normal characters, we have to protect them from the shell.

There is an old saying that both fire and government are dangerous servants and fearful masters. The same can be true of the shell. It is a monster that can take the lines you write and change them. When it does what you want, it gives you great power. But, like summoning a demon from the nether world, if it gets out of control, it will destroy what you were trying to do. Fortunately, the shell is an honest monster. It has a set of rules that it obeys. If you learn its rules, you can control it.

Seeing What the Shell Does

To see what the shell is doing, we use the **echo** command and the **sh** −*x* command. They are also discussed in the chapter on debugging.

The Backslash (\ )

You can protect a single character with the backslash character.

```
$ echo > Message
```

In this command line the shell opens a file called *Message* and writes a single newline into it. This is fine if that is what you wanted. But suppose you wanted to echo the string > *Message*. You have to tell the shell to leave the right-arrow character (>) alone. You can use the backslash like this.

```
$ echo \> Message
> Message
```

Note that the shell now takes the right-arrow character as a normal character and allows **echo** to display it.

Also note that the backslash was removed by the shell. It will honor the backslash, but removes it. So **echo** only sees > *Message,* which it displays on the screen. This is what we want. Otherwise we would get \ > *Message* displayed. Once the quote character has done its work, we want the shell to strip it off. If we want a backslash in our text, we will have to write two of them. The first protects the second and the first is removed, leaving the one we wanted. The backslash is kind of ugly and it only works on one character. Some more quote characters follow.

The Single Quote (')

The single quote is your greatest shield against the shell monster. It protects **absolutely** the characters enclosed within.

```
$ echo 'ha ha, can not get me in here so I can use < > | ? *'
ha ha, can not get me in here so I can use < > | ? *
```

See what happened? The meta characters were safely passed on to **echo** and then to our screen. The shell monster is sulking at our making fun of it. But it is honest, and will not break its rules even when we tease it.

The Double Quote (")

The double quote is similar to the single quote, but will allow the shell monster to get in and do some substitutions. It allows the dollar ($) and the back quote (`) to be seen. The chapter on variable substitution and command substitution explains what these meta characters do.

Here, it is important to know that the double quotes are not as strong as the single quote, but sometimes it is what we need.

```
$ echo "$HOME"
/usr/rod
$ echo '$HOME'
$HOME
$ echo "`date`"
Sat Aug 24 21:58:11 EDT 1985
$ echo "date"
`date`
```

Note that with the double quote, the substitutions were done anyway. With the single quote, they were not done.

The rules for quoting are shown in Table 7. The letter *y* stands for yes, the character is recognized and acted upon by the shell. The letter *n* is for no, the character is ignored by the shell. A blank means the end of the string quoted by the quote character.

Table 7. Quote Character Protection

within	\	$	*	`	"	'
'	n	n	n	n	n	
"	y	y	n	y		n
`	y	n	n		n	n

Note in Table 7 that the single quotes protect every character. The double quotes allow the shell to act on the backslash, dollar, and star. The back-quote, command substitution, protects everything but the backslash.

The awk Command

Passing quoted strings to **awk** is an advanced example. **awk** also uses the double quote for strings and the dollar sign for variables. The problem arises when we need to mix these arguments on an **awk** program command line.

Backslash Quote (\ ")

The best technique is to use double quotes and backslash

```
$ VAR = 'Hello, there '
$ awk − F: "{ print \"$VAR\" \$1 }"/etc/passwd

Hello, there root
Hello, there bin
Hello, there guest
Hello, there marc
Hello, there rod
```

Here we use double quotes around the entire command so that it will be passed as one argument to the **awk** command and to protect the special characters. The double quotes around *$VAR* must get to **awk** so they must be protected. Finally, the dollar in *$1* is intended for **awk** so it must be protected.

Let's use **echo** to see what **awk** sees on its command line.

```
$ VAR = 'Hello, there '
$ echo − F: "{ print \"$VAR\" \$1 }" /etc/passwd
− F: { print "Hello, there " $1 } /etc/passwd
```

Good. That is what we wanted **awk** to see. We are asking that the string *Hello, there* be printed, followed by the first column of the input file. Since the field separation character in the */etc/passwd* file is a colon, we include the *−F* : option.

WINDOW

Some people have discovered another trick. You can create a little *window* in the program in which the shell can do variable substitution. But there is a big problem with this approach. If there is any white space, blank, tab, or newline in the substituted string, **awk** will fail. **awk** then has two string commands because the shell divides its arguments on the white space characters.

In this case there is a blank in *VAR*.

```
$ VAR = 'Hello, there '
$ awk − F: '{ print '$VAR' $1 }'
/etc/passwd
awk: syntax error near line 1
awk: illegal statement near line 1
```

Note that the single quote protection starts at the beginning of the command and then ends right before *$VAR*. Then it starts again and goes to the end. Thus *$VAR* is in a little window without single quote shell protection.

With a little shell script called **seeargs**, that we will show you later, we can see what **awk** saw.

```
$ VAR = 'Hello, there.'
$ seeargs − F: '{ print '"$VAR' "$1 }' /etc/passwd
− F:
{ print "Hello,
there. "$1 }
/etc/passwd
```

You can see that the **awk** program { print "Hello, there. "$1 } was divided into two different arguments because of the white space between *Hello,* and *there.* Therefore **awk** failed. So do not use the window technique unless you are certain that there is no white space in the strings that are being substituted.

MULTIPASS MULTIBACKSLASH

Sometimes the line you write is scanned by the shell and/or other programs more than once. Each time the monster reads your line, it honors the quote protectors, but takes them away. Then the next time the shell parser scans the line, the quotes are gone and the monster can have its way with your defenseless command line. To prevent such unspeakable acts, you need to know how to give your strings added protection for each bout with the shell.

Let's look at some examples first, and then derive the principles.

```
$ echo $1

$ echo \$1
$1
```

Here we want to say one dollar *($1)*, but the shell sees the dollar sign and substitutes its value for dollar one which is null. Therefore we get nothing instead of the string we wanted. The backslash in the second **echo** was honored, but removed.

In the foregoing example, the shell scans and rewrites the line once. In the following example, the monster gets two turns at the string.

```
$ echo `echo \$1`

$
```

The **echo** in back quotes (`) is executed first. It writes the dollar one on to the command line of the first **echo.** Then the shell parser gets its second turn at the string, rewriting it to null which comes out a blank line. We need reinforcements. First, lets add another backslash.

```
$ echo \\$1
\
$
```

What happened? Why didn't double protection work? The first backslash protected the second backslash. Since the second backslash was protected, it could not protect the dollar sign to its right. So the dollar sign was interpreted. The shell monster is chuckling and smacking its lips.

So lets try three backslashes.

```
$ echo \\\$1
\$1
$
```

Why did three work? The first protected the second and the third protected the dollar. Backslashes lose their lives protecting others in this nasty business. The first and third were removed for their efforts, leaving the second backslash to fight another day.

So here are the principles. You must use odd numbers of backslashes. The number of backslashes you need is a function of the number of passes the string must endure. Here is the function: *back slashes = (2 * passes) − 1.*

So one pass is one backslash, two passes are three, and four passes need seven backslashes. This gets out of hand quickly. Fortunately, you usually don't need too many passes.

POSITIONAL PARAMETERS

When you write a shell program you often want to pass data into the program from the command line. Within a shell program you can use *$1* for the first word on the command line, *$2* for the next word and so forth.

```
$ cat cmd
echo First word is $1 and the second word is $2
$ cmd Hi there
echo First word is Hi and the second word is there
```

Here we have a little program that prints out its first two arguments, i.e., the first two words on its command line. Note that when we run it with the words *Hi there,* it substitutes the *Hi* for *$1* and the *there* for *$2*.

```
$ cat print
pr $1 > /dev/lp
$ print file1
```

This **print** command will substitute the filename you give it, in this case *file1,* for the *$1* in the program. So inside the program the **pr** command line will look like this:

```
pr file1 > /dev/lp
```

Sometimes you want to refer to all of the words on the command line. You can do so with a special parameter dollar star ($*).

```
$ cat cmd
echo $*
$ cmd Hello there, you all.
Hello there, you all.
```

Note that the **cmd** command echoes all of the words on the command line.

THE shift COMMAND

The **shift** command is built into the shell rather than being a program called by the shell. It is discussed more in Chapter 17. The **shift** command can be used to shift over the arguments. It throws away the value of *$1* and assigns the value of *$2* to *$1*. Then it sets the value of *$2* to the old value of *$3*. And so forth to the end of the arguments.

```
$ cat cmd
echo The first word is $1
```

```
shift
echo The second word is $1
$ cmd Get Help
The first word is Get
The second word is Help
```

Note that we echoed a message using *$1* which at first is set to *Get*. Then we shifted the arguments over one and echoed the new value of *$1* which now is *Help*.

13

Shell Variables

The shell is a string-oriented computer language. This means that the variables are of type string. Most computer languages have several types. The C language has type *char* for a byte, *int* for integer, *float* for floating-point real number, etc. But the shell variables are only strings of ASCII characters.

Shell variables come into existence simply by assigning a string value to them. They are used by putting a dollar sign in front.

```
$ VAR = string
$ echo $VAR
string
```

Here we have assigned the string *string* to a variable named *VAR*. The shell saw the equal sign in the first word *VAR = string*. It knows that when it finds that equal sign it is not a command to be executed, but a variable assignment. The shell created a variable in its internal buffers. Then when it saw the *$VAR* the shell looked up the variable in its buffers, found the string value, and replaced *$VAR* with its value *string*. Finally, the shell executed the **echo** command which only saw *string* as an argument and echoed it to our screen.

There must not be any white space (space, tab, or newline) around the equal sign.

```
$ VAR = string
sh: VAR: not found
```

In this case, the shell thought we were trying to execute a command called *VAR*. It looked for it and could not find it. So it reported the error *sh: VAR: not found*. The assignment must be jammed together.

QUOTING VARIABLE ASSIGNMENTS

If you need to have white space in your string, you must quote it. This protects it from the shell.

```
$ GREETING = 'Hello, there.    I am your friendly computer.
> And you had better not forget it!'
$ echo $GREETING
Hello, there. I am your friendly computer. And you had better
not forget it!
```

Note that the single quote protected the whole string including the spaces and newline when we were entering them. When we hit newline, the shell knew we were not through, because we had started a single quote protected string, but had not typed the second single quote to end the string. So the shell gave us the secondary prompt > to say: *keep typing*.

But notice a couple of peculiarities in the string that the **echo** command displays. The newline has been replaced by a single space and the two spaces before *I* have been reduced to one space. Why do you think this happened? While you are thinking about it, look at this:

```
$ echo "$GREETING"
Hello, there.    I am your friendly computer.
And you had better not forget it!
```

When we put double quotes around *$GREETING* the newline and double space are preserved. Why? In both cases the shell sees the *$GREETING* and replaces it with the two line string. With double quotes around the new string, **echo** is given just one argument, the whole string, which it sends to our terminal. But in the first case, **echo** was given 14 arguments. Each word was an argument. The newline and double spaces are lost as the shell makes up the 14 word argument list. **echo** displays its arguments with only a single space between each, and has no idea that there were other white space characters in the list.

Thus to get the correct greeting, we have to quote the assignment string and then quote again when we use the variable to keep the shell from breaking the string into separate words and throwing away the white space character we wanted to keep. What if we had put single quotes around *$GREETING?*

```
$ echo '$GREETING'
$GREETING
```

Oops, we overdid it. Remember, the single quote protects absolutely so the shell ignores the dollar sign and does not rewrite the variable. The double quote protection is what we need here.

USING SHELL VARIABLES $VAR

You can use shell variables in many places. Wherever you would put the value of a variable, you can put the variable itself. The shell will rewrite the variable with the value when it sees the variable name following a dollar sign.

As a style recommendation, please capitalize your variable names. It makes it much easer to read your code, to find the variables in one or more source listings with the **grep** command, and will reduce the possibility that you will accidentally use a lowercase reserved word or command.

STANDARD VARIABLES

There are several shell variables which are created when you log in. These standard variables are needed by the shell to do its work. But, since they are variables, you can change them by reassigning another string to them. Several are discussed below. Not all UNIX systems have the same standard shell variables. They are presented below in the order of their most likely appearance on UNIX systems.

HOME—The *HOME* variable is set to the path of your home directory. Your home directory is the directory you are automatically put into when you log in. It is also the directory you go back to when you type the **cd** command without any arguments.

```
$ echo $HOME
/usr/rod
```

This says that my directory, named *rod,* is under the *usr* directory. You can always see the value of a variable with the **echo** command. So try typing *echo $HOME* on your terminal and see what your home directory is.

PATH—How does the shell find a command when you type it? There are thousands of files and hundreds of directories on the system. The shell could go all through the file system to find a command. Then each command would take over a minute to start. That does not sound like a wonderful idea. The shell could have a built-in idea of where commands are, but then all commands would have to be in the same place. Instead, the shell has a flexible way of handling the problem. The *PATH* variable holds a list of directories in which the shell must look for a command.

```
$ echo $PATH
/bin:/usr/bin:.
```

Note that the directories are separated by colons (:). In this case, when you type a command, the shell will first look for it in the */bin* directory, then the */usr/bin* directory, and finally in the current directory represented by a dot (.).

It is not unusual for it to be a long list of many directories. Each software system can have its own directory. You will probably create your own command directories for the programs you write. Be sure to put the full path names of your command directories into the *PATH* variable so that your commands can be found when you type them.

Here is an often used trick:

```
$ PATH = $PATH:$HOME/bin
$ echo $PATH
/bin:/usr/bin:.:/usr/rod/bin
```

We can assign *PATH* first its old value, plus the *bin* directory under our *HOME* directory. *$HOME* is expanded into the path to the home directory and the */bin* directory is added to it.

PS1—*PS1* stands for *prompt string one.* The prompt is the string of characters that the shell writes to the screen to say, Ok, what's the next command. It is usually the dollar sign ($) for the Bell shell and the percent sign (%) for the C shell. We use the *$* as the prompt in this book. But you can set it to anything you want.

```
$ echo $PS1
$
$ PS1 = 'Yes, your worship: '
Yes, your worship:
Yes, your worship: PS1 = '$ '
$
```

This is useful when you have not been getting enough respect. First we echoed the current value of *PS1* which was '$ '. Next we changed the command prompt to *Yes, your worship:* . Then, instead of the dollar prompt, we get the message. We hit the return key and got it again. Then we changed *PS1* back to '$ '. Note that the space is needed so that the cursor is not right up next to the dollar. To keep that space in, you need to quote the dollar space string. Since the double quote would allow the shell to act on the dollar, we must use the single quote or a backslash.

People usually change these prompts to personalize them or to remind themselves where they are. You might write a shell program that prompts for input. Having a different prompt might help you remember that you are talking to that program and not to the shell.

When you become super user (root), it is nice that the prompt reminds you. The super user prompt is usually set to the number sign (#).

PS2—You seldom see the second prompt string, *PS2*. It is displayed when there is a continuation of a command to more lines.

```
$ echo '
> '
```

Here we use a single quote to protect the newline. But the shell knows that there is more input because the closing single quote is missing. The shell issues the secondary prompt to say, "Ok, keep typing." *PS2* can also be changed when you want.

IFS—IFS holds a string of characters that are the interfield separators. These are the characters that the shell looks for to separate words. They are usually called *white space*. Normally, they are the space, tab, and newline characters. It is dangerous to change them, but you may need to for parsing. See the chapter on parsing (Chapter 17) for details and examples.

TERM—TERM holds the name of the terminal. It is not used by the shell. It is used by the **vi** editor and other programs that use the *curses* package of screen handling routines. It is used to look up the terminal in the */etc/termcap* file or the new */usr/lib/terminfo* directory.

*TERMCAP—*The */etc/termcap* entry for your terminal can be assigned to the *TERMCAP* variable. This saves the **vi** program the time of searching for the entry in the */etc/termcap* file.

TZ—TZ is the time zone variable. Set it for your local time. For example, *EST5EDT* means Eastern Standard Time, 5 hours west of Greenwich, modified by Eastern Daylight Savings Time.

LOGNAME—LOGNAME is your login account name.

*CDPATH—*This is the search path for the **cd** command. When you set it to a path of directories, you don't have to type the whole path name to change directories to them.

MAIL—MAIL is the directory that holds your mail files. This is used by the **mail** program.

THE set COMMAND

You can use the **set** command with no arguments to see all of your variables.

```
$ set
HOME=/usr/rod
IFS=

LOGNAME=rod
MAIL=/usr/mail/rod
```

PATH = :/bin:/usr/bin:/etc:/usr/rdb/bin:/usr/act/bin:/usr/rod/bin:

TERM = pc
TZ = EST5EDT

THE env COMMAND

There are really two lists of shell variables maintained by the shell, one local, one environment. The **set** command shows you the local variables. When you assign a variable it goes into this local list. You can see the environment variables with the **env** command. Environment variables are passed to all programs and subshells. Keeping these two lists separate allows you to change a variable in one shell without affecting the programs and subshells, unless you choose.

THE export COMMAND

You can export a variable to the second list, the environment, with the **export** command.

    $ export VAR

Note that in the **export** command you do not put a dollar sign in front of the variable, because the shell would convert it to its value and **export** would not get to see the name of the variable.

THE .profile FILE

Of course you don't want to have to retype variable assignments every time you log in. These you can put in a file called .profile in your home directory. They will be reset on every login. If you put them into the /etc/profile, they will be set for everyone on the system when they log in. Note that this global profile file, in the /etc directory, does not have the dot in front. When a dot is the first character of a file, the filename is hidden from such commands as **ls, rm,** etc.

VARIABLES SET BY THE SHELL

The shell automatically sets certain variables for you. You will be using them a lot in shell programming.

$* All parameters and $# Parameter Count

These first two automatic shell variables were discussed in Chapter 12 under positional parameters. You can refer to all of the command line arguments with the $* variable.

```
$ cat echoargs
echo $*
$ echoargs a b c
a b c
```

$# returns the number of arguments on your command line.

```
$ cat argcount
echo $#
$ argcount a b c
3
```

$? Return Status

When a program exits, it returns a number to the shell that indicates its exit status. Usually the value is zero for a successful return and some other number for an error or unusual condition. It can be used by the **if** and **test** commands. See the chapter on control flow statements (Chapter 14).

$$ Process-id

The process-id is useful in making unique filenames. We use it all the time in making temporary files for shell programs.

```
$ TMP = tmp$$
$ echo $TMP
tmp1488
```

Unique names are important because a shell program may be run by two users at the same time. If they both used the same filename, they would clobber each others' files.

The $ − Variable

This variable carries a list of the shell and **set** options that are current. See the section on shell options in Chapter 17.

$! Background id

If you want to kill the last background job you can use the **kill** command and $!.

```
$ kill $!
```

This saves you the bother of remembering or writing down the process-id of a job you put in background. In a shell program, it saves you from having to keep the process-id in a shell variable.

$@ All Parameters

$@* is the same as *$* except that when surrounded by double quotes, *$@* quotes each word instead of the whole line.

```
"$*" = "word1 word2"

"$@" = "word1" "word2"
```

You can see the difference in this example.

```
$ cat argcount
echo $#
$ set a b c
$ argcount $*
3
$ argcount "$*"
1
$ argcount $@
3
$ argcount "$@"
3
```

Can you follow this? The **argcount** program simply echoes the number of arguments it sees by using the *$#*. The **set** command makes *a, b,* and *c* positional arguments, so that we can use dollar star (*$**) and dollar at-sign *($@)*. When we ask **argcount** for the number of arguments it sees, with *$**, it reports three. With the quotes, however, it only sees one argument. In both the quoted and unquoted *$@* sign shell variable, all three arguments were seen separately. This feature is useful when you need to quote your arguments inside the shell program for protection of special characters.

DEFAULT PARAMETERS

Sometimes we want to give variables default values. The user, for example, could supply a value, but if he or she does not, there would be a normal or default value. This can all be done with the **if test** commands described in Chapter 14 on flow control. But sometimes you might want these shorter, but more cryptic facilities.

${VARIABLE}

First lets look at another way of writing variables. We have been using variables by putting a dollar sign in front of their names, i.e., *$HOME*. But sometimes we want letters after the variable name. To help the shell parser find the end of the variable name, put curly braces ({}) around the variable name, i.e., *${HOME}xyz*. *${VAR}* is just another way of writing *$VAR*.

${VARIABLE:-string}

Sometimes you use a shell variable and cannot be sure that it has been set yet. It could be set by the user from the command line, but it is optional. Or the code in a shell program, before the line you are writing, does not guarantee that the variable is set. You can supply a default value like this.

```
$ echo ${TERM:-dumb}
pc
```

In this example, we want to echo the value of *TERM,* but if *TERM* has not been set, we want the *dumb* terminal to be the default. In this case the *$TERM* had been set to *pc*.

${VARIABLE: = string}

When we use the equal sign (=), we will also set the *VARIABLE* to *string* if *VARIABLE* is not already set.

```
$ echo ${EDITOR: = vi}
vi
```

This code can be used in a shell program that needs to call an editor. If the variable *EDITOR* has been set in the environment of the user to the preferred editor, then it will be used. But if *EDITOR* is not set, it will be set to the **vi** program here.

${VARIABLE:?string}

This is different than the cases above. Sometimes you want to test a variable to see if it has been set. In this case, it is an error for it to not have a value. So if it does not have a value, you want to print an error message and exit the shell program. **WARNING:** Be careful trying this example, for when *PATH* is set to null, no UNIX programs will run, because the shell does not have a path to find them.

```
$ OLDPATH = $PATH
$ PATH =
$ echo ${PATH:?"Not set. Please set PATH."}
sh: PATH: Not set. Please set PATH.
$ PATH = $OLDPATH
```

Here we saved our old path and then set *PATH* to null. The **echo** command never got called because the shell found the error while scanning the command line, printed the message, and exited. Note that we had to quote our error message string, because it has spaces in it.

${VARIABLE: + string}

Finally, we might want to test a variable but use another string.

```
$ echo ${LOGNAME: + "Hello, $LOGNAME."}
Hello, rod.
```

In this example, we want to see if the variable *LOGNAME* is set and has a value. If so, we want to say hello. If not, we want to keep quiet.

If we had just echoed out the message without checking, we would get the following:

```
$ LOGNAME =
$ echo "Hello, $LOGNAME."
Hello, .
```

That looks pretty dumb.

COMMAND SUBSTITUTION

A very powerful trick is to be able to write the output of a command onto the command line. When it is too difficult to type some information on a command line, you can ask the shell to run a program, including piped commands, etc., and put the output in place of the command, on the command line. You are getting the shell to help you write shell programs.

To do this, we use a new ASCII character with several names. It looks like this (`), and is called *back quote* or *single back quote*. The French call it *accent grave* and they use it to change the accent of a syllable in a word from its standard emphasis. Here we will call it the *back quote* to distinguish it from the *single quote* (') and the *double quote* ("). We use it somewhat like the other quotes:

```
$ echo `date`
Fri Jul 26 11:04:20 MST 1985
```

Here, the shell first executed the **date** command within the back quotes. Then it wrote the results on the command line, just as if we had typed:

```
$ echo Fri Jul 26 11:04:20 MST 1985
Fri Jul 26 11:04:20 MST 1985
```

Then the shell executed the **echo** command, with its rewritten command line, and **echo** faithfully printed out its new command line. This is called *command substitution* because we can substitute the output of a command for the command itself. It gives us a powerful new way to input data into a program. Suppose we wanted a program that would send mail to everyone on the system. The problem is that the **mail** program wants a list of receivers on its command line:

```
$ mail rod marc < poisonpenletter
```

The **mail** command uses standard-in to get the message. We can use **sed** to get the list of users on the system from the **who** command.

```
$ who
madonna       tty3         Aug 10 04:53
marc          tty0         Aug 10 04:53
rod           console      Aug 10 04:53
$
$ who | sed 's/ .*//'
madonna
marc
rod
```

The **sed** command took every character starting with the first space and substituted nothing. It removed everything but the first column, which happens to be the names of users who are currently logged in. However, I am also getting my own name. There are tricks to remove it, but for now, I will just get the mail back to confirm that it was sent.

How do we get that column of names onto the command line of **mail?** We do this:

```
$ mail `who | sed 's/ .*//'` < loveletter
$
```

The **who** | **sed** pipe command is enclosed by the back quote ('). It tells the shell to execute the command within the back quotes and write the standard output of the command onto the line replacing all newline characters with spaces.

Let's use **echo** again to see what the shell does to the command line before **mail** sees it.

```
$ echo `who | sed 's/ .*//'`
madonna marc rod
```

echo faithfully reproduces its command line and shows us that the shell did in fact execute the pipe command and wrote the output as a list on the command line.

KEYWORD PARAMETERS

In addition to positional parameters you can also set variables to a value before calling a function.

VAR = val Command

```
$ cat cmd
: cmd sample shell programming command
USAGE = 'usage: cmd'

echo $A $B
$ cmd

$ A = 1 B = 2 cmd
1 2
$
```

Here we have our little **cmd** program echoing variable *A* and *B*. The variables are set on the command line just before the command. This will cause the variables to be set within the program.

This feature is seldom used, because it is more typing for the user, harder to document, and UNIX people are used to employing a flag to specify arguments with commands. But you might use it along with the variable substitution command to provide another method to control a program.

14

Control Flow

Now we get into program control flow. So far we have written shell scripts that execute top-to-bottom just one time. But often we need to repeat a set of instructions for a list of data or files. Or we need to test a condition and execute different code depending upon the result of the test. The commands discussed in this chapter are typical of many programming languages. In fact they are modeled closely on Algol, a language that influenced many modern languages like C, Pascal, BASIC, PL/I, etc. When Steven Bourne wrote the UNIX shell in the early 1970s, few would have imagined that C would become a dominant language. Bourne also chose Algol as his model language. Some of these control statements may look odd to us today, but don't worry, it will quickly become natural to you. Trust us.

if *list* then *list* elif *list* else *list* fi

The **if** command executes a list of commands and, if they all return zero status, e.g., success, it will execute another list of commands. The syntax is **if. . .then. . .else. . .fi,** where **fi** finishes the **if** statement.

```
$ if grep '∧joe:' /etc/passwd > /dev/null
> then
>               echo "joe is in the password file"
> fi
$
```

In this example, the command **grep** is executed to look for the name *joe* as the first field in the password file. We don't want to see the output of **grep.** We just want to check its status code. So we send its output to */dev/null,* a special device that throws characters away. At the end of the day, you can sweep them up from behind the computer.

When **grep** cannot find a match of its pattern in the file, it returns a status code of 1.

```
$ grep '∧joe:' /etc/passwd > /dev/null
$ echo $?
1
```

if considers a nonzero status code a failure and does not execute the **echo.** But if the match is made, **grep** returns a 0 and the **echo** is executed. Since we did not get a message, **grep** must have failed.

Note that the shell knows about **if** statements and gives us the secondary prompt (>) until we enter the **fi** to finish the **if** command. By the way, **fi** is **if** spelled backwards.

Most of the time **if** executes the **test** command to compare variables or check to see if a file exists and can be read, etc.

```
$ if test −r file1
> then
> cat file1
> fi
$
```

In this case the **test** command was run to see if a file named *file1* existed and was readable. If it succeeds, the file will be *cated out,* otherwise not. There must not be a *file1,* because we received no output.

By the way, how do you like these new verbs like "cated out"? Sounds like you went out last night and had a good time. But we shudder to think of what happened if you "greped"!

Sometimes you have more conditions to test. So there is an "else if" statement that is written **elif.**

```
$ if test −r file1
> then
>            cat file1
> elif test −r file2
>            cat file2
> fi
$
```

In this case we should get *file1* if it exists and is readable, or *file2* if it exists and is readable, or nothing. We received nothing, so they both must be missing or unreadable.

Finally, we also have the **else** statement which will execute its list of programs if the tests above it fail.

```
$ if test −r file1
> then
>            cat file1
> elif test −r file2
>            cat file2
```

```
> else
>                          echo "Where are the damned files?"
> fi
$
```

So if the **if** and **elif** fail, we will get a message.

while *list* do *list* done

while will keep executing two lists of commands until the first list fails.

```
$ cat echoreply
: echoreply—just echos what the user types in
while read REPLY
do
   echo $REPLY
done
$ echoreply
Hi
Hi
You sure are dumb!
You sure are dumb!
Is there an echo here?
Is there an echo here?
∧d
```

The **read** command fails when it gets the *control-d* end-of-file character.
   The **until** command is just like **while** except it continues as long as the list *fails*.

```
$ cat greeting
: greeting sends a message to marc when he signs on
until who | grep '∧marc ' > /dev/null
do
   sleep 60
done
echo "Hi, Marc" > /dev/tty3
```

We assume that Marc's terminal is plugged into */dev/tty3*.

for *VAR* in *word* . . . do *list* done

The **for** statement is unusual in that it steps through words in a list instead of incrementing numbers like most languages.

```
$ for I in *
> do
>                              sort < $I > tmp
>                              mv tmp $I
> done
```

This is a useful command. It will sort each of the files in the current directory. The variable *I* is set to each filename which is generated by the star (*). Then each time through the loop that file will be sorted into a temporary file and the temporary file moved back to the original file. There are several UNIX commands that can only work on more than one file by being called in a loop like this.

The **for** command is also good for stepping through the arguments to a shell program. In fact **for I** is the same as **for I in $*** in that they both walk through the positional arguments ($1, $2 . . .) of the program they are in.

```
$ cat multi
: multi—will perform a command on all files listed
USAGE = 'usage: multi command file . . .'
COMMAND = $1
shift
for FILE in $*
do
   eval $COMMAND < $FILE > tmp
   mv tmp $FILE
done
$
$ multi sort *
```

This **multi** program will do the same as the loop above, but saves the work of typing the whole loop.

Note the use of the **eval** command. It is explained in the chapter on built-in commands. It is used here in case there are any meta characters in the command.

case *word* in *pattern) list*;; . . . esac

The **case** statement not only allows the normal multibranching, but is a superpowerful pattern matcher. It is better than C or other languages for letting you test on strings. The C programming language **switch** statement only handles integer numbers and single characters. This power to branch on string patterns, alone, makes the shell the language of choice for programs that must handle strings. Also the **case** statement is built into the shell, so it is very fast.

Here is a big example of a **case** statement that is used to parse the arguments on a command line. It shows the different kinds of patterns that we can match on. The syntax of the command is on the line after *USAGE*. Your job is to match the syntax to the case patterns and actions.

```
$ cat parseargs
: parseargs—is an example of handling command line arguments

USAGE = 'usage: parseargs [ -a -b file -c -d ] reqarg [ file ... ]'
EUSAGE = 1

while test -n $1
do
   case $1 in
   -a)            OPTA = true ;;
   -b)            shift ; BFILE = $1 ;;
   -c|-d)         OPTCD = true ;;
   -*)            echo Option $1 unknown. 1 > &2
                  echo $USAGE 1 > &2
                  exit $EUSAGE
                  ;;
   *.c)           SOURCE = "$SOURCE $1" ;;
   [A-Z]*)        CAPFILE = "$CAPFILE $1" ;;
   esac

   shift
done
```

Here are some hints. The options in square brackets are optional, so we need the **case** statement. Various shell variables are set when certain options are seen. Following are more details.

Pattern Literal String

These patterns are also called regular expressions. The simplest pattern is a literal string. In the foregoing example, the *-a* and *-b* are literal strings to be matched.

Pattern or |—The *or* character (|) means the first pattern or the second pattern. The pattern *-c|-d* means *-c* or *-d* is a match.

Pattern Wildcard *—The star (*) means any number of any character. The *-** pattern above will match any argument that begins with a minus. In this case, since the legitimate options were already tested for, this must not be legitimate. So an error message is printed and the program exits. The last pattern of only *a* * will match anything. It catches all patterns not matched before. It is the default pattern and action.

Pattern [characters]—We can specify a list of characters that can match a single character in the string with the square brackets ([]).

Pattern [range]—We can also save ourselves the bother of typing long lists by using the minus to create a range. So *[A-Z]* means the list of characters from A to Z.

Note the ugly double semicolons to separate the different patterns and actions from each other. They are required. Also note the funny **esac** which is **case** spelled backward. More groans. It is the end of the **case** statement.

Break Out or Continue

If you want to break out of a **for, while,** or **until** loop, you can use **break.**

Also, **continue** is like **break,** but instead of leaving the loop, jumps over the rest of the statements in the loop and goes on to the beginning of the loop. From these sections you can see that the following names are reserved:

if then else elif fi case esac for while until do done {}

So don't use them as the names of the programs you write!

15

Shell Built-in Commands

These commands are built into the shell. Which means that the shell executes its own code when it sees them, rather than calling UNIX or other programs. This is sometimes for speed and sometimes because only the shell has the information needed to execute the command. Some built-in commands control the shell itself.

COMMENT COMMANDS

Comments should be the simplest feature of a language. Unfortunately, things are a bit complicated with the shell comments (plural). That is right, there are two of them.

The colon (:) is the old comment symbol. In the early days of the shell (mid 70s version 6) there was a . . . **goto** statement. This obscenity was expunged, but it had a **label** command that went with it. It looked like this:

    label: goto label

This example is a very efficient way to be very inefficient. It will loop forever. The zero'th principle of structured programming is to burn **goto** and **label** statements at the stake.

Colon (:) Comment Statement

However, the colon (:) was left behind as a do-nothing command. It became a comment statement, with a strange side effect. The shell actually scans and parses the line. It even opens any files indicated! Watch this folks:

```
$ echo This is file1 > file1
$ cat file1
This is file1
$ : this is a comment about > file1
```

```
$ cat file1
$
```

A message is written into a file and the file is cated out to see that the message is there. Then there is a harmless little comment and we cat out the file again . . . hey, what happened to *file1?* It is now empty!

That harmless comment, when scanned by the shell, caused *file1* to be opened for output, which zeroed out its contents. We can hear your screams of outrage. A comment that kills your data? Before you get too upset, let us say that there is a simple fix. Use the single quote to force the shell to ignore the contents of the comment.

```
$ : 'This comment is safe because it is quoted'
```

Oh, but that is so ugly. By the way, there must be a space after the colon, or the shell will think it is one big command.

```
$ :'This comment is safe because it is quoted'
sh: :This comment is safe because it is quoted: not found
```

What a mess.

Number or Hash Sign (#)

More recent UNIX systems use the number, or hash, sign (#), or pound sign on European terminals, for the comment. This is much better because the shell correctly ignores whatever special characters are used in the comment. It would seem that we could just switch over to the number-sign character. Many of you will and should. But there are some reasons to use the colon. One is porting back to older UNIX systems. Some older UNIX systems do not accept the new number-sign comment. The other is the C shell.

C shell Complication

The C shell adopted the number sign as its comment character. It also uses it to execute the program under the C shell, and not the Bell Shell that is also available in Berkeley UNIX. This is a good convention, but forces us to be careful that we do not use the number-sign character as the first character in a Bell shell file, if the program is run by someone under the C shell. We recommend you use a colon as the first character.

Finally, when debugging, the **sh** -*x* trace command will print comments if they start with a colon but not if they start with a number sign. So, if you want to see the comments with your trace, use the colon comment character, otherwise use the hash sign.

We have used the colon as the preferred comment character because it is compatible with older UNIX shells. If you don't have to run your shell programs on older UNIX programs you can use the number or hash symbol (#). Now that you know the whole story, do as you think best.

```
$ : this is a comment
$ : 'this is a comment that is protected'
$ # this is the new comment
```

The break [n] and continue [n] Commands

Sometimes one thinks they need to break out of a **while, until,** or **for** loop. Often, with more thought there is a cleaner way to write the loop, so that the **break** is unnecessary. But when you need it, you can jump out of the loop and go to the code beyond the **done.** You can even jump out of several nested loops by giving a number.

```
$ while :
> do
>           until false
>           do
>           if true
>           then
>                   break 2
>           fi
>           done
>                   echo loop 1
> done
> echo loop 2
loop 2
$
```

Here we have two loops and an **if** statement. Note that the colon (:) and the **true** command always returns a status code of 0 and **false** returns a status code of 255. The **if** statement is not a loop and does not count. If it had, we would have gotten lots of *loop 1* output lines. But the **break 2** took us all the way to the **echo** *loop 2* statement which is all that printed out.

The **continue** command is just like break except you go back to the top of the loop and skip over whatever instructions are left in the loop.

Changing Directories

The **cd** command allows you to change directories. Actually, all that happens is that the shell keeps track of the current directory in an internal buffer and uses it in all relative addressing. But, it is best for us humans to imagine that we are *moving* about the file system. The original name for this command was **chdir,** but people must type it so often that it was shortened to **cd.** New users complain that UNIX commands are too short and cryptic. Frequent users appreciate minimum keystrokes.

The eval Command

The **eval** [*arg* . . .] command allows you to handle a special problem. Sometimes you need the shell to scan and rewrite the line more than once. Suppose you have a substitution that contains another substitution. **eval** will cause a second scan.

```
$ CMD = 'echo $HOME'
$ $CMD
$HOME
$ eval $CMD
/usr/rod
```

Note that the first time the shell scanned *$CMD* and rewrote it as **echo** *$HOME*. **echo** displayed *$HOME* because the shell did not rescan and rewrite the *HOME* variable with its value. But with the **eval** command the *$HOME* variable is rewritten with its value.

The **exec** command has two functions. One allows you to do what is called *chaining*. You can execute another program in place of the current program. The current program is killed in the process. You cannot return to the current program. The UNIX kernel saves a slot in its process table, by replacing the current program with the executed program. The other function is file redirection. You can use the **exec** command to open files and redirect I/O. within the program. The files *standard-in* (0), *standard-out* (1), and *standard-error* (2) are not always enough.

```
$ cat showexec
: showexec

exec 3< file1
cat <&3
$ showexec
Line 1 file1
```

Here we opened a file for input and assigned it to file number 3. Then we read from file number 3 with *<&3*.

Reading a File

The problem with the **read** command is that it can only read from the standard-in (0). But we can get it to read another file with the **exec** command.

```
$ cat execread
: execread—demo exec and read commands

exec 3< file1
exec 0<&3
read LINE
echo $LINE
$ execread
Line 1 file1
```

Here we open the file *file1* as file number 3 as before. But then we equate file number 3 to file number 0. Then when the **read** command reads from file number 0, it gets number 3. **read** assigns a whole line to the variable *LINE*. Finally **echo** displays what the **read** command got. In this way you can open files and read from them just as most computer languages allow you to do.

The exit Command

You can leave a program immediately with the **exit** command. With a number, *n,* you can set the return status ($?) variable.

```
$ cat exiterror
: exiterror—exit with a status code of 1
exit 1
$ exiterror
$ echo $?
1
```

The export Command

There are two lists of variables kept by the shell. A local list that can be displayed with the **set** command and an environment list that can be displayed by the **env** command.

```
$ A = showexport
$ set
A = showexport
HOME = /usr/rod
$ env
HOME = /usr/rod
$ export A
$ env
A = showexport
HOME = /usr/rod
```

Note that the variable *A* did not get to the environment list until it was exported.

The newgrp [arg . . .] Command

This command allows you to change to another group. UNIX protects files and directories at the owner, group, and system level. Group gives an intermediate protection. It lets several people access a file without making it available to everyone.

```
$ newgrp topsecurity
```

The read [name . . .] and readonly [name . . .] Commands

This **read** command is for reading the next line from the standard-in (0). **read** assigns what it reads to the variable name that follows it.

```
$ cat sayhello
: sayhello
echo Who are you?
read ANSWER
echo Hello, $ANSWER.
$
$ sayhello
Who are you?
Rod and Marc
Hello, Rod and Marc.
$
```

In this **sayhello** program we prompt with an **echo** command, then read from the standard-in. Whatever the user types is assigned to *ANSWER*. Then we use the *ANSWER* variable.

If you give the **read** command more than one variable, it will assign the first word to the first variable, the second word to the second variable, and all remaining words to the last variable.

```
$ cat intro
: intro

echo Please enter your first and last name:
read FIRST LAST
echo Hello, $LAST. May I call you $FIRST.
$
$ intro
Please enter your first and last name:
Rod Manis
Hello, Manis. May I call you Rod.
$
```

Sometimes you want to assign a value to a variable and not let it be changed by subsequent commands. For this you use the **readonly** command.

```
$ PARM = important
$ readonly PARM
$ readonly
readonly PARM
$ PARM = unimportant
sh: PARM: is read only
```

When we type **readonly** without arguments we get a list of variables that have been previously marked. We also get an error when we try to reassign the protected variable.

The set [—ekntuvx [arg . . .]] Command

The **set** command has several uses. Kernighan and Pike correctly call it overworked.

List Local Variables—If you type the **set** command with no arguments or option, you get a list of your local variables.

```
$ set
HOME = /usr/rod
IFS =

LOGNAME = rod
MAIL = /usr/mail/rod
PATH = :/bin:/usr/bin:
TERM = pc
TZ = EST5EDT
```

This is a nice fast way to see how the shell sees you.

Parse String—If you have a string following **set,** then **set** will assign the first word to the positional parameter $1, the second word to $2, and so on. You can then use them.

```
$ date
Mon Aug 19 22:46:46 EDT 1985
$ set `date`
$ echo $2 $3, $6
Aug 19, 1985
```

We picked out the second, third, and sixth words to make another date format from the date line. The back quotes after the **set** command execute the **date** command and write the date line on the line before **set** sees it. Then **set** assigns each word to positional variables. Finally, the **echo** command displays them.

Change Shell Options—Within a shell program you can change an option. This is usually done for debugging. When you run a shell program you can set the *-x* option to see all of the statements after scanning and rewriting but before execution. But on a long program, you may only want to see a few lines. You can turn the *-x* option on before the lines, and off after. The other options are discussed in the chapter on shell options (Chapter 17).

The shift Command

We can walk through a list of positional variables (*$1, $2,* etc.) with the **shift** command.

```
$ cat seeargs
: seeargs—displays its arguments on separate lines
USAGE = 'seeargs arg1 arg2 ...'
while test -n "$1"
do
```

```
        echo $1
        shift
done
$ seeargs we are arguments
we
are
arguments
```

We keep listing out *$1,* but after each **shift** command the arguments shift to the left. So *$1* comes to equal each of the arguments in turn.

The test Command

The **test** command used to be a separate UNIX program, but in System V UNIX it was built into the shell for speed. It is usually used with the **if, while,** and **until** statements to test some condition. It can test file conditions, strings, and numbers.

```
$ if test "$#" -eq 0
> then
> echo "We ain't got no arguments."
> fi
We ain't got no arguments.
```

The time Command

The UNIX **time** command displays the read, user, and system time of a single command or pipe. If you want total times, use **times.**

```
$ times
13m42s 6m3s
```

This shows, in a smashed format, the user and system times of all of the subprocesses of the current shell.

The trap [arg] [n] Command

The **trap** [*arg*] [*n*] command allows us to catch interrupts. We can then execute some instructions. Finally we can exit the program or return to what we were doing. In the style chapter we show a standard shell program skeleton. There the **trap** command removes temporary files if the program is interrupted.

```
$ trap "rm -f /usr/tmp/$$*" 0 1 2 3 15
```

This is rather complicated, so let's go through it step by step. First, the **trap** command has three parts: the command name, a list of commands separated by semicolons (;) and enclosed in double quotes, and finally a list of interrupt signal numbers.

The argument is the line of commands that are executed whenever the program gets one of the interrupt signals listed in the last part.

```
"rm -f /usr/tmp/$$*"
```

First we remove all of the temporary files we may have created in the */usr/ tmp* directory. The **rm** remove command with the *-f* option means to remove the files if they are there, but not to complain if there are no files to remove. */usr/tmp* is the preferred directory to use as a temporary directory according to the System V Interface Standards from AT&T.

We have listed four signals to catch.

0	normal exit
1	hangup
2	interrupt
3	quit
15	software termination signal

When any of these occur, including normal exit, we will remove the temporary files.

There is nothing sacred about this list, you can create your own. The idea is to catch the more *normal* interrupts and remove the temporary files. But for the more extreme signals, to leave the files for possible help in debugging. See the **signal(2)** UNIX system call for a complete list of signals.

The umask [*nnn*] Command

The **umask** command [*nnn*] allows you to set the default permissions when files are created. You can enforce a policy of openness or closedness. If you really need security, use:

```
$ umask 777
```

With this setting all permissions are turned off when a file is created. Even the owner cannot read or write the file without running the **chmod** command. Such a policy is a terrible nuisance when you have work to do. So if you don't need security, set the mask to 0.

The wait Command

The **wait** command lets you wait for background processes to complete before continuing. You can run a large job in the background, do some other processing, then wait till the background job is finished before executing code that needs the output of the background process.

```
$ bigjob > file1 &
$ littleprog
$ wait
$ useoutput < file1
```

16

More Shell Meta Characters

BACKGROUND OR BATCH PROCESSING

With a single ampersand character (&) you can make a command list run in the background, also called batch processing.

```
$ nroff bigfile > bigfile.out &
1345
$
```

The ampersand (&) at the end of a command will cause it to be run independently of your terminal. The process-id number (1345) of the process is returned. Then you get a prompt because the shell is ready for you to type more commands. This is the big advantage of running processes in the background. It frees up the terminal for other work. **nroff** is a utility for formatting text files that are relatively large which you might not want to wait for.

Killing Background Processes

You can use the number returned to kill the background process.

```
$ kill 1345
1345 Terminated
```

You can also use the special character *$!*.

```
$ kill $!
1345 Terminated
$
```

You can use the process status command to see what is running.

```
$ ps
ps
```

```
PID   TTY        TIME   COMMAND
1203  console    0:00   sh
1345  console    0:59   nroff bigfile
1604  console    0:00   ps
```

The number under the *PID* column is the process-id number to use to kill the process.

If the process resists your efforts to kill it, use the -9 option.

```
$ kill –9 1345
1345 Terminated
```

-9 is an uncatchable interrupt. It terminates with extreme prejudice.

SUBSHELLS

Sometimes you may want to run a subshell. For example, you may want to change to a directory, do some work and then come back to your current directory.

```
$ pwd
/usr/rod
$ (cd /etc ; ls –l termcap)
–rw–r--r--   1 bin      bin      10215  Aug 10 08:43 termcap
$ pwd
/usr/rod
```

First we checked to see where we were with the **pwd,** *present working directory,* command. Then we changed directories and executed a command. Afterward we found that we were still in the original directory. Why were we not left in the */etc* directory? Because the parentheses around the command ran the command list in another shell. The present working directory of that *other* shell changed, but not the one of the shell we are in. Therefore, when the other shell exited and died, we were then talking to our original shell which had not changed directories.

You can also use this trick to change shell variables in a subshell without affecting the shell variable of this shell.

```
$ ( VAR = string ; echo $VAR )
string
$ echo $VAR
$
```

In the first line we created and assigned a variable and echoed it out in a subshell. But the parent shell knows nothing about the variable.

Inserting Data in a Stream

Another useful trick that can be done with subshells is to insert data into a stream. This gives us multiple input to a pipeline.

```
$ cat table | (cat Head ; echo — ; cat ) | pr
```

First the **cat** command sends a table through the pipe. The subshell within parentheses executes three commands in turn. First it cats the file *Head*. Then it echos the dash lines. Finally it calls **cat** which reads from standard-in, the pipe on the left, and writes to standard-out, the pipe to the right. The **pr** print command sees the contents of the *Head* file first, followed by the dash line, followed by the table. The **pr** command then puts out its input in a nice page format ready for a line printer.

Input Into the Shell With Dot (.)

The opposite of creating a subshell is to read a file into the current shell. A common use of this trick is to read in the *.profile* file. If you have just modified it and do not want to log out and log back in, you can just type:

```
$ . .profile
```

This will change variables in the current shell.

And Or

You can execute a command or command list and, depending whether it executes successfully, execute another command list. This can be done in two ways. One way is with the **if** and other control statements. Here is another way.

And &&

If you place the double ampersand (&&), *and,* between two command lists, the second list will only be executed if the first succeeds.

```
$ ls file1 && cat file1
file1 not found
$ ls file1
file1 not found
$ cat file1
cat: cannot open file1
```

Since the **ls** command failed to find the file *file1* the **cat** command was not executed. To prove to ourselves that we were getting the error message from the first command and not the second, we ran each of them separately.

Or ||

Or (||) is the same as *and* (&&) except that the second command list will only be executed if the first *fails*.

```
$ cat file1 || cat data/file1
cat: cannot open file1
This is from file1
```

The first **cat** command failed to find the file, but the second one was successful and displayed the single line from *data/file1*.

CHAPTER

17

Shell Options, Inputting Data, and Parsing

The shell, like many UNIX programs, has command line options, also called *flags*. These options change the way the shell operates. Some of them you will seldom, if ever, use. Others, like -x, you will use all of the time. Some of the options can also be turned on within a shell script, with the **set** command.

COMMAND LINE ONLY

If you put a filename on the command line, the shell will take its instructions from it.

```
$ echo who > file
$ sh file
rod           console     Aug 21 10:07
```

This is like executing a shell program, except we explicitly execute a shell to do it. There are two differences. One, we do not have to make the file executable. Readable is good enough. Two, the *PATH* variable is not consulted. So unless you give the exact path to this file, the shell will not be able to find it. The shell treats it as a file, not a command.

With the -c option you can specify the input on the command line.

```
$ sh –c 'set `date` ; echo $6 $2 $3'
1985 Aug 21
```

This is a trick to use the **set** command to parse a string in a subshell without affecting the positional variable (*$1, $2,* etc.) of the current (parent) shell. Note that we used a single quote so that the *$6, $2,* and *$3* would not get substituted from the current shell, but would be substituted by the subshell after the **date** command.

The -s option will do three things:

1. Cause the arguments to be assigned to the positional variables.
2. Take input from standard-in, and
3. Send shell messages to standard-error.

```
$ sh -s a b < file
```

The *-i* option makes the shell interactive, which outputs the prompt. This is the kind of shell you are typing to on your terminal.

The *-r* option makes the shell restrictive. You may want to do this when setting up inexperienced users or data entry operators who are not supposed to roam about the system. You can put this in the *.profile* file in their home directories. Then when the operator signs on, they are restricted to their directory and perhaps to a single entry program. This increases security on the system and protects against inadvertent errors.

COMMAND LINE AND SET COMMAND OPTIONS

The following options can be used on both the shell command line and within the shell program with the **set** command. These options are turned *on* with a *minus* and *off* with a *plus*. So *-x* turns on the execution trace and *+x* turns it back off. You may sprinkle this through your shell program with the **set** command, to see what is going on.

The *-e* option makes the following lines very sensitive to error. If one command fails, the shell exits. This is useful when you do not want to keep going if there is an error. You might also use it in debugging to stop on each bug and let you try to isolate and fix it before continuing. It will also stop further processing of the files that you might want to see before they are modified.

The *-k* command will put all of the keywords into the environment for a command, not just the keywords that precede the command.

```
$ A = x cmd B = y
```

In this case the keyword-value pair $A = x$ would be passed to **cmd** in the environment. Ordinarily the keyword-value pair $B = y$ would not be passed as a keyword, but as a positional parameter. But with the *-k* option, it would be passed to the environment along with variable A.

The *-n* is another debugging aid. With this option the shell will scan the command lines and do substitutions, but will not execute the programs. If the program is big, or its effects are hard to reverse, this will let you debug its command lines before you let it run on real data.

The *-t* option says to exit after executing the next command. Again, for debugging, you can stop after one command and check to see what is going on. This is like single-stepping with an on-line debugger. If you don't know what that is, you are lucky. It comes from our painful past and will not be needed with languages like the shell.

The -*u* option is used for more debugging and safety. Usually, if a variable is not set, a variable substitution will simply substitute nothing, which causes some commands to fail strangely and perhaps dangerously. They might destroy a file. This option catches such errors and exits.

The option -*v* stands for verbose. This causes each command line to be displayed before substitution. It lets you watch your program, or a few lines, run.

The -*x* option is the biggy of debugging discussed in the chapter on debugging. It displays each line *after* the shell has done all of its rewriting (file, variable, and command substitutions).

The − − *(double minus)* option is used to protect an argument that is not an option that begins with minus (−). The double minus means the end of the option list. If a subsequent argument starts with a minus, it is not an option but an argument like a filename. Even so, avoid leading minuses in filenames.

INPUTTING DATA

There are several ways to input data into a command. We are discussing them together in this chapter to help you remember them when you are programming. Sometimes you need to get data into a command in an unusual way. For example, a command that produces the data writes to standard-out, but the command that needs the data gets it from its command line. How can we write the standard-out to a command line? For the answer, see *Command Substitution* later. You need to know that, on UNIX, you can always get data from anywhere and send it to anywhere. If you forget, you will get stuck.

No Input

Just for completeness, we should mention that several commands do not require input, at least from the user. The **pwd** command finds out the *present working directory* from the shell. **ls** gets a list of the current directory from the directory file. The **date** command gets the date and time from clock system calls. These are the trivial or zeroth data input situations. You might also write a C or other language program that gets data from the system.

File Direct

Another way to input data is for a command to read a predefined file. Some of your shell programs can do this. The most usual case is the temporary files that you write and then read.

Command Line

Many programs get data from their command lines. With the positional parameters (*$1, $2,* etc.) you can access the arguments that were typed on the command line by the user or the calling program.

```
$ cmd file
```

File In and Pipe

A program can also read from a file that was directed into the program by the caller and opened by the shell. The program just reads from standard-in.

```
$ cmd < file
```

A program can get data from a pipe also by reading from standard-in.

```
$ cmd1 < file | cmd
```

Here Files

A program can read data from the shell file that calls it. It still reads from standard-in.

```
$ cmd <<EOF
here comes the data
and more data
EOF
```

Interactive

You can just type the name of a command that reads its input from standard-in. It will read in each character you type till you type the end-of-file character, control-d.

```
$ cmd
type in data
and more data
^d
$
```

mail is a good example of this:

```
$ mail marc
Let's meet for lunch.
^d
$
```

The file that is sent to marc is the lines after the **mail** command and before the ∧d.

Sometimes when a program hangs and nothing is happening, try the control-d. It could be reading from standard-in, your keyboard, and it will wait forever for an end-of-file character.

Command Substitution

Remember our problem of how to write standard-output of one file to the command line of another? Here is how. Command substitution will write the output of a command in place of the command itself.

```
$ cmd1 `cmd2`
```

Here **cmd2** will be executed and the output will be written on the command line in place of `cmd2.`

See the section on *Command Substitution* in Chapter 13 for examples.

In summary you can stick data into a command every way you will ever need to. And don't you forget it.

STRING CONVERSION

One of the most frequent things we do in programming is to transform one string into another. UNIX has a wonderful set of tools for doing this job. We bring many of these tools together here in this section. Seeing them here together should help you when you have strings to transform. There is almost always a UNIX command, or a pipe of them that can do what you need.

No Conversion

To start with the simplest case, **echo** and **cat** are the zero-level string converters, in that they do not convert at all. We include them here, just for completeness.

Single Character Conversions

The converter **tr** will convert one character to another. You give it two strings of characters. **tr** will convert the first character of the first string into the first character in the second string when it finds the character in the input character stream. And so forth.

```
$ tr '[A-Z]' '[a-z]' < FILE > file
```

This will convert all uppercase letters in *FILE* into lowercase letters, and put them into *file*.

113

dd for ASCII to IBM and Byte Swap

The UNIX **dd** program is usually used for reading tapes, but it can process any file or stream of characters in a pipe. It can convert ASCII to and from IBM code, convert uppercase characters to or from lowercase, insert new lines at the end of fixed-length records, swap bytes for the DEC VAX computers, deblock and reblock data, etc.

Strings and Regular Expressions

A regular expression is a short way of writing a string. We can give regular expressions to many UNIX programs. They will scan for a string of characters that matches the regular expression. Then they will act depending upon the program.

There are two systems of regular expressions in UNIX (Table 8). One comes from the old **ed** text editor. The other comes from file substitution.

Table 8. Regular Expression Meta Characters

ed	file	Meaning
a	a	Literal Character Means Itself
*	.*	Any Number of Any Character
?	.	Any Character Matches One Character
[ ]	[ ]	List of Characters That Match One Character
[-]	[-]	Range of Characters That Match One Character
^		Beginning of Line–File Must Match Whole Word
$		End of Line–File Must Match Whole Word

The commands **ed, sed, awk, grep, lex,** etc., use the **ed** regular expression meta characters. The shell and the **case** *(pattern)* use the file substitution meta characters.

sed for String Substitution

sed looks for regular expressions and substitutes other strings into a stream of characters. It fits nicely in pipes.

ed for Files in Place

The **ed** command will also substitute one string for a regular expression in a file where it sits on the disk. It also can find lines relative to other lines, which **sed** cannot do.

m4 for Word Substitution

m4 does macro substitution. It knows what a word is and will substitute a string for a word. It uses an input file of define statements.

awk for Numbers and Strings

The **awk** command can do math on number strings and can look for regular expressions in columns, instead of the whole line. It can also use its **printf, sprintf, substring,** and **split** built-in functions for formatting and manipulating the strings it finds.

case for Command Execution

The shell **case** statement will match a string to regular expressions and execute programs. You can write programs that are driven by input strings.

lex for Complex Strings

lex uses C language actions and has much more extensive pattern recognition facilities than any other command.

yacc for Context Sensitive

Yet another compiler compiler, **yacc,** is the most powerful, and the most work. It can recognize a string in a very complex text by building a finite state machine with a stack and shift-reduce mechanism. You not only can write a compiler or a language translation system, but you can drive a complex system with it and interact intelligently with a user. Mainly because it knows what has come before and the context of a string. **yacc** has its own Bachus-Naur style input grammar.

Now you can stand at the bar and shout, "I can beat any conversion problem."

STRING PARSING

To parse a string means to break it up into its parts, usually words. We often have to get a word or substring out of a string. The shell has several powerful, and easy to use, ways of breaking up a string to let us access any part of it.

set String

The principal method, unfortunately, is almost undocumented. Certainly difficult to find. We didn't find it for years, and today seldom meet anyone who knows it. Once you know it is there, you can find a brief mention under the **set** command in the built-in commands section of the **sh** (1) manual page.

If you type:

```
$ set a b c
```

the **set** command will assign the first word to *$1*, the second word to *$2*, the third word, here *c*, to *$3*, and so on. Then you can use them just as if they were command line arguments. By the way, the *$1*, etc. are no longer pointing to the command line arguments, so you should save them in shell variables before you call the **set** command.

Let's use this method to parse the date line and format the date the way we want it. The date command puts out a line like this:

```
$ date
Sun Aug 11 08:41:50 EDT 1985
```

Let's make a normal US date:

```
$ set `date`
$ echo $2 $3, $6
Aug 11, 1985
```

Note the back quotes around *date*. They cause the shell to execute the **date** command and write its output on the command line of **set.** Then the **set** command finds the six fields of the **date** output as arguments. The **set** command assigns *Sun* to *$1*, *Aug* to *$2*, and so forth. We then access the words we want with the **echo** command.

IFS and Delimiters

Note that the whole time string (08:41:50) is one word because there are no spaces within the time string. It is delimited, or separated by colons (:). Suppose we want to parse the time string, and get rid of the seconds. How can we change the shell's idea of what a word or field separator is? It turns out to be very easy.

There is a standard shell variable called *IFS*. That stands for *interfield separator*. Normally it points to a string of three characters: space, tab, and newline. These three characters are called *white* space. We now can parse the time string two ways. One way is as follows.

```
$ IFS = :$IFS
$ set `date`
$ echo "It is now $4 o'clock and $5 minutes."
It is now 09 o'clock and 04 minutes.
```

We added the colon to the *IFS* characters to parse the time string along with the other strings of the date line all at the same time.

Another way is to save the time string and just parse it:

```
$ set `date`
$ TIME = $4
$ IFS = :$IFS
$ set $TIME
$ echo "It is now $1 o'clock and $2 minutes."
It is now 09 o'clock and 04 minutes.
```

By the way, you can use **sed** to strip off leading zeros, like this:

```
$ echo It is now `echo $4 | sed "s/∧0//"` o \ 'clock \
and `echo $5 | sed "s/∧0//"` minutes.
It is now 9 o'clock and 29 minutes.
```

Here we passed the hours and minutes through a pipe to **sed** which looked for leading zeros and replaced them with nothing. If we had not used the up arrow or hat character (∧), we would have turned 10 into 1. We only want to strip off leading zeros.

WARNING : Be careful with *IFS*. If you change *IFS* for this parsing, and do not change it back, things can really get messed up. The shell will use the new *IFS* for regular command string substitution. If you change *IFS* to colon (:) for example, the shell will look for colons to separate commands from their arguments. The principle is to change *IFS*, use it, and change it back to its original value as soon as you can. So here is a good technique. It adds a little more work, but just get used to doing it.

```
$ OLDIFS = "$IFS"
$ IFS = :
$ set $SOMETHING
$ IFS = "$OLDIFS"
$ echo The hour is $4.
```

Here we save the value of *IFS* in a new variable called *OLDIFS* before we change *IFS* to a colon. Then as soon as we can, after the **set** command, we return *IFS* to its old value. Then we can safely go on. Be sure to note that we have to put double quotes around *IFS* and *OLDIFS* because they have spaces and tabs and things that must be protected from the shell which would otherwise throw them away. You can also do this in a subshell.

```
$ ( IFS = ":$IFS" ; set `date` ; echo The hour is $4. )
The hour is 10.
```

We have changed the *IFS* variable in the subshell, but it dies right away. Bad variables in dead shells won't hurt us. Another way of parsing uses the **for** control statement and is covered in the chapter on control flow.

117

PARSING WITH THE sed COMMAND

We can also do other types of parsing with the **sed** command. We can strip off characters or strings, convert characters, explode the whole string, etc.
First lets strip off leading and trailing characters.

```
$ echo abcde | sed 's/.//'
bcde
```

The **sed** command stripped off the first character, regardless of what it was, because the dot (.) matches any character. It was replaced with the null string *(///)*. Let's get rid of the seconds by stripping off the last three characters of the time string.

```
$ set `date`
$ echo $4| sed 's/...$//'
09:38
```

The dollar sign means the end of the line, so we replace the last three characters, before the end of the line, with nothing.

Separator Conversion

Without messing with the *IFS* variable we can use **sed** or **tr** to convert special characters into the normal white space separator.

```
$ sed 1q /etc/passwd | sed 's/:/ /g'
root 0 0 /
```

The second **sed** substituted a space for all of the colons. Put this in a command substitution of a **set** command line and you won't need *IFS*. However, be warned that there may be spaces and tabs in the data fields of the file which should create extra fields when **set** parses the line. Only if you are sure that this won't happen can you use **sed** in this way.

Explode

The **sed** command can even explode the entire string and put spaces between each character.

```
$ echo abcde | sed 's/./& /g'
a b c d e
```

The dot matches any character and the ampersand means whichever character matched. The *g* stands for globally or the whole line. So, in English we have told **sed** to take each character on the line and replace it with itself and a blank. Lay that on the **set** line and you can walk through each character.

PARSING WITH A CALL TO ANOTHER PROGRAM

Just like the **set** command assigns each word in a string to a positional variable, so too does the shell when a program is called. You can call a program with a string and the program can walk through its arguments.

PARSING WITH for AND case

The **for** and **case** statements can also be used to parse a string. The **for** control statement will set a variable to each word in a string and the **case** statement can match patterns and take actions depending on what it finds.

PARSING WITH lex AND yacc

For parsing with the power to build compilers and complex systems, there are the UNIX **lex** and **yacc** programs. They handle the hardest cases. **lex** has more complex patterns that it can match, than anything mentioned so far. **yacc,** yet another compiler compiler, can handle situations where you only want to convert a string when prior or subsequent strings are found. You can build a complex state machine and handle almost anything with **yacc.**

PART

III

SHELL PROGRAMS

- Administration
- Recursion
- Style
- Handling Arguments
- Relational Database Example
- Screen Entry Forms
- Portability and Speed

CHAPTER

18

Administration

This chapter discusses various techniques for managing the shell programs that you develop. Often an environment must be set up for less experienced users. It is not enough to just write the programs.

MENU

Users can execute your programs, the same way the developer does, but there are advantages to having a menu. First, it helps show the user what programs are available. Second, it saves typing. It is easier to type the number, or short name of a command, than the whole command. Thirdly, you can prompt the user for required and optional arguments to the command and do validation and help. Some commands may take a lot of tedious typing of options. Menu options can simplify this. Menus are easy to do with shell programming. In the User Manual section of this book is a sample **menu** program that you can edit for your own menus.

At this point, we would like you to turn to the **menu** pages in the User's Manual in the back of this book. In the last part of the **menu** pages is the source for making a menu in the shell. At some point in time, you will want to make your own menus, and we encourage you to use our **menu** program as a boilerplate.

Validation means testing the answers the user types and doing something if they make errors. For example the user may choose an item from the menu to do something to a file. You can prompt the user for the name of the file. Then you can test the string that the user types to see if it is a legitimate file. If not, you can advise the user and let her or him enter another filename. The code below can be edited into your **menu** shell script.

```
echo "Enter file name: " \\c
while read FILENAME
do
    if test –r "$FILENAME"
    then
```

```
            cmd $FILENAME
            break
        else
            echo "$FILENAME does not exist or is not readable"
            echo "Type Control-d to return to menu or,
            echo "Enter another filename: " \\c
        fi
    done
```

There are several ways to code this kind of prompting and testing. Each has it advantages and disadvantages. Above, the user is prompted for a filename using the backslash-c option to **echo** to suppress the carriage return. This leaves the cursor on the same line as the prompt. The double quotes are needed to keep the shell from throwing away the last space in the **echo** command line. The **while** command will keep testing the **read** command and will exit the loop when the **read** command gets an end-of-file. This allows the user to get out of the loop with a control-d, if he or she wanted to go look for the right filename or decided to give up trying. Be sure to always let the user escape from the normal sequence.

Then the string that the user types is assigned to *FILENAME* and tested for existence and readability. If it is ok, the command that uses it is executed and we break out of the **while** loop. Otherwise we advise the user, telling her or him the option to break out and reprompting for the filename.

bin AND PATH

All of the programs you write should go into some *bin* directory. The */bin* and */usr/bin* are for UNIX programs. You are forbidden to put your programs in them. UNIX will let you, but it is a very bad practice. You may clobber a command by the same name. Also, when you get a new UNIX release, you will have the painful job of separating your programs from UNIX programs.

You should create your own *bin* directory. While you are doing development, you might have a development directory or use *$HOME/bin,* a bin in your home directory. For your system, you might use */usr/lbin,* a standard at Bell Labs. *lbin* stands for local bin. Or */usr/local/bin,* the Berkeley name. Whatever bin you create, and load with your programs, must be executable and listed in the *PATH* variable of every user who may run your programs.

PERMISSIONS AND GROUPS

Use **chmod** to make programs and directories executable and readable by users.

```
$ ls -l /usr/lbin /usr/lbin/yourprog
-rw-rw-r--    1 root    super    50 Sep 29 15:10   /usr/lbin/yourprog
/usr/lbin:
total 0
-rw-rw-r--    1 root    super    50 Sep 29 15:10   yourprog
$ chmod +x /usr/lbin /usr/lbin/yourprog
$ ls -l /usr/lbin /usr/lbin/yourprog
-rwxrwxr-x    1 root    super    50 Sep 29 15:10   /usr/lbin/yourprog


/usr/lbin:
total 0
-rwxrwxr-x    1 root    super    50 Sep 29 15:10   yourprog
$
```

Note that before the **chmod** command the directory and file were not executable, i.e., had no x in the first 10 characters of the line. After the **chmod** command, they are executable. The permission string now has x 'es.

The name *root* is the owner of the file and *super* is the group. You can make your users belong to groups. Give members of one group permissions that other users do not have by editing the */etc/group* file.

```
$ cat /etc/group
super::0:root,rod,marc
bin::2:root,bin,daemon
sys::3:root,bin
visitor::100:guest,madonna
```

You set the starting group of a user in the */etc/passwd* file. It is the number after the third semicolon:

```
$ grep madonna /etc/passwd
madonna::101:100:Ms. End User:/bin/rsh
```

In this case, the group is 100. But the user can change to any other group with the **newgrp** *group* command, if their name is listed after the group in the */etc/group* file. So you can let some users get access to different groups of files.

$HOME/.profile

Use the *profile* files to set the *PATH* variable for each user.

```
$ cat $HOME/.profile
PATH = /bin:/usr/bin:/usr/lbin:.
export PATH
```

The *profile* file sets up environments for a user. It contains shell commands that are read and executed when the user logs on. The *profile* is very useful for application systems, because you can completely control the powers of the users. To keep the user from accidentally, or deliberately, harming anyone else's work, you can control which programs are available and what permissions the user has.

Shell Variables for Custom Environments

In every user's home directory, you can put a *.profile* file which will set up the environment for that user. You should set any variables that your shell programs need. For example, if a program wants to know the preferred text editor you can assign it to the *EDITOR* shell variable in the *.profile* file.

```
EDITOR = vi
export EDITOR
```

export puts the *EDITOR* shell variable into the environment where it can be seen by child processes. In Chapter 13, you also learned about setting default values for shell variables, such as in *EDITOR = :vi*.

Any setup that you wish to apply to all users who sign on the system, you can put into the */etc/profile* file. Note this *profile* has no dot before it. The purpose of the leading dot in home directories is to hide the file from the **ls, rm,** and other commands. They ignore files that start with a dot. To see all titles in a directory, you can type *ls -a*.

CONTROLLING THE USER

Sometimes you want to be more than helpful, you need to control the user. For example, you may want the data entry clerks to enter employee time-cards, without looking at wage rates or paychecks.

The menu, exit, and trap Commands

You can give users a menu that only lists and gives access to the programs you want them to run. Put this menu in the users' *.profile* file and it will come up automatically on login. Here is a sample controlled user *.profile*.

```
$ cat /usr/user/.profile
PATH = /bin:/usr/bin:/usr/lbin:.
export PATH
trap 'trap 0; exit' 1 2 3 4 5 6 7 8   11 12 13 14 15
Menu
exit
```

The **exit** command, after the menu in the *.profile,* causes the user to be logged off of the system when he or she leaves the menu. The **trap** command keeps the user from breaking out of the menu program to get to the UNIX shell. In the example above, the trap command catches all traps and throws the user off the system. The **trap** 0 command turns off the **trap** interrupt command so that trying to exit will not cause an infinite loop. Be sure not to give the user access to any UNIX programs that allow the user to escape to the shell, such as **vi, ed, ex, pg,** etc.

Restricted Shell and Traps Command

If you want to get really tough with the user, give him or her the restricted shell **rsh.** This really limits what the user can do. Put */bin/rsh* in the */etc/ passwd* file:

```
$ grep madonna /etc/passwd
madonna::101:100:Ms. End User:/bin/rsh
```

This will keep her from stealing your heart, or anything else you leave in your computer system.

MAN DOCUMENTATION

Will you please break down and document your programs. We know it isn't fun and exciting like programming. It is actually a lot like work. It does not stimulate you intellectually. It will not impress your peers. Everyone knows that *real* programmers don't document anything. They figure it out from encrypted core dumps, printed with a wornout ribbon, and passed through a shredder.

But please give the poor user more than a few cryptic remarks, even if it breaks a hallowed UNIX tradition. Much of your work is done for you. A UNIX manual style page can be copied into your directory and edited for the programs you write. See the */usr/man* directory on your UNIX computer or the *yourprog* manual page at the end of this book. Then you can use **nroff** or **troff** with the *-man* option to generate beautiful manual pages. They will look so nice, few will notice that you can't write. Please, do a manual description for each program you write. And do it before, during, or right after writing the program. We know you want to run on to the next program, but in a week you will have no idea what the program *xkhiusnz* does. It will no longer matter how jiffy keen and superfast it was. No one will be able to appreciate your brilliance if they can't understand your program. We are fully aware that this plea will be totally ignored.

19

Recursion

Recursion is a popular programming technique in which a program or routine calls itself. Many languages allow it, and some, like lisp, depend on it. Our advice is to avoid recursion. First, you can always replace recursion with a loop. Loops are easier to code and debug than recursion. Secondly, recursion builds a stack in memory. Therefore, memory will eventually be exhausted and the program will fail unpredictably. A loop can usually go on forever, as most programmers discover by accident.

However, if you are addicted, here are a few samples. Recursion is easy in the shell, because it is so easy to call another program, including the same program.

DIRECTORY TREE SEARCH

Tree searching is a natural for recursion and the UNIX directory system is an easy tree to search.

```
$ cat dir
: dir—displays directory tree starting at given directory
USAGE = 'usage: dir [ directory ] [ indent ]'
: default is current directory
DIR = ${1:-`pwd`} export DIR
: put indent before directory name
echo "$2$DIR"
: add new tab to indent
INDENT = "$2      "
: go to the directory
cd $DIR
: loop through files and directories in the current directory for DIR in `ls`
do
    if test -d "$DIR"
```

```
        then
            dir $DIR "$INDENT"
        fi
    done
    $
    $ dir /usr/lib
    /usr/lib
        acct
        cron
        ctrace
        help
            lib
        lex
        macros
        spell
        tabset
        term
        terminfo
            P
            c
            p
            src
        tmac
        uucp
    $ cd /usr/spool ; dir
    /usr/spool
        cron
            atjobs
            crontabs
        lp
            class
            interface
            member
            model
            request
            lp1
            plot
        uucp
        uucppublic
            receive
```

This can also be done with the **find** command.

TOWERS OF HANOI

Another old favorite from the game playing division of artificial intelligence is the Towers of Hanoi puzzle. Imagine three pegs and a stack of disks on one. Each disk on the peg is smaller than the one below it. The task is to move the disks, one at a time, to another peg so that they are stacked in the same order, small to large. You may move the disks to the third peg, but you may not ever put a larger disk on a smaller, or put a disk anywhere but on a peg.

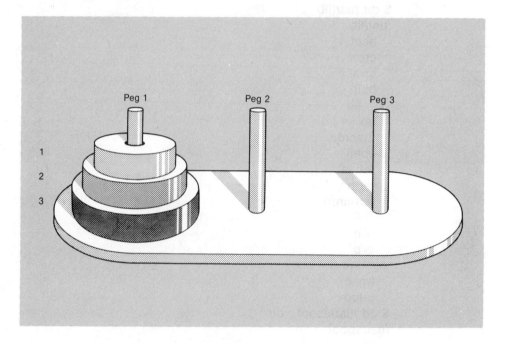

You must move all of the disks from peg 1 to peg 2. To solve the problem, realize that the *last* step is to put disk 1 onto peg 2. Therefore, we have reduced the problem to getting disks 2 and 3 to peg 2. By backing up from the solution we can determine which peg to move disk 1 to, on the first move.

The following shell program does this by recursively descending to the solution and backing up to the start.

```
: towers—plays towers of hanoi game
: inspired by Dolotta and Mashey, Proceedings of IFIPS Working
:    Conference on Command Languages, September 10-14, 1979.
USAGE = 'usage: towers disks from to spare'
EUSAGE = 1
EOK = 0

if test "$#" –lt 4
then
    echo $USAGE 1 > &2
    exit $EUSAGE
elif test "$1" –lt 1
```

```
then
    exit $EOK
fi

DISKS = `expr "$1" - 1`
FROM = $2
TO = $3
SPARE = $4

towers $DISKS $FROM $SPARE $TO
echo "Disk $1 from $FROM to $TO"
towers $DISKS $SPARE $TO $FROM
$ towers 3 1 2 3
Disk 1 from 1 to 2
Disk 2 from 1 to 3
Disk 1 from 2 to 3
Disk 3 from 1 to 2
Disk 1 from 3 to 1
Disk 2 from 3 to 2
Disk 1 from 1 to 2
$ towers 4 A B C
Disk 1 from A to C
Disk 2 from A to B
Disk 1 from C to B
Disk 3 from A to C
Disk 1 from B to A
Disk 2 from B to C
Disk 1 from A to C
Disk 4 from A to B
Disk 1 from C to B
Disk 2 from C to A
Disk 1 from B to A
Disk 3 from C to B
Disk 1 from A to C
Disk 2 from A to B
Disk 1 from C to B
```

If you like recursion so much, you can figure out how this works. Have fun.

Since we are on UNIX, we can have more fun with this. Let's see how many moves are needed for different numbers of disks.

```
$ for I in 1 2 3 4 5 6 7 8 9 10
> do
> echo "$I          `towers $I 1 2 3 | wc -l`"
> done
1          1
```

```
2          3
3          7
4         15
5         31
6         63
7        127
8        255
9        511
10      1023
$
```

By inspecting this table you can see that the formula for the number of moves is 2 raised to the number of disks, minus 1. See how much fun UNIX is?

CHAPTER

20

Style

Here we propose some style conventions. These are purely personal. There are no standards in shell programming and that is why so many shell programs are so messy. You will doubtless develop your own style. But consider these conventions.

SAMPLE PROGRAM

First lets look at a sample program that we will call **yourprog.**

```
: %W% SCCS Information

: yourprog—a description of the command
: any further comments about the command
: this is a sample program for you to copy and modify

: edit the line below to represent the syntax of your program
USAGE = "usage: yourprog -o arg ... [ oparg ... ] < filein > fileout"

: the above is standard, below is optional

: if you have abnormal exit status codes, define them here

: error—bad syntax or usage
EUSAGE = 1

: error—other error messages and return codes with increasing numbers
MOTHER = 'Error: other error message.'
EOTHER = 2

: if you are going to use temporary files, include this line for each
TMP = /usr/tmp/$$yourprog
TMP1 = /usr/tmp/$$1yourprog

: be sure to trap interrupts and remove the temporary files
```

```
trap "rm -f /usr/tmp/$$*" 0 1 2 3 15
: if you have required options, you can test for them here
: be sure to send error messages to standard-out
if test "$#" -lt 1
then
    echo $USAGE 1>&2
    exit $EUSAGE
fi
: here is a crude sample of argument parsing
for ARG in $*
do
    case $ARG in
    -a) OPTIONA = true ;;
    -o) OPTIONO = true ;;
     *) OPARG = "$OPARG $ARG" ;;
    esac
done
: finally this program code simply echoes the name of this program
echo $0
```

You may be shocked at so much overhead. Every shell program does not need all of this. But let's discuss each section. You can copy this sample into a file, modify it to suit your tastes, and grab a copy every time you start writing a new program. It is easier to chop out parts you don't need, than to type in the ones you do.

SCCS INFORMATION

SCCS is the name of a group of programs that manage source code. If you write a lot of programs, and/or more than one person is modifying the code, you will need *SCCS* to protect it. See the UNIX documentation on *SCCS*. This line is needed by the *SCCS* programs.

Please put a description of your program at the top so that others can tell what this program is for. Even you will forget in a few weeks or months. Of course a *real* hacker never documents, but studies the code to figure out what the program does. Save us from hacker macho. Perhaps real hackers have lots of time for this because they can't get a date.

USAGE

The *USAGE* variable shows the syntax of the program. It serves two purposes. It documents, at the top of the program, the syntax. Thus it is easy to find. Secondly, it is used later when syntax errors are detected to display a standard message. It should also be copied to the *SYNOPSIS* line of your manual documentation. Note how the syntax is described. You will have to edit this *USAGE* line to reflect the syntax of the program you are writing. Be sure to re-edit whenever you change the syntax.

usage:—The term *usage* to mean syntax has been used by a lot of UNIX programs and is continued here. Think of it as how to use this command.

options—Options are the letters and words preceded by minuses.

args—Args are the required arguments. We test to see that they are there.

oparg—Opargs are the optional arguments which may or may not be there.

. . .—The ellipses indicate that one or more of the preceding arguments may be present.

[]—The square brackets surround items that are optional. Meaning they do not have to be there.

< filein > fileout—This is not usually done in UNIX documentation, but you can indicate the kind of source and destination the program expects.

Single Quotes—Note that single quotes enclose the whole *USAGE* line to protect all of the special characters.

EXIT STATUS CODES

The **exit** command allows you to return status codes. A zero is a successful normal exit. Other numbers are available for error codes. Please list the codes at the top of your program so that they are easy to find. Then you can call them in the program when you need them.

You can also copy them over to your documentation. Yes, we are still harping on documentation. If we make it supereasy, almost automatic, will you do just a little bit? No, probably not.

THE TMP FILE

TMP is a temporary file that may be used in the program. For example, you may need to sort:

```
$ sort file > $TMP
$ mv $TMP file
```

You have to do it this way because if you type:

$ sort file > file

you will clobber the file.

/usr/tmp—TMP is being created in */usr/tmp*. This is the new standard. However, many UNIX computers do not yet have */usr/tmp*. If your system does not have it, make the */usr/tmp* directory with the **mkdir** command. You may have to be the superuser.

$$yourprog —The two dollar signs, *$$*, will be replaced by the unique process-id for the program when it is run. If two users run the program at the same time, they will each get different files (different numbers) in */usr/ tmp*. Putting the program name in the temporary filename makes it easier to find the leftover files, if the program aborts. They may help you debug the program. So the temporary filename might look like this:

/usr/tmp/1349yourprog

THE trap COMMAND

The **trap** command will catch any interrupts and execute the command within double quotes. In this case it will remove the temporary files. So, when the program exits, the temporary files will be cleaned up. See the chapter on built-in functions for more information on **trap**.

test ARGUMENTS

If certain arguments are required, we will need to test that they are there before we do any more processing. Here the **if test** commands are used. If an error is found, you can display the *USAGE* message and exit with a non-zero *EUSAGE* number. A program calling this program can then test the status code *$?* with an **if** test or **case** statement and detect that an error or unusual condition occurred. The **for** and **case** statements are used to test for arguments.

COMMENTS

Please comment each section of your program. Otherwise it is even more difficult to fix or modify.

If you are a programmer who works for someone, don't comment your code. Then they can't fire you. If you are a manager, fire any new programmers who do not comment their code, before they can pull this trick on you.

Make all of your variables in capital letters so they will be easier to see in the code. Also, please write long pipes down the page for easier reading and editing.

SYSTEM V INTERFACE DEFINITION

AT&T has issued an *Interface Definition*[5] which is an attempt to state the minimal standard for UNIX that software developers can hope will be available on all UNIX computers. It is almost the same as the */usr/group* user organization's standards. It deals mostly with UNIX system calls and libraries, which are of interest to C language programmers. However, there is one page (343) that discusses command syntax standards. Here are the rules that they put forth for command-line syntax. You will probably want to follow them for your shell programs, for they point to the future. No reasons are given for the rules, although many are obvious.

Command Names 2 to 9 Characters—Forbidding one character commands leaves these short command names for the user. We are not sure why they chose 9 characters as the limit. UNIX allows 14 characters for program (or any file) name. If it is a C language program, it will end in a *.c,* which takes up two characters. The **SCCS** programs add an *s.* to the beginning of the source code they control. So a program may look like: *s.program.c,* if it was a C program under **SCCS** control. That takes up another four characters. This gets us down to 10 characters. Nine characters will allow a two-character suffix. We do not see any reason why a shell program could not be 12 characters long, since they seldom have suffixes, except that is a lot of typing for a user.

Command Names Lowercase and Digits Only—UNIX allows you to name files, and therefore commands, with almost any character, even nonprinting characters. But things can get very messy if you use such characters. This is a good rule that is easy to follow.

Option Names Single Character in Length—There are several UNIX commands that break this rule. The **dd** command has options like *if* for *input file,* etc. This rule aims at putting a stop to such irregularities.

All Options Delimited by Minus (−)—**dd** and **tar** do not use the minus to indicate an option. This rule says, let's start all of our options with minuses.

---

5. D.E. Kevorkian, Editor, "System V Interface Definition," *AT&T,* Spring 1985, Issue 1.

Options Without Arguments Can Be Grouped After Minus—This makes possible two forms: **cmd -xy** and **cmd -x -y**. To parse the first is more difficult in the shell, because you must *walk down* the list of characters. It is easier to do in the C language than in the shell.

If there are not too many options, you can list the combinations like this:

```
case $ARG in
-x)          X = true ;;
-y)          Y = true ;;
-xy|-yx)     X = true ; Y = true ;;
esac
```

If there are many, you can walk through the option string with **sed.**

```
: remove the leading minus
ARG = `echo $1| sed 's/.//'`
while test ! $ARG  = ''''
do
   case $ARG in
   x*)        X = true ;;
   y*)        Y = true ;;
   z*)        Z = true ;;
   esac
   # remove option from front of list
   ARG = `echo $ARG| sed 's/.//'`
done
```

Separate Option and Arguments by Space—Some commands jam together the option and its arguments. For example:

```
$ cu -s9600
```

is the **call** *UNIX* command with speed set to 9600 baud. Future programs should expect to see:

```
$ cmd -x 1234
```

where *-x* is the option and *1234* is the option's argument, with a space between.

Options Arguments Not Optional—This rule makes it easier to parse the command line. If an option has an argument, it must be there. Otherwise, you will have to try to figure out if the next argument is for the option or for the command, which can be difficult and error prone.

Option Arguments Separated by Commas, or Space and Quoted—This rule allows the following:

```
$ cmd -x 1,3,8
$ cmd -x '1 3 8'
```

but prohibits:

```
$ cmd -x 1 3 8
$ cmd -x1 3 8
```

All Options Before Operands—Some UNIX commands allow you to mix options with operands and some don't. This rule says that you should list all options first and then the rest must be operands. Again this makes parsing easier.

This is ok:

```
$ cmd -o -x file
```

This is not allowed under the new rules, although many UNIX commands accept it:

```
$ cmd file -o -x
```

Two Minuses (−−) Indicate End of Options—A new convention to separate options from operands is to use the double minuses (−−).

```
$ cmd -x -yz -- file1 file2
```

is an example. This allows us to have arguments that start with a minus, without confusing the program into thinking they are options.

Options Acceptable in Any Order—Options can come in any order. There should be no difference between these two invocations:

```
$ cmd -x -y
$ cmd -y -x
```

Use a **case** statement in your shell program to parse the options because a **case** does not care which order its patterns come in.

Operands May Be Position Related—However, you can also make the operands positional. For example, the **cp** copy command insists that the first file be the source and the second file the destination.

```
$ cp fromfile tofile
```

In your shell program you can use these positional parameters:

```
$ cp $1 $2
```

Minus Alone Means Standard Input—Several UNIX commands already use this convention:

```
$ tbl text | nroff –mm localmacros - endstuff
```

This allows you to send to **nroff** the output of **tbl** between the *localmacros* file and the *endstuff* file. **nroff** will read *localmacros,* then the standard input to **nroff,** which will be the pipe to the left from **tbl,** and finally will read from *endstuff.*

21

Handling Arguments

When the user types the name of our shell program, followed by various arguments, we need to see those arguments in the program and take different actions depending upon what the arguments are. Inside of a shell program there are several shell variables to help us parse the command line.

$# ARGUMENT COUNT FOR REQUIRED ARGUMENTS

One test, that is often made first, is to check the number of arguments the user has typed. This is stored in an automatic shell variable: *$#*. Here is a typical test:

```
if test "$#" –lt 1
then
    echo $USAGE 1>&2
    exit $EUSAGE
fi
```

This code demands that there be one or more arguments. This is used to guarantee that the required minimum number of arguments has been typed in. For example, the shell program might need the name of the directory to look in, or the name of a file to process, etc.

USAGE is a shell variable that is assigned the syntax of the program at the top of the code. The syntax for required arguments is arguments without square brackets.

```
USAGE = 'usage: cmd requiredarg [optionalarg] [manyoptargs . . .]'
```

Here, only *requiredarg* must be typed in. The others are optional arguments. The *$#* is an automatic variable that is set by the shell when the program is cranked up. But it is best to put the double quotes around it. Just make it a habit to always double quote the **test** strings. Then you will not forget when it is important. Why double quotes, and not single quotes? Single quotes would protect the string absolutely and the $# would not be converted into a number.

$1, $2. . .POSITIONAL ARGUMENTS

The shell does another big job for us. It assigns each argument word to $1, $2, etc. This allows us to pick off positional parameters.

```
USAGE = 'usage: cmd directory file'
DIRECTORY = $1
FILE = $2
if test ! –d "$DIRECTORY" –o ! –f "$FILE"
then
    echo $USAGE 1 > &2
    exit $EUSAGE
fi
```

The syntax of this program requires that the first argument be a directory and the second argument a readable file. So we test to see if they are. The position of the arguments is important for knowing which argument is the directory and which is the file. Only use positional parameters when you must, because they are a little more burden on the user to get the arguments in the right order. These positional parameters are very similar to the *argc* and *argv* variable in C programming.

$* ARGUMENT LIST

Sometimes you need to grab all of the arguments. The automatic shell variable *$** holds them. One common trick is to grab the first, or first few arguments, shift and then use the rest of the arguments.

```
USAGE = 'usage: cmd directory file . . .'
DIRECTORY = $1
shift
cp $* $DIRECTORY
```

This program reverses the usual order for the **cp** copy command. Here we get the first argument, which is the directory. Then we shift the arguments over so that we only have files as arguments. Finally, we copy the files to the directory.

OPTIONS

When you must look for options in your arguments, these are the **case** and **pattern** commands.

```
USAGE = 'usage: cmd [-o -a] file'
for I in $*
do
  case $I in
  -o)        OPTION = true ;;
  -a)        OPTION = true ;;
  *)         FILE = $I ;;
  esac
done
```

Here the *OPTION* shell variable is turned on when we find *-o* or *-a* in the arguments, otherwise (*), the *FILE* variable is set to the argument. This allows any number of combinations to be correctly handled. Notice that we *walked through* the arguments in the **for** loop using $*.

UNSET ARGUMENTS

Sometimes an argument is missing. Here is how to test a variable to see if any value has been assigned to it.

```
if test -z "$FILE"
then
    echo $FILE unset 1>&2
    exit $NOTSET
fi
```

LAST ARGUMENT

Picking up the last argument is often a challenge. Here is one way. It uses *$#* to find out the last argument, then grabs that positional parameter.

```
"Getting Last Argument"
$ cat lastarg
LAST = `eval echo \\\ $$#`
echo $LAST
$ lastarg a b c
c
$
```

Looks weird? The dollar number *($#)* is the number of arguments. On the first scan it is converted into the number of the last argument. It becomes 3 in this example. We want **echo** to see dollar-3 *($3)*, so another pass is needed. **eval** makes the shell re-evaluate the line, converting *$3* into the last argument, letter *c*. Let's use the shell trace option *(-x)* to see what happens.

```
$ sh -x lastarg a b c
+ eval echo $3
+ echo c
LAST=c
+ echo c
c
$
```

We assumed that you wanted to assign the last argument to a shell variable, in this case *LAST*. It is even simpler, if you don't have to grab it.

22

Relational Database Example

UNIX has most of the tools for managing a relational database. Many are easy to use, some are a little tricky. We will show you how to have a relational database on UNIX—at least some of the basics. But we must admit that some things are hard to do. That is why we developed a relational database management package called **/rdb** that is available from several sources. See software sources.

TABLES

The basic idea of a relational database management system is that all information can be stored in tables. Here is a small inventory table example:

```
$ cat    inventory
Item    Amount    Cost    Value    Description
1          3        50     150      rubber gloves
2        100         5     500      test tubes
3          5        80     400      clamps
4         23         9     437      plates
5         99        24    2376      cleaning cloth
6         89      1471    3083      bunsen burners
7          5       175     875      scales
```

Note that we have the name of each column at the top, followed by a dash line and that we are using a tab character to separate each column. This kind of table can be typed in and updated with a text editor. As long as the tabs and headers are there the relational commands below will work.

In our commercial database system, special editors are available to do form editing and validation on this kind of table.

Once we have our data in tables, we can get it out in many convenient ways. Relational database theory shows that we can convert any query into project, select, and join commands.

Project

A project cuts out only the columns we want from the table. We can use **awk.** Suppose we want a new table consisting of only the *Amount* and *Description* columns.

```
$ awk 'BEGIN {FS="   "; OFS="   "}{ print $2,$5 }' < inventory
```

Amount	Description
3	rubber gloves
100	test tubes
5	clamps
23	plates
99	cleaning cloth
89	bunsen burners
5	scales

The *BEGIN* pattern is used to set the input *(FS)* and output *(OFS)* field separators to tabs. The single quotes (') are needed to keep the shell from messing with the special characters. This is more typing than we want to do so let's make a **project** program.

```
$ cat project
: project cuts out requested columns from a table
USAGE="usage: project 'columnnumber,...' < table"

awk "BEGIN {FS=\"  \"; OFS=\"  \"} { print $* }"
$
```

Let's try it out.

```
$ project '$2,$5' < inventory
```

Amount	Description
3	rubber gloves
100	test tubes
5	clamps
23	plates
99	cleaning cloth
89	bunsen burners
5	scales

Note that the column numbers must be within single quotes to protect them from the shell. Also, the comma is necessary for **awk** to separate the columns with tabs on output. If we only have spaces, they would be jammed together.

This is still not as nice as we want. In **/rdb,** for example, the **project** command looks like this:

```
$ project Amount Description < inventory
```

We wanted to be able to name the columns and let the **project** program decide what column numbers they are. In System V UNIX, a command called **cut** will do the same thing as **project**, but much faster.

Select

We can select only those rows that meet some logical condition with **awk.**

```
$ awk 'BEGIN {FS = ""; OFS = ""} NR < 3 || $2 < 10' < inventory
```

Item	Amount	Cost	Value	Description
1	3	50	150	rubber gloves
3	5	80	400	clamps
7	5	175	875	scales

Note that the *NR < 3* will list the first two header lines. *NR* means number of record. The double pipe symbols (|) is logical *or.* The *$2 < 10* matches all rows in which column 2 (Amount) is less than 10. Since there is no action in curly braces ({}), **awk** does the default action of printing the whole row. That is a lot more typing than we want so let's write a **select** command.

```
$ cat select
: select displays only the rows in a table that meet condition
USAGE = "usage: select 'condition' < table"

awk "BEGIN {FS = \" \"; OFS = \" \"} NR < 3 | $* "
$
$ select '$2 < 10' < inventory
```

Item	Amount	Cost	Value	Description
1	3	50	150	rubber gloves
3	5	80	400	clamps
7	5	175	875	scales

Note that now we only have to type in the condition. But what we really want to type is:

```
$ select 'Amount < 10' < inventory
```

Using named columns is the way **/rdb's select** command works.

147

PIPING

Now that we have the **project** and **select** commands we can also pipe them together.

```
$ project '$2,$5' < inventory | select '$1 < 10'
```

Amount	Description
3	rubber gloves
5	clamps
5	scales

Here a report is created with a single line. That line can be saved in a file, the file can be made executable, and the report can be produced by simply typing the name of the file.

```
$ cat myreport
project '$2,$5' < inventory | select '$1 < 10'

$ myreport
```

Amount	Description
3	rubber gloves
5	clamps
5	scales

We might want this report to see which items in our inventory are low and may need to be reordered.

THE join COMMAND

There is a UNIX **join** command. Joining two tables, based on a common column, is fundamental to relational databases. However, if you give *join* tables with headlines, it will not work. You will have to remove the headlines before you join them, then put the headlines back on. Use **tail** +3 to remove headlines.

COMPUTE AND VALIDATE

You can also use **awk** to compute all kinds of equations on tables. And you can use it to validate a file. You can test for conditions that are illegal and print messages when they are found.

TERMINOLOGY

A table shows that a *relation* exists between each column, thus the name relational database. The terminology comes from mathematics and logic set theory. If you are a nonmathematician, you may find the literature on relational databases incomprehensible. The main problem is the terms used. Different terms are used by mathematicians, computer people, and other humans. We try to use human terms throughout the **/rdb** documentation. We ignore the mathematicians, since they seem to ignore us. But we love them. Without them we would not have relational theory. Table 9 will help each group translate terms used by another group.

Table 9. Relational Database Terminology Translation

Most Humans	Computer People	Mathematicians
table	file	relation
column	field	attribute (domain)
row	record	tuple
number of columns	number of fields	degree
number of rows	number of records	cardinality
list of tables	schema	data model
user's tables	user view	data submodel
simplified	simplified	normalized
no repeated columns	no multi fields	normalized
one concept per table		3rd normal form
get rows	get records	select
get columns	get fields	project
combine tables	concatenate	join
new command	shell script	view

23

Screen Entry Forms

You can put forms on the screen and handle user entry from shell programs. It is seldom done, because most programmers assume that they must write C or other language programs to handle screens. On older, slower UNIX computers it may not be fast enough. But the new computers and the fast UNIX System V, Release 2 shell is quite satisfactory.

TERMCAP AND TERMPUT

When Bill Joy wrote the **vi** text editor, he developed a terminal capability facility to handle different terminals. There is a file called */etc/termcap* on every UNIX that supports **vi.** That is most UNIX computers today. The file has an entry for each terminal it knows. It uses two-letter codes for each capability. For example *cl* means clear the screen. Following the code is a string of characters, which, when sent to the terminal screen, will perform the action. For example the IBM PC/XT™ terminal might have the following entry in the termcap file.

Termcap Entry for the IBM PC

```
cpc|pc|PC|ansi standard pc console:\
  :al = \ El:cd = \ E[lbrktJ:ce = \ E[K:cl = \ E [0;0H \ E[2J: \
  :cm = \ E[%2;%2H:co#80:dl = \ EL: \
  :li#25:nd = \ E[C:pt:sr = \ EM:up = \ E[A: \
  :ku = \ E[A:kl = \ E[D:kr = \ E[C:kd = \ E[B:kh = \ E[H: \
  :k0 = \ ED:k1 = \ E;:k2 = \ E < :k3 = \ E = :k4 = \ E > :k5 = \ E?: \
  :k6 = \ E:k7 = \ EA:k8 = \ EB:k9 = \ EC: \
  :se = \ E[m:so = \ E[7m:us = \ E[4m: \
  :if = /usr/lib/tabset/std: \
  :sf = \ ED:
```

By the way, these entries are not always correct. You can correct them with a text editor. Use *the termcap* description, usually in section 5 of your UNIX manual, and the manual for your terminal.

The **termput** command in the manual at the end of this book finds these entries and sends them to the screen. It is similar to the **tput** command in UNIX System V, Release 2, but uses *termcap,* which is more widely available than *terminfo*.

CLEAR SCREEN

Note that on the second line, clear is defined as *cl=\E[0;0H\E[2J.* The backslash-E (\E) means the escape character. If that string is sent to the terminal, the screen will be cleared. If you have the **termput** program you can type:

```
$ termput cl
```

to clear the screen.

For speed, you should get the string once in your *$HOME/.profile*. Add a line like this:

```
CLEAR = 'termput cl'
export CLEAR
```

Then you can clear the screen in a shell program with one of the following, depending on which **echo** command you have.

```
$ echo $CLEAR
$ echo -n $CLEAR
$ echo $CLEAR \\c
```

This should be ten times faster than using **termput** each time you need to send a string of characters to the screen.

CURSOR MOVEMENT

Moving the cursor is a little trickier than the other terminal commands, because the string must have the column and row number inserted. Note that the entry above for *cm,* cursor movement, is *cm = \E[%2;%2H.* The percent two (%2) means that two digits should be inserted representing the row and column respectively. You could write a shell program to move the cursor:

```
$ cat cursor
USAGE = 'usage: cursor row column'

echo "^[[$1;$2H" \\c
```

151

This takes the two arguments and plugs them into the string and sends the string out without a newline. This will put the cursor on the screen where you want it. However, this hardwires a single terminal's cursor movement string. In this case the PC. To make it more general, you must be able to handle any terminal. One way is to use the **tgoto** function in the **cursor** library of subroutines. See the chapter on System V, Release 2.

OUTPUT WITH echo AND INPUT WITH read

If you can move the cursor to where you want on the screen, you can use **echo** to write anything you want there. So you can paint the screen and prompt the user with cursor moves and **echo** prompts.

```
$ cursor 10 20 ; echo "Please enter your name: "
```

Then you can move the cursor to where you want and use the **read** command to read in a shell variable.

```
$ cursor 10 45 ; read VAR
```

Once you have the input, you can validate it or write it into a file.

You can also write the output of any shell command or pipe to any position on the screen. For example:

```
$ cursor 5 40 ; date
```

This writes the date line on the screen at the indicated location. You might enjoy playing with these features.

24

Portability and Speed

The word *port* is a contraction of the word transport. It has come to mean moving a program from one computer system to another. There are some problems with porting shell programs. Some that work on one UNIX system may not work on others. The authors have ported both C and shell programs to over 30 different computers in the last few years. We have shell programs running on IBM PC/XT's and Cray 2's and many computers in between. The good news is that there are very few problems. Compared to other systems, these problems are trivial. But UNIX people are lazy and are annoyed with having to deal with any portability problems at all. Also, these problems stand out against a background of almost perfect portability.

The bad news is that they are unnecessary and could have easily been avoided. AT&T is spending millions of dollars trying to make their UNIX the standard, yet their hackers created most of the nonstandard features. The idea that Bell Labs creates the standard for UNIX ignores the fact that there are lots of UNIXes out in the world and people are writing programs on them. These are the same people who have made UNIX such a success.

New features naturally introduce portability problems. But this is acceptable. We want the new features. And we all have a choice. The new features can be used, if we do not have to port to other UNIX systems. When we write software that must be ported, we avoid the nonportable features. Changing syntax is intolerable. This makes life very difficult for users. AT&T has made a few syntax changes in often-used commands that complicate the job of porting.

BELL VS. BERKELEY

When the Berkeley people enhanced UNIX, they were very careful to not interfere with programs that ran on other UNIX systems. But, the people at AT&T Bell Labs have made needless changes. They have broken the zero'th

153

principle of Bell Labs: *"If it ain't broke, don't fix it."* Engineers love to fiddle with things. The management of the Labs tried to put a stop to incessant fiddling with working systems, with mixed results.

The Labs could have adopted the Berkeley enhancements, but instead—took a few, changed the syntax of others, rewrote some more, and left out many. What a waste of money and good people's efforts.

Termcap and Terminfo

The */etc/termcap* file was a brilliant invention of Bill Joy. When he wrote the screen oriented text editor **vi**, he needed to handle any computer terminal screen. So he developed a language for describing terminal characteristics and saved each terminal's capabilities in the */etc/termcap* file. He wrote the *curses (/usr/lib/libcurses.a)* screen handling routines to manage the screen. Device independence has become one of the most attractive features of UNIX utilities, as seen in the *plot* filters for graphics, or the printer handling of device-independent *troff*.

Bell Labs UNIX did not have a screen editor as late as System III. It did not make much sense to have such a powerful system as UNIX and still no screen editor. The old **ed** text editor is powerful, but very painful to use because it is a line editor. Companies which ported UNIX to other systems simply added **vi** and most of the other Berkeley enhancements. Only in System V did Bell Labs add **vi** and the */etc/termcap* file.

Unfortunately, Bell Labs developed the *terminfo* system instead of enhancing the *termcap* system. Many new capabilities have been incorporated into *terminfo*, and the authors surmise that the labs figured that the amount of information that would have to be kept in ASCII format under *termcap* was too large, and a binary version of all that data made more sense. Hence, *terminfo*. However, having a new system makes it very difficult for users and administrators. Most programs which handle the terminal screen, like word processors and editors, and menu programs, use *termcap* and now have to convert to *terminfo*.

Having two systems greatly complicates porting. The good news is that both systems, *termcap* and *terminfo,* are being delivered so that we have a choice. Let the better system prevail.

The new *terminfo* has more capabilities, but they could and should have been added to *termcap*. There is also an effort to be faster by compiling the terminal entries and putting them in a hash directory. Hashing is a trick for finding an entry quickly by looking at the key. For speed, they created directories (Figure 3) for each first letter of the terminal type. This reduces the directory search time. To find file *pc* in */usr/lib/terminfo* look in directory *p*.

All of this results in a rather modest increase in speed. However, *termcap* has a faster trick. By assigning your *termcap* file entry to the shell variable *TERMCAP,* **vi** can find it superfast in its own environment. So it seems that the new *terminfo* incompatibility does not buy us anything.

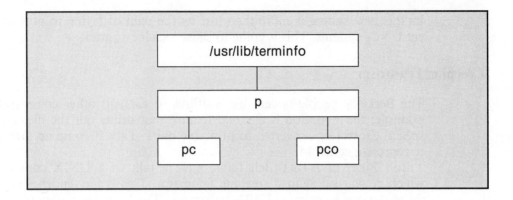

Figure 3. Hash Directory for Speed

Renamed Commands

Some programs are renamed. The Berkeley **more** command was rewritten as **pg** in the Bell UNIX Systems (Table 10).

Table 10. A Program by Any Other Name . . .

Bell	Berkeley
pg	more
sed 10q	head

Command Options

Some of the UNIX commands have different options on different systems.

echo Options—The old **echo** command with a *-n* option suppressed the newline character at the end of the line. This made it possible to issue a prompt to the user and leave the cursor at the end of the prompt.

```
$ echo -n "Enter your name: "
Enter your name: __
```

The new **echo** has more editing capabilities, but changed syntax.

```
$ echo "Enter your name: " \\c
Enter your name: __
```

The backslash, backslash-c *(\\c)* is the new way. The first backslash is needed to protect the second backslash from the shell. Whatever is gained by this new system is more than lost by the pain of trying to port to different UNIX systems. This is going to cause us a lot of grief.

Creeping Featurism

The Berkeley people added new features to **cat** and other commands. For example, the **-v** option is a *visual* feature that prints out the file(s) with all special characters converted to printable pairs. Tabs become up arrow I (∧I) to represent control-i.

Bob Pike, of AT&T Bell Labs, gave a talk to a UNIX convention in which he warned against creeping featurism. This is the tendency of adding more options to existing UNIX programs. The Berkeley group added many useful features. But Pike contends that this is a mistake. That each tool should be kept simple. We agree. It is easier to work with a screwdriver, a hammer, and a wrench, than a funny looking thing that tries to be all. The idea is for UNIX commands to be simple and elegant, and to do one job very well. As each command starts taking on the functions of other commands, things get very confusing and inefficient. It is better to write new commands than to change the syntax of old commands if we ever hope to write shell programs that can be ported to other UNIX computers.

UNIX PROGRAMS OF MAJOR UNIX SYSTEMS

Table 11 is a recap of UNIX programs showing which systems they are in. The table can be used in several ways to help you write portable shell programs. Each UNIX system has a different set of commands. Fortunately, the most used commands are in all the systems. They are shown as italics in Table 11. This will help you find commands that are on all UNIX systems. For the history of these UNIX systems see Chapter 25.

Table 11. Programs on Different UNIX Systems

PWB	Programmers Workbench or System 1.0
V7	Version Seven UNIX
4.1BSD	Berkeley Enhanced and Supported UNIX
4.2BSD	Latest and Greatest Berkeley UNIX
SysIII	System III From AT&T (S3.0 Internally)
SysV	System V From AT&T (S5.0 Internally)
SysV.2	System V, Release 2 From AT&T (S5.2 Internally)
yes	Program exists on that system
blank	Program does not exist in that UNIX system

Program	PWB	V7	4.1BSD	4.2BSD	SysIII	SysV	SysV.2
300					yes	yes	
300s					yes		
4014					yes	yes	
450	yes				yes	yes	
ac		yes	yes				
acctcom					yes	yes	
accton		yes					
adb	*yes*	*yes*	*yes*	*yes*	*yes*	*yes*	*yes*
addbib				yes			
admin	yes				yes	yes	yes
analyze			yes				
apl			yes				
apply				yes			
apropos			yes	yes			
ar	*yes*	*yes*	*yes*	*yes*	*yes*	*yes*	*yes*
arcv		yes			yes	yes	
arff			yes				
arll			yes				
as	*yes*	*yes*	*yes*	*yes*	*yes*	*yes*	*yes*
asa						yes	yes
at		yes	yes	yes			yes
awk		yes	yes	yes	yes	yes	yes
banner	yes				yes	yes	yes
bas	yes	yes					
basename		yes	yes	yes	yes	yes	yes
bc	*yes*	*yes*	*yes*	*yes*	*yes*	*yes*	*yes*
bdiff	yes				yes	yes	yes
bfs	yes				yes	yes	
biff				yes			
binmail			yes	yes			
bs			yes		yes	yes	
cal	yes		yes	yes	yes	yes	yes
calendar		yes	yes	yes	yes	yes	yes
call			yes				
cat	*yes*	*yes*	*yes*	*yes*	*yes*	*yes*	*yes*
cb	*yes*	*yes*	*yes*	*yes*	*yes*	*yes*	*yes*
cc	*yes*	*yes*	*yes*	*yes*	*yes*	*yes*	*yes*
ccat			yes	yes			

Program	PWB	V7	4.1BSD	4.2BSD	SysIII	SysV	SysV.2
cd	*yes*	*yes*	*yes*	*yes*	*yes*	*yes*	*yes*
cdb	yes						
cdc					yes	yes	yes
cflow						yes	yes
chdir	yes						
checkcw					yes		
checkeq				yes	yes		
checknr				yes			
chfn			yes	yes			
chghist	yes						
chgrp	yes	yes			yes	yes	
chmod	yes		yes	yes	yes	yes	yes
chown	yes	yes	yes		yes	yes	yes
chsh			yes	yes			
clear			yes	yes			
clri		yes	yes				
cmp	*yes*	*yes*	*yes*	*yes*	*yes*	*yes*	*yes*
col	*yes*	*yes*	*yes*	*yes*	*yes*	*yes*	*yes*
colcrt			yes	yes			
colrm			yes	yes			
comb	yes				yes	yes	yes
comm	*yes*	*yes*	*yes*	*yes*	*yes*	*yes*	*yes*
compact			yes	yes			
convert						yes	
cp	*yes*	*yes*	*yes*	*yes*	*yes*	*yes*	*yes*
cpio	yes				yes	yes	yes
cpp						yes	yes
cprs						yes	
cpx	yes						
cref	yes				yes		
crontab							yes
crypt	yes	yes	yes	yes	yes	yes	
csh			yes	yes			yes
csplit	yes				yes	yes	yes
ct					yes	yes	
ctags			yes	yes			yes
ctrace							yes
cu		yes	yes		yes	yes	yes

Program	PWB	V7	4.1BSD	4.2BSD	SysIII	SysV	SysV.2
cut					yes	yes	yes
cw					yes	yes	
cxref						yes	yes
date	*yes*	*yes*	*yes*	*yes*	*yes*	*yes*	*yes*
db	yes						
dbx				yes			
dc	*yes*	*yes*	*yes*	*yes*	*yes*	*yes*	*yes*
dcheck		yes	yes				
dd	*yes*	*yes*	*yes*	*yes*	*yes*	*yes*	*yes*
ddate			yes				
delta	yes				yes	yes	yes
deroff	*yes*	*yes*	*yes*	*yes*	*yes*	*yes*	*yes*
df	yes	yes	yes	yes	yes		
diction				yes			
diff	*yes*	*yes*	*yes*	*yes*	*yes*	*yes*	*yes*
diff3	yes	yes	yes	yes	yes	yes	
diffdir			yes				
diffmark	yes						
diffmk					yes	yes	
dircmp					yes	yes	
dirname					yes		
dis						yes	
dmesg			yes				
dpd						yes	
dpr						yes	
dsw	yes						
dtree				yes			
du	*yes*	*yes*	*yes*	*yes*	*yes*	*yes*	*yes*
dump		yes	yes			yes	
dumpdir		yes	yes				
echo	*yes*	*yes*	*yes*	*yes*	*yes*	*yes*	*yes*
ed	*yes*	*yes*	*yes*	*yes*	*yes*	*yes*	*yes*
edit			yes	yes			yes
efl					yes	yes	yes
egn		yes					
egrep	yes	yes			yes	yes	
enable						yes	yes
enroll		yes		yes			

Program	PWB	V7	4.1BSD	4.2BSD	SysIII	SysV	SysV.2
env					yes	yes	yes
eqn	yes		yes	yes	yes	yes	
erase							yes
error				yes			
ex			yes	yes		yes	yes
exit	yes						
expand			yes	yes			
explain				yes			
expr	*yes*	*yes*	*yes*	*yes*	*yes*	*yes*	*yes*
eyacc				yes			
f77		yes	yes	yes	yes	yes	yes
factor		yes			yes	yes	
false		yes		yes	yes		
fc	yes						
fd2	yes						
fed				yes			
fgrep	yes	yes		yes	yes		
file	*yes*	*yes*	*yes*	*yes*	*yes*	*yes*	*yes*
find	*yes*	*yes*	*yes*	*yes*	*yes*	*yes*	*yes*
finger			yes	yes			
flcopy			yes				
fmt			yes	yes			
fold			yes	yes			
fp				yes			
fpr				yes			
from			yes	yes			
fsend						yes	
fsplit				yes		yes	yes
ftp				yes			
gath	yes						
gcat						yes	
gcore				yes			
gcosmail						yes	
gdev						yes	
ged						yes	
get	yes			yes	yes	yes	yes
getopt					yes	yes	yes
gets			yes				

Program	PWB	V7	4.1BSD	4.2BSD	SysIII	SysV	SysV.2
goto	yes						
gprof				yes			
graph	yes	yes	yes	yes		yes	yes
graphics						yes	
greek					yes	yes	
grep	*yes*	*yes*	*yes*	*yes*	*yes*	*yes*	*yes*
groups				yes			
gsi	yes						
gutil						yes	
head			yes	yes			yes
help	yes				yes	yes	yes
hostid				yes			
hostname				yes			
hp	yes				yes	yes	
hpio						yes	
hyphen					yes	yes	
icheck		yes	yes				
id					yes	yes	yes
if	yes						
indent				yes			
indxbib				yes			
install				yes			
iostat		yes	yes	yes			
iperm							yes
ipcs	yes						
iul			yes				
join		yes	yes	yes	yes		yes
kas					yes		
kill	yes	yes	yes	yes	yes		yes
kun					yes		
last			yes	yes			
lastcomm			yes	yes			
ld	yes	yes	yes	yes	yes		yes
learn		yes	yes	yes			
leave			yes	yes			
lex	*yes*	*yes*	*yes*	*yes*	*yes*	*yes*	*yes*
line					yes	yes	yes
lint		yes	yes	yes	yes	yes	yes

Program	PWB	V7	4.1BSD	4.2BSD	SysIII	SysV	SysV.2
lisp			yes	yes			
list						yes	
liszt			yes	yes			
ln	yes	yes	yes	yes	yes		yes
lock			yes	yes			
login	*yes*	*yes*	*yes*	*yes*	*yes*	*yes*	*yes*
logname					yes	yes	yes
look		yes	yes	yes			
lookbib		yes		yes			
lorder		yes	yes	yes	yes	yes	yes
lp						yes	yes
lpq			yes	yes			
lpr			yes	yes	yes	yes	
lprm			yes	yes			
lpstat						yes	yes
ls	*yes*	*yes*	*yes*	*yes*	*yes*	*yes*	*yes*
lxref				yes			
m4	*yes*	*yes*	*yes*	*yes*	*yes*	*yes*	*yes*
machid						yes	yes
mail	*yes*	*yes*	*yes*	*yes*	*yes*	*yes*	*yes*
make	*yes*	*yes*	*yes*	*yes*	*yes*	*yes*	*yes*
makekey						yes	
makewhatis			yes				
man	yes	yes	yes	yes	yes	yes	
mesg	*yes*	*yes*	*yes*	*yes*	*yes*	*yes*	*yes*
mkconf		yes					
mkdir	*yes*	*yes*	*yes*	*yes*	*yes*	*yes*	*yes*
mkfs		yes	yes				
mknod		yes					
mknode			yes				
mkstr			yes	yes			yes
mm	yes				yes	yes	yes
mmchek					yes		yes
mmt					yes		
mnt						yes	
more			yes	yes			yes
mount		yes	yes				
msgs			yes	yes			

Program	PWB	V7	4.1BSD	4.2BSD	SysIII	SysV	SysV.2
mt				yes			
mv	yes	yes	yes	yes	yes		yes
mvt					yes		
ncheck		yes	yes				
neqn	yes	yes		yes	yes		yes
net			yes			yes	
netcp			yes				
netlog			yes				
netlpr			yes				
netmail			yes				
netq			yes				
netrm			yes				
netstat				yes			
nettroff			yes				
newaliases				yes			
newform						yes	yes
newgrp	yes	yes	yes		yes	yes	yes
news					yes	yes	yes
next	yes						
nice	*yes*	*yes*	*yes*	*yes*	*yes*	*yes*	*yes*
nl					yes	yes	yes
nm	*yes*	*yes*	*yes*	*yes*	*yes*	*yes*	*yes*
nohup	yes	yes		yes	yes	yes	yes
nroff	yes	yes		yes	yes	yes	yes
nscstat						yes	
nsctorje						yes	
nusend						yes	
od	*yes*	*yes*	*yes*	*yes*	*yes*	*yes*	*yes*
onintr	yes						
pack					yes	yes	yes
page				yes			
pagesize				yes			
passwd	*yes*	*yes*	*yes*	*yes*	*yes*	*yes*	*yes*
paste					yes	yes	yes
pc				yes			
pcat					yes		
pcc		yes			yes		
pdx			yes	yes			

Program	PWB	V7	4.1BSD	4.2BSD	SysIII	SysV	SysV.2
pi			yes	yes			
pix			yes	yes			
plot		yes	yes	yes			yes
pmerge				yes			
pr	*yes*	*yes*	*yes*	*yes*	*yes*	*yes*	*yes*
primes					yes		
print			yes	yes			
printenv			yes	yes			
prmail			yes	yes			
prof	*yes*	*yes*	*yes*	*yes*	*yes*	*yes*	*yes*
prs					yes	yes	yes
prt	yes						
ps	*yes*	*yes*	*yes*	*yes*	*yes*	*yes*	*yes*
pstat		yes	yes				
pti			yes	yes			
ptx	*yes*	*yes*	*yes*	*yes*	*yes*	*yes*	*yes*
pump	yes						
pwd	*yes*	*yes*	*yes*	*yes*	*yes*	*yes*	*yes*
px			yes	yes			
pxp			yes	yes			
pxref			yes	yes			
quiz	yes						
quot		yes	yes				
quota			yes				
ranlib				yes			yes
ratfor		yes	yes	yes	yes	yes	
rc	yes						
rcp				yes			
refer		yes	yes	yes			
reform	yes						
regcmp					yes	yes	yes
regcomp	yes						
renice			yes				
reset			yes	yes			
restor		yes	yes				
rev		yes	yes	yes			
rewind			yes				
rgrep	yes						

Program	PWB	V7	4.1BSD	4.2BSD	SysIII	SysV	SysV.2
rjestat	yes					yes	
rlogin				yes			
rm	*yes*	*yes*	*yes*	*yes*	*yes*	*yes*	*yes*
rmail				yes	yes		
rmdel	yes				yes	yes	yes
rmdir	yes	yes		yes	yes		
roff	yes	yes					
roffbib				yes			
rsh	yes			yes	yes		
ruptime				yes			
rwho				yes			
sa		yes	yes				
sact					yes	yes	yes
sadp			yes			yes	
sag			yes			yes	
sar			yes			yes	
scat			yes			yes	
scc					yes	yes	
sccs					yes		
sccsdiff	yes				yes	yes	yes
script			yes	yes			
sdb			yes		yes	yes	
sdiff					yes	yes	
se						yes	
sed	*yes*	*yes*	*yes*	*yes*	*yes*	*yes*	*yes*
see			yes				
send	yes					yes	
sendbug				yes			
sh	*yes*	*yes*	*yes*	*yes*	*yes*	*yes*	*yes*
shift	yes						
size	*yes*	*yes*	*yes*	*yes*	*yes*	*yes*	*yes*
sleep	*yes*	*yes*	*yes*	*yes*	*yes*	*yes*	*yes*
sno					yes	yes	
soelim			yes	yes			
sort	*yes*	*yes*	*yes*	*yes*	*yes*	*yes*	*yes*
sortbib			yes	yes			
spell	*yes*	*yes*	*yes*	*yes*	*yes*	*yes*	*yes*
spellin			yes	yes			

Program	PWB	V7	4.1BSD	4.2BSD	SysIII	SysV	SysV.2
spellout				yes			
spice			yes				
spline	yes	yes	yes	yes		yes	yes
split	*yes*	*yes*	*yes*	*yes*	*yes*	*yes*	*yes*
ssp			yes				
stat						yes	
stlogin						yes	
strings			yes	yes			
strip	*yes*	*yes*	*yes*	*yes*	*yes*	*yes*	*yes*
struct		yes	yes	yes			
ststat						yes	
stty	*yes*	*yes*	*yes*	*yes*	*yes*	*yes*	*yes*
style				yes			
su	*yes*	*yes*	*yes*	*yes*	*yes*	*yes*	*yes*
sum	*yes*	*yes*	*yes*	*yes*	*yes*	*yes*	*yes*
switch	yes						
symorder			yes	yes			
sync	yes	yes	yes			yes	yes
sysline				yes			
tabs	*yes*	*yes*	*yes*	*yes*	*yes*	*yes*	*yes*
tail	*yes*	*yes*	*yes*	*yes*	*yes*	*yes*	*yes*
talk				yes			
tar	*yes*	*yes*	*yes*	*yes*	*yes*	*yes*	*yes*
tbl	*yes*	*yes*	*yes*	*yes*	*yes*	*yes*	*yes*
tc		yes	yes	yes	yes	yes	
tee	*yes*	*yes*	*yes*	*yes*	*yes*	*yes*	*yes*
telnet				yes			
test	*yes*	*yes*	*yes*	*yes*	*yes*	*yes*	*yes*
time	*yes*	*yes*	*yes*	*yes*	*yes*	*yes*	*yes*
timex						yes	yes
tip				yes			
tk		yes	yes	yes			
toc						yes	
touch		yes	yes	yes	yes	yes	yes
tp	yes	yes	yes	yes			
tplot						yes	
tput							yes
tr	*yes*	*yes*	*yes*	*yes*	*yes*	*yes*	*yes*

Program	PWB	V7	4.1BSD	4.2BSD	SysIII	SysV	SysV.2
tra			yes				
trman			yes	yes			
troff	*yes*	*yes*	*yes*	*yes*	*yes*	*yes*	*yes*
trouble						yes	
true		yes	yes	yes	yes	yes	yes
tset			yes	yes			
tsort		yes	yes	yes	yes	yes	yes
tty	*yes*	*yes*	*yes*	*yes*	*yes*	*yes*	*yes*
typo	yes						
ul			yes	yes			
umask					yes	yes	yes
umount		yes					
uname	yes				yes	yes	yes
uncompact			yes	yes			
unexpand				yes			
unget					yes	yes	yes
uniq	*yes*	*yes*	*yes*	*yes*	*yes*	*yes*	*yes*
units	yes	yes	yes	yes	yes	yes	
unpack					yes		
uptime				yes			
users			yes	yes			
uucp		yes	yes	yes	yes	yes	yes
uudecode				yes			
uudiff			yes				
uuencode				yes			
uulog				yes	yes		
uuname					yes		
uupick					yes		
uusend				yes			
uustat					yes	yes	yes
uuto					yes	yes	yes
uux		yes	yes	yes	yes	yes	yes
val					yes	yes	yes
vc						yes	
vfontinfo				yes			
vgrind			yes	yes			
vi			yes	yes			yes
vlp				yes			

Program	PWB	V7	4.1BSD	4.2BSD	SysIII	SysV	SysV.2
vmstat			yes	yes			
vp	yes						
vpac			yes				
vpq			yes	yes			
vpr			yes	yes	yes	yes	
vprint			yes	yes			
vprm			yes	yes			
vtroff			yes	yes			
vwidth				yes			
w			yes	yes			
wait	*yes*	*yes*	*yes*	*yes*	*yes*	*yes*	*yes*
wall		yes	yes	yes			
wc	*yes*	*yes*	*yes*	*yes*	*yes*	*yes*	*yes*
what	yes			yes	yes	yes	yes
whatis			yes	yes			
whatsnew	yes						
whereis			yes	yes			
which			yes	yes			
while	yes						
who	*yes*	*yes*	*yes*	*yes*	*yes*	*yes*	*yes*
whoami			yes	yes			
write	*yes*	*yes*	*yes*	*yes*	*yes*	*yes*	*yes*
xargs					yes	yes	yes
xget		yes		yes			
xref					yes		
xsend		yes	yes	yes			
xstr			yes	yes			yes
yacc	*yes*	*yes*	*yes*	*yes*	*yes*	*yes*	*yes*
yes				yes			

PROGRAMMER TIME VS. COMPUTER TIME

In the old days, computers were terribly expensive relative to programmer salaries. Many programmers would spend much of their time making programs run faster. Today computers are cheap and programmers are expensive. Efficiency today means saving programmer time. This is why UNIX and shell programming are so valuable. It is important that speed considerations not become an obsession. If they do, you will start slowing down your productivity which is a much greater loss than seconds on the computer.

However, we include here several tips on speeding up shell scripts. The biggest improvements have come from the new faster computers and the recent speed up of the System V, Release 2 shell.

Time Commands

The first tool you should become familiar with when you start speeding up programs is the **time** and the newer **timex** commands. The two commands will time a program and print out a list of user, system, and clock time. Here is one of our favorite benchmarks to see how fast a UNIX computer is. It times the reading and counting of all of the characters in the UNIX kernel.

```
$ time wc /unix
    589   1172   68821 /unix
real        2.6
user        1.1
sys         0.3
```

The UNIX kernel is */unix*. We can see that there are 68821 characters in the file. It took 2.6 seconds of clock time to execute the command, of which 1.1 seconds went to doing user work, i.e., reading and executing the command and 0.3 second doing system work like opening the file, etc. The rest of the time the computer was doing other things. This is a pretty good measure of system performance on a UNIX computer because the real bottleneck is reading from and writing to the disk. CPU cycles only matter in number crunching applications. These can often be speeded up more cheaply by adding floating point and array processors.

Process Files, Not Lines

The shell has the ability to process files a line at a time. The **read** and **line** commands can be used. However, if you process large files with them, they will take a long time. They are really only appropriate for small files of a few or a few dozen lines.

You should always try to use the UNIX commands to process whole files at a time. This will require new thinking if you have a traditional programming background. On other systems we are used to thinking in line or character at a time processing. Now it is much faster to pipe commands together that do all of the processing with one read and/or write of a file.

Built-Ins

The built-in commands are much faster than the other UNIX commands. Use them when you can. When you pipe together commands, try to reduce your data as soon as possible.

```
$ sort < bigfile | grep STRING
$ grep STRING < bigfile | sort
```

The second command line is much faster then the first for the same size file input: *bigfile*. The second command put **grep** first, which matched only a few lines in *bigfile* and passed them to **sort.** Therefore, **sort** had much less to sort.

Fast grep

There is a fast **grep** called **fgrep.** It will only match literal strings. There is also a slower **egrep** (extended grep) that matches more complicated patterns. Use the fastest one that does the job.

PATH

Give some thought to how you set up your *PATH*.

```
$ PATH = .:/usr/home/bin:/usr/lbin:/bin:/usr/bin
$ PATH = /bin:/usr/bin:/usr/lbin:/usr/home/bin:.
```

The second *PATH* is much faster then the first, ordinarily. The most frequently called commands are in */bin*. In the second case it is looked at immediately. In the first case, the current directory (.) is looked at first. Therefore, for most commands we will waste a lot of time looking in directories unsuccessfully.

Background and Wait

Sometimes you can get a little pseudo-parallelism by throwing some of your commands in the background, executing others in the foreground and waiting for the background programs to finish. We say *pseudo* because one CPU can only be doing one thing at a time. However, with several programs to run, it might be waiting for a disk access and have time to work on another program.

25

History of UNIX Shells

The shell has grown with UNIX. Table 12 shows some important dates. Until System V, AT&T Bell Labs had two versions of UNIX, one internal and one external. The idea was to debug the internal UNIX inhouse and ship the old version out. This proved too difficult, so today everyone has the same release. The names are still different, as you can see in Table 12. BSD stands for Berkeley Software Distribution.

Table 12. UNIX History

Year	Public	Bell	Berkeley	Comment
1968				Multics work declines
1969				Ken Thompson first UNIX on PDP-7
1970				Kernighan proposes the name UNIX
1971				Ritchie starts the C language
1972				Pipes added
1973				UNIX kernel in C
1974				First article in CACM
1975	V6	V6		Sent to many universities
1976				
1977	PWB	S1.0		Many new shell features
1978				Bourne Shell
1979	V7	S2.0	3.0BSD	Version 7 widely distributed
1980		S3.0	4.0,4.1BSD	Berkeley supports BSD
1981				AT&T new UNIX prices
1982	SysIII	S4.0		Many UNIX computer companies
1983	SysV	S5.0		AT&T divested
1984	SysVR2	S5.2	4.2BSD	Many books and mags on UNIX
1985				First books on shell programming

Brief History

The following information was pieced together from many different sources and may not be completely reliable. It should indicate some interesting milestones.

1969—Bell Labs had cooperated with others in the development of Multics, a much larger and more ambitious operating system. Problems led to the Labs withdrawing from the project. Dennis Ritchie credits Ken Thompson, himself, D. McIlroy, and Joseph F. Ossanna as the *most involved in the beginnings of UNIX.* The file system, including device files, was one of the earliest parts designed. Ritchie[6] recalls that Thompson wrote a game called *Space Travel* that simulated the movement of the major bodies of the Solar System *with the player guiding a ship here and there, observing the scenery, and attempting to land on the various planets and moons. . . .a game cost $75 for CPU time on the big computer. It did not take long, therefore, for Thompson to find a little-used PDP-7. . .* The file system and some basic programs to copy, print, delete and edit files were developed on the PDP-7. Many of the basic features of UNIX including system calls were added.

1970—Brian Kernighan suggested the name UNIX as a take-off on Multics. Official approval and funding of UNIX development had been turned down. Joe Ossanna proposed that a word-processing system be funded by the Labs. That got approval. They got a PDP-11 with a 24K memory and a half meg disk. How quickly we get spoiled.

1971—**roff** was copied from Multics, which had copied it from **runoff** on CTSS. The Patent Office, at Bell Labs, adopted UNIX because they could do line numbering.

1972—Pipes were added.

1973—Most of the basic features of the shell were in this version of the shell. The **if, goto,** and **exit** commands were independent UNIX programs. The shell was less than 20 pages of C code.

1974—First article on UNIX appears in the Communications of the ACM. Thompson travels to several universities to install UNIX.

1975—String variables, trap and *PATH* were added. One of the authors of this book first worked with UNIX at UC, Berkeley, a fact of absolutely no historical significance.

---

[6] Ritchie, Dennis M., *The Evolution of the UNIX Time-Sharing System,* **Language Design and Programming Methodology, Proceedings of a Symposium,** 10-11 September 1979.

1976—The flow control commands were moved into the shell to speed them up. The shell was about 40 lines of C code.

1977—The Programmers Workbench idea was primarily pushed by John Mashey, who probably saw most clearly the importance of the software tools approach, and urged keeping UNIX programs consistent with interchangeable use. There was a Mashey shell, but it lost out to the Bourne shell. The PWB shell was very primitive. It only had one-character shell variables. Much of the power for programming was introduced with Version 7. The **goto** and **label** features of PWD shell were dropped in going to Version 7.

1978—The shell was redesigned and grew to 100 pages of C code. UNIX was now widely used at Bell Labs and university campuses.

1979—Berkeley enhances Version 7 UNIX and supports it on PDP-11's and Vaxes. The shell we know today was pretty much finished by 1979 with the Version 7 UNIX.

1980—Bell Labs switches to System 3.0 internally.

1981—AT&T announces the availability of UNIX with attractive prices.

1982—At least 80 computer companies with UNIX operating systems emerge.

1983—UNIX becomes widely discussed and recognized. New UNIX organizations emerge.

1984—AT&T divested January 1st. Announces UNIX computer line. The changes for System V, Release 2 have greatly sped up the shell, but left its syntax and function the same.

1985—Bell announces System V, Release 2.2 with demand paging. The first shell programming books are published and their readers go on to do great things.

26

Grammar

Here is a Backus-Naur grammar for the shell in **lex/yacc** format style. **lex**
and **yacc** are UNIX software tools for developing language lexical analyzers
and compilers. We have made it a little more readable than what would be
necessary for **lex/yacc.** It would take work to make it a real **lex/yacc** script.

The idea here in Table 13 is that we define a term on the left side by giving possible combinations of terms on the right side.

Table 13. Shell Grammar in Backus-Naur Notation

Leftside	Rightside
program	: command-list
	;
command-list	: command
	| command-list newline
	| command-list ";"
	| command-list "&"
	| pipeline
	| andor
	;
andor	: command-list "&&" command-list
	| command-list "||" command-list
	;
pipeline	: command
	| pipeline "|" command
	;
command	: simple-command
	| (command-list)
	| [command-list]

Table 13 (Continued).

Leftside	Rightside
	| "for" name "do" command-list "done"
	| "for" name "in" word . . . "do" command-list "done"
	| "while" command-list "do" command-list "done"
	| "until" command-list "do" command-list "done"
	| "case" word "in" casepart . . . "esac"
	| "if" command-list "then" command-list elsepart "fi"
	;
casepart	: pattern ")" command-list ";;"
	;
pattern	: word
	| pattern "|" word
	;
elsepart	: empty
	| else command-list
	| elif command-list then command-list elsepart
	;
empty	:
	;
simplecommand	: item
	| simplecommand item
	;
item	: word
	| inputoutput
	| name " = " string
	;
inputoutput	: ">" file
	| "<" file
	| ">>" file
	| "<<" word
	;
file	: word
	| "&" digit
	| "&" -
	;
string	: ascii-characters
	| string ascii-character
	;

Table 13 (Continued).

Leftside	Rightside
word	: non-blank-char | word non-blank-char ;
name	: letter | name letter | name digit | name underscore ;
non-blank-char	: ascii-character NOT space tab newline ;
ascii-character	: [\000-\177] ;
letter	: [A-Za-z] ;
digit	: [0-9] ;
underscore	: "_" ;
whitespace	: space | tab | newline ;
space	: " " ;
tab	: [\010] ;
newline	: [\012] ;

CHAPTER

27

UNIX System V Shell

System V is the name for AT&T's newest version of the UNIX operating system. There is a series of releases under the System V umbrella, and different release versions have been provided to different machines. Like past versions of UNIX before it, System V fixed bugs in the older software and added a number of new utilities and features.

THE IMPORTANCE OF SYSTEM V

However, System V has far more significance than bug-fixing and new commands. In fact, System V has been something of a watershed in UNIX history. The reason for this is represented in a document called the *System V Interface Definition*. It specifies standards or guidelines for UNIX software on issues such as operating system services, the error conditions and return codes from executed commands, the types of values of signals, library routines, environmental variables, data files, and the way arguments are passed to and interpreted by commands.

The significance of these standards is profound. All future UNIX systems software will follow these standards. Or at least that is what AT&T says. Further, software developers now have a set of guidelines for building their own applications, and we hope this will make it far easier to combine packages from different vendors.

As mentioned earlier, there have been many versions of AT&T UNIX, Berkeley UNIX, and probably a dozen other UNIX lookalikes over the past ten years. To the commercial world, UNIX has been anarchy! AT&T's push behind the System V standard is changing this perception. System V provides a predictable environment and programming guidelines that standardize how end users see UNIX commands and how software developers build applications in areas such as terminal interfaces and command syntax. If you are in the market to buy UNIX, System V UNIX, or at least System V compatibility, is without question the way to go. It doesn't even matter whether System V has better features than 4.2BSD or UNIX lookalikes; all the large manufacturers and large buyers are targeting System V because, quite simply, it is now "the standard." At the time of this writing, even the major Berkeley 4.2 vendors are putting "System V compatibility," at the system call level, into their software. This includes Digital Equipment Corporation (with Ultrix™), and Sun MicroSystems.

In terms of functionality, there are substantial gains in System V. First, the terminal input/output interface has been completely revamped and improved. For programmers, this was always one of the standouts in Berkeley UNIX, and now, System V has comparable capability. Second, System V has provided powerful mechanisms for interprocess communications. This is important primarily for sophisticated applications in scientific and factory environments. Third, System V has record-locking, a feature that will be of immense value to applications developers targeting commercial markets. Fourth, System V has added dozens of new utilities. Some of these utilities are only for programmers. Others can help all of us. For example, a set of commands called *Source Code Control System* allows for archiving of ASCII files, providing version numbers, description of changes, and the ability to retrieve any past version. Programmers use this for their source files, documenters for their writing, and even applications developers for maintaining databases and audit trails. The Documenter's Workbench, an extra package that can be purchased with System V, also includes a range of utilities for formatting text and equations. In short, there is a lot more UNIX in System V.

Not all is rosy with System V. A major feature that is still missing, for example, is a scheme for memory management called *demand paging,* something that other large computer operating systems have implemented for faster performance in multiuser, multiprocess situations. The AT&T UNIX has always relied on "swapping," where entire jobs or processes are moved in and out of available memory. Paging slices individual processes into smaller segments. Under situations where multiple users are running programs that can "share" certain "pure" or re-entrant code segments, the benefits of paging can be substantial. Berkeley UNIX, in fact, has already implemented paging. Expect paging to come out of AT&T within the coming year. An analogous situation to paging is in the area of communications. Berkeley has had system call level subroutines, generally called *sockets,* for opening paths to different computers to read and write data. Bell Labs is expected to release a variation of this technology which goes by the name of *streams.* Clearly, the people at Berkeley have paved the way for Bell Labs in memory management for large computers and networking.

THE BOURNE SHELL

The System V Bourne shell also has significant improvements, over older shells, in both speed and functionality. At the same time, for the most part, it is "upward compatible" with the previous Bourne shells. The shell scripts written in Bourne shell for Version 7 or System III UNIX systems will work under System V. The System V shell is faster when it executes shell scripts. The reason for this is that several important commands that are commonly used in shell programming have been built into the Shell, and no longer require a separate **exec** to run. These include the **echo** and **test** commands. The internal buffer for the environment has also been doubled in the System V shell. This is not usually a factor, except when very long strings are assigned to shell variables and are then manipulated. Lastly, although not strictly part of the Shell, System V has a number of new utilities or separate programs that can be very handy in shell programming. In this chapter, we will examine several important new features of the shell and a set of new utilities.

Built-Ins

echo—The simple step of building echo into the shell does more to improve the speed of executing shell scripts than anything else. The **echo** command is the same as in older systems, except for the way that one specifies *Don't put out a new line.* Before, this was done with the $-n$ flag to echo. Now, you leave out the $-n$ flag and put "\\c" after the last character of the string to be echoed. Here's a quick example:

```
echo "What's your name? \\c"
read NAME
```

Which, when executed, will print the string and leave the cursor after the question mark. Otherwise, a new line is printed, and the cursor is left at the beginning of the next line.

test—Another reason why shell scripts will run faster on Systems V is because the **test** command is built into the shell. While all old **test** expressions will work in the new shell, there is also a different way to state expressions that is somewhat terser and stylistically more elegant. The **test** command is awkward and un-UNIX like. It looks like something out of Fortran. The folks at Bell Labs sought to pretty it up a little. Should you bother to learn this new format? You have to consider portability to older systems.

Let's look at some examples. First, here is a simple shell program with a test statement to see if a file exists in our *HOME* directory. The shell program is called with an argument, which is the name of the file we want to look for, and it is substituted into the expression at $1.

```
# lookup: Let's look for the file
if test -z "$1"
then
   echo "usage: lookup filename"
   exit 126
fi
```

```
if test − f "$1"
then
   echo "$1 is a regular file"
   if test − r "$1"
   then
      echo "It is readable. . ."
   fi
   if test − w "$1"
   then
      echo "It is writable. . ."
   fi
   if test − x "$1"
   then
      echo "It is executable. . ."
   fi
   exit 0

elif test − d "$1"
then
   echo "$1 is a directory!"
   exit 1
else
   echo "The file is a special device, or named pipe!"
   exit 1
fi
```

For example, if we typed:

```
$ lookup $HOME/.profile
```

the result would be:

```
/usr/marc/.profile is a regular file
It is readable. . .
It is writable. . .
```

You should already be familiar with the **if, then, elif, else, fi** type expressions in the shell. Similarly, a program can be exited with different values, so that the exit status of a program can then be used to do other things. Here's an example of how we can use the exit status of the shell script of above to do other things:

```
lookup $HOME/.profile
case $? in
0)       echo "Do you want to look at the file? \\c"
         read Z
         if ["$Z" = "y" ]
```

```
                then
                                cat $HOME/.profile
                fi
                ;;
   *)           ;;
esac
```

Here is how a slightly modified version of the **lookup** program looks in the new System V syntax:

```
# lookup: A new test format

if [ ! − n "$1" ]
then
   echo "usage: lookup filename" 1 > &2
   exit 1
fi

if [ − f "$1" ]
then
   echo "$1 is a regular file"
   if [ − r "$1" ]
   then
     echo "It is readable. . ."
   fi
   if [ − w "$1" ]
   then
     echo "It is writable. . ."
   fi
   if [ − x "$1" ]
   then
     echo "It is executable. . ."
   fi
   exit 0
elif [ − d "$1" ]
then
   echo "$1 is a directory!"
   exit 1
else
   echo "The file is a special device, or named pipe!"
   exit 1
fi
```

You can see that the test is automatically invoked with an expression enclosed in brackets. In other words, you don't have to type **test** all the time if you don't want to. One word of caution, however. There must be at least one blank space after the open square bracket ([), and at least one blank space before the closing square bracket (]). Lastly, in the second shell script, the first test expression is an example of the (!) or unary operator in the test command. The *(− z)* flag, and the (! *− n)* are equivalent in functionality.

Now here's the rub. An important feature of programming in the shell is that it has been highly portable across different UNIX machines, in fact, more portable than any other language. For example, the authors were working on one particular project, leading a team developing several dozen distinct applications for a federal government user. The development work started on Intel-based desktop computers. Half way through the job, the hardware environment was changed entirely to AT&T 3B2s. All we had to do was **uucp** (the communications program) our data files and shell scripts over to the new computer, clone the directory structures from one machine to another, and set up the new user profiles. Everything was in ASCII text and it took a day. We were fortunate, however, that the desktop microcomputers and the 3B2s were both running System V, because we used the new test syntax, and many features of the **tput** command to be described below. If the new environment had been VAXes running 4.2BSD, for example, probably a hundred shell scripts would have had to be re-edited to remove System V dependent statements. Therefore, the point is clear: if you suspect that you will be running in a non-System V UNIX environment, be cautious about using the new features of the System V shell.

pwd and set—The **pwd** command has also been built into the shell, so it is fast! Here's a little shell script that gets the last component of the current working directory from **pwd.**

```
# dirname: current directory name

OLDIFS = $IFS
IFS = "/
"
set `pwd`
IFS = $OLDIFS

while [ "$1" ]
do
   LAST = $1
   shift
done

echo "$LAST"
```

This command script saves the original Interfield Separator and resets it to '\'. Then, the **set** breaks up the path output by **pwd**. Next, we walk through the positional parameters, which are the directories in the path to the present working directory, always shifting one position to the right, until we reach the last one. At this point, the value of the parameter will be saved in the variable called *LAST,* and we will break out of the **while** loop, print out the value of *LAST.* Of course there are a couple of faster ways to get the last word of the **pwd** string. Hint: use $#.

The **set** command also has a new flag, the −*f* flag, which turns off metacharacter expansion in the shell. This can be most useful if you want to pass an asterisk (*), for example, to a shell script as an argument, and don't want it expanded into a filename. For example, the command

```
cd /; echo *
```

produces the following output:

```
adm bck bin dev doc etc lib lost+found mnt prog stand tmp
unix usr
```

which is a listing of all the file or directory names at the root level. On the other hand, the command:

```
cd /; set −f; echo *
```

produces only the asterisk

```
*
```

The *set* −*f* disabled the wildcard expansion.

***The* getopt *command*—**The **getopt** command is specifically used to parse command-line options given to a shell script. By specifying the legal flags that can be given to the command, **getopt** will parse the command line, detect errors, and provide greater flexibility to the user for typing the command. In the example below, a sample shell script using **getopt** is shown. Note that the first thing that we do is define a *USAGE* string that can be used later on. Next, a **set** is performed on the **getopt** command output. We pass to **getopt** the valid flags, *a,b,?,* and lastly *c.* The colon means that *c* must be used with one argument. If **getopt** cannot parse the user's command line correctly, it exits with a nonzero status. The test condition will pick this up ($? always gets the exit status of the last command run) and will print out an error message. In the **case** statement, we look to see what flags were given on the command line and print out simple messages to show that the parsing worked. Again, you might want to type this shell script into your computer and experiment with it.

```
USAGE = "prog −[ab] −[c file]"

set − `getopt abc:? $*`
if [ $? != 0 ]
```

```
        then
            echo $USAGE 1>&2
            exit 1
        fi

        for I in $*
        do

            case $I in
            −a)         echo "The −a flag"
                        shift
                        ;;
            −b)         echo "The −b flag"
                        shift
                        ;;
            −c)
                        ARG=$2
                        echo "The −c flag has an argument with it: $ARG"
                        shift 2
                        ;;
            −\?)
                echo $USAGE
                exit 1
                ;;
            esac

        done
```

The **set −** is a special feature of the **set** command which tells **set** to use the minus (−) to separate flags. Note also that inside the **case** statement, shifts are performed to keep the positional parameters ($1, $2, etc.) current for each loop with a new flag. Only in this way, for example, can *ARG* be assigned to the argument specified with the −c flag to the shell script. In other words, the shifts allow us to access that argument specifically as $2.

Once you get used to **getopt,** you will find that it provides a useful standard for parsing command line options in your shell scripts. Further, it will make your shell scripts interpret command line options just like all the UNIX utilities. For example, two valid ways of running the shell script above are:

```
    $ program −a −b −c arg
    $ program −ab −c arg
```

Both of which will generate:

```
    The −a flag
    The −b flag
    The −c flag has an argument with it: arg
```

More on stdin, stdout, stderr, and read—Let's review a few basic principles for a moment. UNIX commands employ the concepts of *stdin, stdout,* and *stderr* all the time. *stdin,* which stands for standard input, is where the commands typically receive their data for processing. As we described earlier, UNIX commands usually take input that is redirected from existing files or that is piped from other commands. The following command line demonstrates both types of *stdin.* It is an example from the graphics that are available under UNIX.

```
graph < data | plot —T4014
```

The **graph** command uses data files that are *x,y* pairs, which are contained in the the file *data.* The output of the **graph** command must then be piped into the **plot** filter, which, using the device specified with the —*T* flag, knows which type of output device to send the graphics output to. If we were using a Tektronix 4014 terminal, we would have a graph! *stdin* can also be typed from the keyboard, followed by a control-d *(CNTL-d),* which means end of input for the command. Borrowing the example above, we might type:

```
graph | plot
1   2
3   4
4   10
2   1
```

The **graph** command knows to look for input from the keyboard because none was supplied by redirection from a file or by a pipe from another command.

While there is only one input channel going into UNIX commands, *stdin,* there are two for output. The first output channel is called *stdout.* The second is called *stderr.* There is a convention in all UNIX programming that error messages are written to *stderr,* and that the normal output of commands is sent to *stdout.* This can be most useful when you want to save error messages and regular output in different files. The way to do this on the command line is to refer to *stdin* as 1, and *stderr* as 2. The general format to save *stdout* and *stderr* in different files is

```
program < data 1> file1 2> file2
```

This means that *stdout* is saved in *file1,* and *stderr* in *file2.* If you don't redirect output, both will just come to the screen, mixed together.

Just as it is convenient to have two separate output channels built into UNIX, you just might run into the need for having two different channels for input. Here's a simple case where two types of input are needed. Let's say we have a shell script that formats a text file and can send it off to the printer. One input requirement is to redirect the textfile as the *data* for the shell script. The other input requirement would be to ask the user for data. You might ask, "How are they going to pull that one off? There is only one input channel, *stdin.*" Well friends, we can achieve two effective *stdin* streams by faking out the shell. The following shell script, **look,** shows an example of this.

```
# A script to show that using piped stdin into a program
# and getting keyboard response is a little tricky

echo "Let's take a look at your file.
Type 'c' for cat, 'p' for pg, or 'q' to quit
- > \\c"

read ANS < /dev/tty
case $ANS in

   [Cc]) cat <&0
      ;;
   [Pp]) pg <&0
      ;;
   *)
      ;;
esac
echo "Bye now!"
```

The way to execute the command is simply

```
$ look file
```

The purpose of this shell script is to allow the user to pick how he or she wants to look at a text file. The first two lines simply echo out a question, and the user will type *'c'* to employ the **cat** command, or *'p'*, to use the **pg** command. When we do a **read** from the shell, it normally reads from *stdin.* In this case, that would be a problem, because *stdin* is the file that is specified on the command line. To get the input from the keyboard, we make **read** take its input directly from the keyboard, which can be referred to as */dev/tty* inside shell scripts. The next part of the shell script is a simple **case** statement, that does a switch on what the user types as a response to the **echo** question. The next important thing to note is that when we execute either **cat** or **pg** inside the shell script, we force the commands to take their input from the formal *stdin,* by redirecting into them the address of *stdin,* where the & stands for *address,* and 0 stands for *stdin.*

Cursor Control: **tput**—This is one area that System V is substantially different in implementation than older versions of UNIX. The basic design concept for dealing with terminals is that there should be a database of terminal information. Then editing programs, spreadsheets, and any other interactive program can clear the screen, scroll text, set highlight mode, insert and delete lines, and so forth. With such a terminal information database, the application program can be *device independent*.

In older versions of UNIX, and still under Berkeley 4.2, life was simple: the terminal information database was an ASCII text file that you could easily edit and understand as a programmer. There were two drawbacks, however. First, the information for all terminals is contained in a single file, called */etc/gtermcap,* and so for large multiuser systems, the file could be immense (with entries for hundreds of terminals). The second drawback is that you had to program in C to access and use the */etc/gtermcap* capabilities. (However, the **termput** program in the Manual at the back of this book shows how to get at those entries with a shell program.) You could do this in two ways: either through a higher level screen management library called *curses,* or, with a little more work, through a lower level library containing a few routines called *termlib.*

Under System V, life has changed quite a bit, perhaps for the better, perhaps not. On one hand, under System V, you can access a myriad of terminal information and use it inside shell scripts. With this capability, you can use **echo, read,** and a new command called **tput,** to build sophisticated dialogs all from within the shell! On the other hand, the implementation of the terminal information database is more complicated from a systems administration point of view. One has to make a *source* for the terminal description, then compile it with a command called **tic** (terminfo compiler), and make sure that this binary data is placed in the proper directory under */usr/lib/terminfo.* Someone at Bell Labs thought it would make the initiation of big editor programs much faster by reading in one binary file rather than scanning the */etc/gtermcap* database.

terminfo, has many more types of terminal characteristics and can be accessed from the shell, but it is also harder to set up. That's unfortunate, because the power of UNIX has always been in its elegance, simplicity, and modularity. Now, let's see how to use *terminfo* from the shell. We hope that you are on a terminal now.

If you turn to Section 4 in any System V Documentation Set, and look up *terminfo,* you will see a listing of several hundred individual terminal descriptive capabilities. Many of the characteristic descriptors are not useful to you in shell programming. Some are, however. For example, under old versions of the shell, if we wanted to clear the screen and "home the cursor" at the top of the screen, we would **echo** an *ESC-H ESC-J* from the shell, as in:

```
echo ∧[H∧[J
```

The control square bracket (∧[) is what an escape looks like if you enter it with the quoting mechanism in **vi.** To get a real **ESC** using **vi,** you must type a **CNTL-V** first, then the **ESC** key. Under System V, to accomplish a clear screen, use the **tput** command and type:

```
$ tput clear
```

The command will work only if a terminal description has been set up under */usr/lib/terminfo* for your particular terminals, and your *TERM* parameter has been correctly set in your *.profile*. This is an important point: using the terminfo capability inside shell scripts introduces a degree of nonportability to the shell scripts. If you plan to move your shell scripts to different UNIX installations, it still is worth using *terminfo,* because the System V standard is becoming dominant. But you may have to put the **tput** commands inside of an **if test** statement that tests a system variable that has been set up in the start of the application. For example:

```
VER = SYS5

# later

if test "$VER" = "SYS5"
then
   tput clear
fi
```

Now, let's look at some more features of **tput.** Let's ring the bell three times.

```
echo "Three chimes for our side"
for I in 1 2 3
do
   tput bel
done
```

And, there is standout mode:

```
tput smso
echo "Hello there"
tput rmso
```

smso turns on reverse video, and *rmso* turns it off. Another way of accomplishing the same end is to assign a shell variable to escape sequences sent by the **tput** command. In the example below, we play with standout mode and blink mode. *sgr0* is the global return-to-normal-mode sequence. Also, **tput cols** and **tput lines** get the number of columns and lines for your terminal.

```
BOLD = `tput smso`
BLINK = `tput blink`
OFF = `tput sgr0`

echo " ${BOLD}Goodbye!${OFF}"
echo " ${BLINK}Later!${OFF}"
```

```
echo "Your terminal has ${BOLD}`tput cols`${OFF} columns
and ${BLINK}`tput lines`${OFF} lines!"
```

Assigning shell variables to tput sequences can be very handy when an application consists of a top shell script calling many other shells scripts. The variable can be assigned at the top shell and then exported, so that other shell scripts can use it.

```
BOLD=`tput smso`
OFF=`tput sgr0`
export BOLD OFF
```

There are several other neat tricks you can play with **tput.** In the example below, a string is echoed to the screen, the shell sleeps for several seconds, and then we move the cursor up one line with the *cuu1* string and erase to the end of the line.

```
echo "
This line has got to go!"
sleep 2
tput cuu1
tput el
echo "And its gone!"
```

To erase to the end of the display from the current cursor position type:

```
tput ed
```

To see how this works, you might try the following:

```
ls −l /usr
tput home
tput ed
```

The shell program **termput** is included in the Manual section in the back of the book. **termput** is like **tput,** except it looks up terminal capabilities in */etc/termcap.* Therefore, it is portable to all UNIX systems with **vi.**

Moving the Cursor

There is one important thing that you cannot do with **tput** directly: move the cursor to a particular column and row position. There is a capability to set up x,y cursor movement in **tput,** but **tput** does not take that last step of interpreting the character sequences and moving the cursor. Here is a sample program, written in C, that will do this for you. The command is called **cursor,** and the source code for it is called *cursor.c.*

```
/*
cursor - moves the cursor to row and col on the screen
*/

#include <stdio.h>

#define USAGE"usage: cursor row col [ CURSOR ]\n\
Where CURSOR is the cm entry in /etc/termcap.\n\
If the shell variable CURSOR has not been set,\n\
use 'tput cup', etc.\n"

#define EUSAGE 1

#define NOCURSOR "%s: No CURSOR argument nor $CURSOR shell \
variable\n"
#define ENOCURSOR 2

#define ROW 1
#define COL 2
#define CURSOR 3

char *tgoto ();
char *getenv ();

main (argc; argv) int argc; char *argv [];
{
    char *cm;

    if (argc < 3) {
        fprintf (stderr, USAGE);
        exit (EUSAGE);
    } else if (argc = = 3) {
        if (cm = getenv ("CURSOR")) {
            printf ("%s", tgoto (cm, atoi(argv[COL]), atoi(argv[ROW])));
        } else {
            fprintf (stderr, NOCURSOR, argv [0]);
            exit (ENOCURSOR);
        }
    } else {
            printf ("%s", tgoto (argv[CURSOR], atoi(argv[COL]),
                            atoi(argv[ROW])));
    }
}
```

Type this text into a file called *cursor.c* on your computer and then type one of the following:

```
$ # For System V
$ cc cursor.c − o cursor − Iterminfo
$ # For Other UNIX Systems
$ cc cursor.c − o cursor − Itermlib
```

which will compile the command. You might then want to move the command to a bin directory in your *PATH*. Now, we can have some fun. To move the cursor to column 10, row 10, we can type:

```
cursor 10 10 '"tput cup'"
```

The command **tput cup** sets up the correct cursor movement string needed by the terminal. The **cursor** command takes that, and two more arguments that are put into the cursor movement string so that the cursor can be repositioned. A faster way of doing this, particularly if you are going to use **cursor** frequently in a shell script, is to assign the shell variable *CURSOR* to the output of **tput cup** as follows:

```
CURSOR = '"tput cup'"
export CURSOR

cursor   10   10   ; echo "Hi there gang"
cursor    1    1   ; echo "Here I am again"
cursor   23   60   ; echo "See you later!"
```

One last refinement is to get rid of our normal shell prompt so that the **cursor** command and **tput** can be used to build a data entry screen or dialog. In the example below, we reassign *PS1* to null. The script is an example of a trivial dialog, but it shows how cursor motion and dialog actions can be used in the shell.

```
PS1 =
CURSOR = 'tput cup'
export CURSOR
tput clear
echo "Its Time for Wine

What is your name ?  \c"
read NAME

cursor   15    0
tput smso
echo"
```

```
---------------------------------------------
|                                           |
|                                           |
|                                           |
|                                           |
|                                           |
|                                           |
|                                           |
|                                           |
|                                           |
|                                           |
|                                           |
|                                           |
|                                           |
|                                           |
|                                           |
---------------------------------------------
"
tput rmso
cursor   16    2
echo "What wine do you like (red, white, rose)? \ c"
read TYPE
case $TYPE in
    re*)
        cursor 6 20
        echo "A sponge no doubt. "
        TYPE = r
        ;;
    w*) cursor 6 20
        echo "Pretty fancy, ug ug."
        TYPE = w
        ;;
    *) cursor 6 20
        echo "The stuff of peasants. "
        TYPE = R
        ;;
esac

    cursor   17    2
    echo "And what type of food (meat, fish, veggies, twinkies)? \ c"
read FOOD
```

```
cursor  20   2
echo "Well $NAME, happy eats and better drinks!"
```

If you type this shell script into your computer and run it, you will see that a question box, placed in reverse video, is created in the middle of the screen. Different responses are then placed above the question box depending on what the user answers, as evaluated in the case statement. Obviously, the potential for building specialized dialogs, more serious than the one above, and perhaps not, is unlimited.

Named Pipes

Named pipes were first introduced in System III UNIX, and have been carried forward into System V. What is a named pipe, and can it be useful in shell programming? The purpose of named pipes is to provide the ability to have independent processes "share" data without having to be linked in a single command pipeline, or having one program write data to a file, and a second one read from that file. In other words, before named pipes, if you wanted two programs to share data from the shell, you would type either:

```
command1 | command2
```

or

```
command1 > datafile
command2 < datafile
```

The problem with writing temporary files is the time they take. UNIX is disk bound. We want to have the shell save our short interprocess messages in a memory buffer. Named pipes create such a buffer for our programs to communicate with.

Now let's say that you wanted to have the second command be invoked at some earlier point in time, and wait around until **command1**, fired up later on, has some data to give to **command2.** The way we used to do this in UNIX, from the shell, was to to have **command2** periodically check a temporary datafile to see if anything has been deposited in it.

```
while true
do
   if test — s file
   then
      command2 < tmpfile
      break
   fi
   sleep 5
done
```

Presumably, *command1* will leave some data in the *tmpfile* "mailbox," and the shell script will see that the *tmpfile* is greater than 0 in size and then call *command2* using *tmpfile* as the standard input.

A named pipe gets around temporary "mailbox" file creation, and the looping and checking shown above. The basic strategy is to use the **mknod** command in UNIX to create a special file, the named pipe, to which data may be sent. Then, any command can read from that pipe as standard input. Since the named pipe is like a file, the read write permissions shown in an *ls −l* command apply to who can read data from it. Also, once a reading command, **command2** in the example above, encounters an end-of-file (EOF) character in the data stream from the named pipe, that command terminates itself, and must be reinvoked to receive more data from the name pipe.

To make a named pipe, type:

```
$ /etc/mknod npipe p
```

The name of the pipe can be any nonexistent filename in the working directory. An *ls −l* of a named pipe directory entry is distinguished by the little *p* in high bit of the permissions data.

```
$ ls −l npipe
prw-rw—     1 marc     prog     0 Oct 19 15:45 npipe
```

Now we can set up a program to read data from the named pipe. Let's use the **wc** (word count) command as a simple example.

```
$ wc < npipe &
```

The ampersand (&) places the command line in background. This is necessary because *wc* will not exit until it receives some data and encounters an end-of-file (EOF). Next, let's write some data to the named pipe.

```
$ ls −l /bin > npipe &
```

Putting the process in background is necessary only if you are not sure that another process is waiting to read data from the named pipe. If one did not exist, the *ls* command above, for example, would just sit there and not exit. However, since we already invoked the **wc** command before, the background operation wasn't really essential.

Now, as soon as we type the command line above, output from the previous **wc** command will appear on the terminal. The operating system had immediately detected that the named pipe had received data and that it was time for **wc** to get to work! A sample of **wc**'s output will look like:

```
92   821   5359
```

28

The Korn Shell

The new Korn shell, **ksh,** introduces many great new features. Developed by David G. Korn, at AT&T Bell Labs, Murray Hill, New Jersey, it has all of the Bell Shell features and the best C shell features. As of the writing of this book it is available from AT&T in the "tool chest," a group of UNIX programs that you can buy individually. The Korn shell is the best seller in the group. We are praying to the gods of UNIX that it will become the standard Bell shell in a future release of UNIX. If it does, shell programming will increase rapidly, because the new features are just what are needed.

Here we will discuss briefly what is new. In general some of the best features of the C shell were added to the Bell shell; such features as history, aliasing, arrays, jobs, and new features like arithmetic, menus, variable attributes, more input and output facilities, and many more features.

Keep in mind that, for a few years, these new features will not be portable until many more UNIX computers are updated to the newer UNIX systems. We are sorry that we can only briefly describe the new features. We want to give you a glimpse into the future of shell programming, but a more detailed treatment will be needed if the Korn shell spreads to many UNIX systems.

NEW SYMBOLS AND COMMANDS

A new pipe symbol (|&) runs the preceding pipe in the background and connects a two way pipe to the parent shell. Foreground jobs can then pipe data to this background job and receive output from it.

New Commands

select *name [in word . . .]* **do** *list* **done**—This is a new menu command. The list of *words* is displayed on the screen with numbers in front, i.e., a menu. The user types one of the menu numbers and the associated word is assigned to *name.* Then the *list* of commands is executed. The command loops until a break or **CNTL**-*d* is entered. The user input is assigned to the shell variable *REPLY,* which can be used in the commands of the *list.*

function **name** { *list ;* } and *name ( )* { *list ;* }—This defines a function and calls it. The System V, Release 2 shell already introduced the shell functions. They give you the ability to write subroutines within your shell program, instead of having to have a separate shell program to call. Functions are nice for collecting your code in one file. It is also more natural to programmers who are accustomed to functions.

Aliasing

As in the C shell, commands can be created as another name for an existing command and, usually, some of its flags. For example, you can alias **l** to be the same as typing **ls -l.**

Tilde Substitution

The C shell feature, ~*user* in a path name is substituted with the path to that user's home directory. ~*guest/file* means the same as */usr/guest/file,* if */usr/guest* is the home directory of *guest.*

New Variable Substitution

Two new variable substitutions are added to *${VAR:-word},* etc: *${variable#pattern}* the number-sign (#) means delete the *pattern* from the beginning of the value of the *variable.* In *${variable%pattern}* the percent-sign (%) is the same, except that it deletes the *pattern* from the end of the variable's value.

New Automatic Variables

$% Process ID of Parent—Many child processes die young. This symbol, for a parent **process-id,** is useful when a command wants a more lasting process-id number than its own.

$. Last Argument of Previous Command—This lets you grab the last argument of the last command and saves you the effort of retyping it.

New Standard Shell Variables

In addition to *HOME, PATH, PS1,* etc., there are several new standard shell variables. Check this list and be careful not to use these names in ways that will conflict in the future with the Korn shell.

PWD—This keeps the present working directory path.

OLDPWD—This holds the path to the last directory you were in and is nice for getting back there:

```
$ cd $OLDPWD
```

RANDOM—This is a random number generator with a different, pseudo random value each time it is used.

REPLY—See the **select** command above.

EDITOR—This keeps the name of your favorite text editor. It lets a shell program call your preferred editor when editing is needed.

ENV—This is like the *.profile* file, but it is executed when the Korn shell is invoked.

FCEDIT—This is your favorite editor for the **fc** command. See **fc** below.

HISTFILE—This holds the history of the commands you type.

HISTSIZE—This variable holds the number of commands you want to have remembered and stored in the *HISTFILE* variable. In other words, the number of commands you can go back to, perhaps re-edit, and re-execute.

MAILCHECK—This is the number of seconds between the times that the shell checks for the arrival of mail.

MAILPATH—This is the list of paths to the mail directories that are searched like the *PATH* shell variable.

PS3—This third prompt string is used by the **select** command, and doubt-lessly more in the future.

SHELL—This holds the path to the shell.

Arithmetic Evaluation

This is an important addition, because in the standard Bell shell one must call either the **expr** or the **bc, dc, awk** programs to do math. These, pro-grams, like all programs, must be cranked up, which takes a while. Usually one to several seconds. Embedded in a loop, these programs can really slow down a shell program. This new facility significantly speeds shell scripts and is easier to use. Unfortunately, it only does long integer arithmetic, not floating-point. So you will still have to use **bc** for floating point math. See the **let** command below for specifics.

Job Control

This facility lets you get at those programs that you ran in the background. A job number is assigned to each background job and you can kill the job or bring it to the foreground. In the foreground you can interact with the program because its input is reconnected to your terminal.

Inline Editing Options

This is a great improvement. Have you ever made a mistake typing a command? We sure have. It is good typing practice to have to retype the whole line, but we would just as soon forego the privilege. This facility lets you edit the last command line as if it were a one line window of a text editor. You can move back and forth on the line and fix the command up. It can give you both the **EMACS** as well as the **vi** Editing Modes.

New Built-In Commands

Here are some of the new commands built into the Korn shell.

alias *[-tx] [name[= value] . . .]*—This lets you assign a string to *name*. Then when *name* is used, the value is executed.

bg *[%job]*—This command will put the current foreground job, or the specified job, into the background.

cd *old new*—This lets you substitute the *new* string for the *old* string in the *present working directory*. This is a quicker way to edit yourself into another directory without having to type the whole path. What a nice idea. The present working directory is just a string in the shell.

```
$ pwd /usr/rod/book/sh/tut
$ cd tut man
$ pwd /usr/rod/book/sh/man
```

Here the *tut* directory was changed to the *man* directory. You can also change the path further up the tree.

fc *[-e ename] [-nir] [first] [last]*—This command lets you edit the commands saved in the history of your commands. It lets you grab an earlier command and edit for re-execution. All of this is to save you typing. The Korn shell uses this command, whereas the C shell used the exclamation mark to indicate previous command editing and re-execution.

fg *[%job]*—This command brings a background process to the foreground, i.e., connects its input to the current shell.

jobs *[-l]*—Type this command and you will get a list of background jobs.

let *arg* . . .—This is the new arithmetic command. It is a lot like the BASIC language **let** command.

```
$ let A = 2 + 2
$ echo $A
4
```

Operators are, in order of precedence:

Table 14. Korn Shell Arithmetic Operators

(())	quotes the enclosed strings like double quotes ('''')
()	execute operants with first
-	unary minus
!	logical negation
* / %	times, divide, modulo
+ −	add and subtract
<= >= <>	logical less than or equal to, greater than or equal to, less than and greater than.
== !=	logical equal and not equal
=	assignment value on right on to variable on left

print *[-npru[n]] [arg. . .]*—This new command has several uses, but most importantly, it is used to send input to the pipe command with the |**&** symbol. In short, you can write into a background job. This makes possible co-routines with programs that take a while to start up. You can keep sending them data to process in the background instead of having to crank them up each time you need them.

read *[-pru[n]] [name?prompt] [name . . .]*—This adds a *prompt* to the standard **read** command.

return *[n]*—This ends execution of a function.

Set Options—Several new set options are added.

substring *[-1L lpat] string [rpat]*—This command deletes subpatterns from *string,* leaving the remaining string.

typeset *[-LRZaeilprtux [name[= value]] . . .]*—This command lets you format a string in many ways like left and right justification, write into two way pipe and many more. It lets you pretty print strings without calling **awk, sed,** or other commands.

We hope the Korn shell is quickly adopted so that we can all start using these new features.

29

The C Shell

The C shell changes so much of the shell that another book of this size is necessary to cover it. Learning the two together makes it very hard to learn either. We don't want to confuse you, so don't read this unless you have to work with the C shell.

If all other things were equal, we prefer the syntax and added features of the C shell. But things are not equal. We are convinced that the future is in the faster Bell shells which are being constantly improved. Plus, any shell programs that must run on every UNIX must be written in the Bell shell. So we will just mention some highlights of the C shell.

THE csh COMMAND

To get into the C shell you can type **csh.** You usually get the percent sign (%) prompt instead of the dollar sign ($). On some systems you are automatically in the C shell. It can be set in your entry in the */etc/passwd* file.

history

The *history* feature is the best part of the C shell. It makes the C shell remember your commands so that you can repeat them with only a few keystrokes. For example, you can re-execute the last line you typed with:

    % !!

You can also re-edit a previous line by substituting one string for another. This feature has been included in the Korn shell. Of course you can also do this in the **vi** editor as we explained in Chapter 6.

history is also a built-in command that will list the previous commands that you have typed. Followed by a number, it lists that many previous commands. To turn the history mechanism on you must type:

    % set history = 20

This tells the C shell to keep the last 20 commands you type. Note that the C shell needs spaces around its equal sign.

First Character of C shell Program

The first character of a C shell program must be the number sign (#). This is used to distinguish between a C shell and a Bell shell. Even when you are in the C shell, it will assume that all shell programs are for the Bell shell, unless you put the number sign as the first character on the first row. If you forget, the Bell shell will try to execute your C shell program, and will usually die when it finds new syntax. Often it is the parentheses that kill it. They delimit word lists in the C shell and subshells in the Bell shell.

C Syntax

foreach *var (wordlist) cmdlist* **end**—The shell **for** command is replaced with the **foreach** command. Note that word lists are in parentheses and the **end** statement replaces the **do, done** statements of the shell.

if *(expression) command*—This replaces the shell **if** command. Note the *expression* is in parentheses.

if *(expression)* **then** *cmdlist* **endif**—**endif** replaces **fi.**

elseif *(expression) cmdlist*—**elseif** replaces **elif.**

else *cmdlist*—This stays the same.

switch *string* **case** *string: cmdlist* **breaksw endsw**—**switch** replaces the **case** statement. **case** *string:* now replaces *pattern*) of the Bell shell.

default: *cmdlist* **breaksw**—This replaces the *) pattern of the Bell shell.

while *(expression) cmdlist* **end**—Note the parentheses around the expression and that **end** replaces the **do, done** begin and end of the shell as in **foreach** above.

if or while test—The C shell has a prettier test expression for the **if** and **while** commands.

Built-Ins

alias *[name [wordlist]] and* **unalias**—**alias** lets you give other names to commands. By itself it lists the aliases you have. With a name, it lists what it converts that string to.

```
% alias ls ls -p
```

Table 15. Shell and C shell Test Expressions

sh Test	csh Expression
number1 -eq number2	number1 = = number2
number1 -ge number2	number1 >= number2
number1 -gt number2	number1 > number2
number1 -le number2	number1 <= number2
number1 -lt number2	number1 < number2
number1 -ne number2	number1 != number2
string1 = string2	string1 == string2
string1 != string2	same
expression1 -a expression2	expression1 && expression2
expression1 -o expression2	expression1 | expression2

From now on when you type **ls** the *-p* option will automatically be turned on as if you had typed it. You can remove an alias with the **unalias** command.

goto—What can we say?

limit *and* **unlimit**—This allows you to set limits on things like *cputime* and *filesize*.

login *and* **logout**—These explicit commands are useful in C shell programming.

onintr—This replaces the **trap** command of the shell.

popd *and* **pushd** *and* **dirs**—When you go to another directory with **cd** you often want to come back to the directory you started in. These commands remember your old directory. **dirs** will list the stack of directories you have been in.

rehash *and* **unhash**—To speed up command execution (marginally) the directories in your *PATH* are hashed for faster lookup of the files in them. The problem is that when you put new programs into the directories, and try to execute them, they cannot be found. You have to type the **rehash** command. Turn off this mechanism with the **unhash** command.

set *and* **unset**—This is like the shell **set** command, but the variable substitution has changed.

```
% set path = (/bin /usr/bin)
```

replaces

```
$ PATH = /bin:/usr/bin
```

unset removes a variable from the C shell's internal list.

setenv *and* **unsetenv**—Instead of **export** *PATH* you type **setenv** *path* *(/bin / usr/bin).*

source *[-h] file*—This command will read code from the *file* as if you had typed it in. It replaces the dot command of the Bell shell.

suspend—This command, along with CNTL-Z (∧Z) will stop a foreground job in such a way that the **bg** command can throw it into the background. Very nice when you suddenly realize that a program you ran is going to take awhile.

.login *and* **.cshrc**—*.login* replaces the Bell shell *.profile* file. Each file must be in the user's home directory and contain a list of commands that are read on **login.** When **csh** starts up it first reads commands from *.cshrc.* All of these files must be in your home directory.

Job Control

Like the Bell shell, the C shell runs programs in the background as well as in the foreground. The C shell gives you more facilities. You can put a running program into the background with the **bg** command and you can bring a background job to the foreground with the **fg** command. **jobs** will list your background jobs and **kill** *% job* will stop the job with the number *job*.

The Math Command

Instead of the ugly **expr** command of the shell, the C shell has a math command. These two commands have the same effect:

```
% A = $A + 1
$ A = `expr $A + 1`
```

BERKELEY ENHANCEMENTS

There are a few dozen commands that the Berkeley people added to UNIX. They are called the *Berkeley enhancements.* Many UNIX porters have added these enhancements to their versions of UNIX. Bell Labs has also picked up some of these functions, but for some perverse reason, renamed them.

The Berkeley **more** command became the **pg,** for page. command when the Bell Labs people wrote it. Both display a file one full screen at a time so that it doesn't run past you.

Software Sources

Program Examples Available

The authors are available for consulting and can be reached through the following:

Bill Hamilton
Knowledge Quest
19762 MacArthur
Irvine, CA 92715
(714) 833-2930

Peter Vizel
MultiNational Computer Software Corporation
9595 Wilshire Blvd., Suite 502
Beverly Hills, CA 90212
(213) 276-3999
TX: 294191

/rdb

/rdb is a relational database management system for UNIX. It consists of over 100 C language and shell language programs which can be piped together with UNIX commands. They use flat ASCII UNIX files.

It is fully relational and offers a complete package of facilities to develop software applications on UNIX that is fully compatible with UNIX.

/rdb is available from several distributors, including those listed below.

Schmidt Associates

Schmidt Associates has an excellent menu shell application development system with windows and over fifty built-in commands. The developer uses the menu and form system to set up an application. When it is set up, it is compiled for high speed. It uses **/rdb** as its database.

Schmidt Associates is one of the oldest UNIX software companies. More copies of their menu software have been sold than any other UNIX add-on software package.

Schmidt Associates
7 Mount Lassen Road
San Rafael, CA 94903
(415) 499-8001

UNIPRESS Software

A wide range of excellent UNIX software is available from UNIPRESS in addition to **/rdb**.

UNIPRESS Software
2025 Lincoln Hwy., Suite 209
Edison, NJ 08817
(800) 222-0550

Robinson Schaeffer Wright

This company has added **ve** a form editor with the same syntax as the UNIX **vi** text editor.

Robinson Schaffer Wright
711 California Street
Santa Cruz, CA 95060
(408) 429-6229

PART

V

User Manual

The following examples are real shell programs. They are in UNIX manual format style and arranged in alphabetical order. Each manual page gives:

Table 16. Manual Sections

NAME	One Line Description of the Program
SYNOPSIS	The Syntax of the Program
DESCRIPTION	Description of the Function of the Program
OPTION	Any Options
EXAMPLE	One or More Examples of the Use of the Program
AUTHOR	Who Wrote the Program
SOURCE	The Shell Program Listing for You To Study and Copy
DISCUSSION	Discussion of the Source Code, Algorithms and Tricks

Name

ask—prompts questions, validates and writes answerlist

Synopsis

ask   questiontable answerlist

Description

ask will prompt the user with questions from the question table, validate the answers from information in the question table, and write out the answers in a list formatted file.

To use the ask program, simply edit the question table for your application. The *Var* column contains the name of the field you wish to enter.

The *Valid* column contains the validation criterion. A *number-number* value will cause ask to test to see if the user's answer is within that range. A filename here will cause ask to grep through the file for a match of the answer that the user types. Anything else in the *Var* column will cause ask to accept anything the user types.

The *Question* column contains the literal question to be asked.

Example

First let's look at the question file:

```
$ cat questions

Var              Valid               Question
name             LETTERS             What is your name?
sex              sex                 What is your sex?
weight           0-1000              What is your weight in pounds?
eye              eye                 What is the color of your eyes?
```

Now let's run the ask program

```
$ ask questions answers
What is your name? (LETTERS)
Rod Manis
What is your sex? (choose from list below)
female
male
```

```
male
What is your weight in pounds? (0-1000)
160
What is the color of your eyes? (choose from list below)
black
blue
brown
green
hazel

hazel
$
```

Finally, let us see the answers as they have been put into list format.

```
$ cat answers
```

```
name        Rod Manis
sex         male
weight      160
eye         hazel
```

Technical

ask is a shell program that you can modify for your own use. Note that it uses **read** to read from the question file, as well as the standard-in. This is done by saving the standard-in in a spare slot in the file table under file descriptor 4. Then standard-in can be switched back and forth between the questions file (3) and the user (4).

Author

Rod Manis

Source

```
: %W% SCCS Information

: ask—asks questions from a table and writes out the answers

USAGE = 'usage: ask questions answers'
EUSAGE = 1
```

```
MACCEPT = 'Error: Cannot find a file named $ACCEPT'
EACCEPT = 2

if test "$#" -ne 2
then
   echo $USAGE
   exit $EUSAGE
fi

: get filenames

QUESTIONS = $1
ANSWERS = $2

: start answer list if it does not exit

if test ! -w $ANSWERS
then
   echo > $ANSWERS
fi

: read questions from file descriptor 3 so we can get replies from 1

exec 3< $QUESTIONS

: save standard in file table entry

exec 4<&0

: save standard IFS, so that we can add tabs

OLDIFS = $IFS

: first skip question table headlines

exec 0<&3
read HEAD
read DASH

: read each line from question table, and switch back to stdin

read LINE
exec 0<&4

: big loop ask question, get reply, validate, write out

while test -n "$LINE"
```

```
do

    : parse question table row

        OLDIFS = $IFS
        IFS = '      '
        set $LINE
        IFS = $OLDIFS
        VAR = $1 ; ACCEPT = $2;  QUESTION = $3

    : test if domain or range

        if test "$ACCEPT" = "$VAR"
        then
           echo "$QUESTION (choose from list below)"
           cat $ACCEPT ||( echo $MACCEPT ; exit $EACCEPT )
           echo
        elif test "$ACCEPT" = "ANY"
        then
           echo $QUESTION
        else
           echo "$QUESTION ($ACCEPT)"
        fi

      : get answer from user

      ANSWER =
      while test -z "$ANSWER"
      do
         read ANSWER

         : validate answer

         case "$ACCEPT" in
         ANY) : accept anything
            break
            ;;
         [0-9]*-[0-9]*) : this a numeric range
            IFS =
            set $ACCEPT
            IFS = $OLDIFS
            LOW = $1
            HIGH = $2
            if test "$ANSWER" -lt "$LOW" -o "$ANSWER" -gt"$HIGH"
            then
         echo Sorry, but your answer must be between $LOW and $HIGH.
```

```
                echo Please enter another answer.
                ANSWER =
            fi
            ;;
        *) : this is a domain, check against table
            grep "∧$ANSWER\$" $ACCEPT 2> /dev/null 1> /dev/null
            if test "$?" −ne 0
            then
                echo Sorry, but the acceptable answers are:
                cat $ACCEPT
                echo Please enter another answer.
                ANSWER =
            fi
            ;;
        esac
    done

    : write out answer and get next question

    echo "$VAR    $ANSWER" ≫ $ANSWERS

    : switch to question file and than back to stdin

    exec 0< &3
    read LINE
    exec 0< &4
done

: add one blank line as record separator

echo ≫ $ANSWERS
```

Discussion

ask—asks questions from a table and writes out the answers

This is a large and complicated shell script. It comes first because these manual pages are in alphabetical order. We recommend that you skip this program and go and study the other programs first. Many are only a few lines. Come back here last.

```
    USAGE = 'usage: ask questions answers'
```

Here is the usual setup stuff, modified for this program.

```
    : get file names
```

This picks up the first and second command line arguments and assigns them to shell variables to be used later.

: start answer list if it does not exit

This puts a blank line into the answer file and throws away everything else. If you want to append to the file, use the double right arrows ($\gg$).

: read questions from file descriptor 3 so we can get replies from 1

We need to use file descriptor 3, because the user will be answering our questions on file descriptor 0, the standard input attached to the keyboard. But we need to read the question file, which means we need another input file. We need file descriptor to hold the standard in entry in, while standard in is diverted to file descriptor 3. We also need to write the answer list into a file which will take another file descriptor. All together we will have five files open, two files for input, and two for output, and one to save the standard in. One set of I/O for the user and another for the question and answer files.

: first skip question table headlines

Just throw away the first two headlines of the question file

: read each line from question table

We start switching standard in from 3 to 4 to get first a line from the question table and then a line from the user. This tricks **read** into reading first from the question file, then from standard in.

: big loop to ask question, get reply, validate, write out

We will keep looping as long as there are rows in the question table.

: parse question table row

Here we get the question and the validation from the current line read from the question table. We use the **set** command to parse the line. *VAR* is the name of the field we are seeking. *ACCEPT* is a code for validation. *QUESTION* is the question we will display to the user.

: test if domain or range

A *domain* is a list of words in a file. The user's answer must match one of the words. A *range* is a numeric range into which the user's answer must fall.

: get answer from user

We use the **read** command to get the user's answer and store it in a shell variable.

: validate answer

This **case** statement will do the validation of the answer. There are three cases.

ANY): accept anything

If the word *ANY* is in the *ACCEPT* validation file, we will accept anything the user types. This is for names, address, etc. Things we cannot validate.

[0–9]*–[0–9]*)　: this is a numeric range

Here we test to see if the *ACCEPT* field has numbers followed by a dash (–), followed by more numbers. If so, it is a range, and parse the range into its high and low number using the minus as the field separator. Then we test to see if the number typed in by the user is within this range.

*)　: this is a domain, check against table

In the case of a domain, which is anything else, we assume that there is a file listing the possibilities for the answer. We **grep** through the domain file for the answer the user gave us. If it is not there we ask the question again and show the possible answers. If this list gets long we will need to make columns using **lc** or **pr -t -5**

: write out answer and get next question

We now have an acceptable answer so we can write it and its variable name to the answer table. Then we read the next question from the question table with the **read** command, switching back to standard-in.

: add one blank line as record separator

This throws one more blank line to the end of the answer file to separate this set of answers from the next set. This makes a file that is list formatted.

Name

cashflow—computes balance column of cash table

Synopsis

cashflow   < cashtable

Description

cashflow will compute a running balance in a *Balance* column (3) from the *Amount* column (2) of a special table that you can use to manage your cash flow.

Example

With an editor, create a table, which we will call *cashtable,* that looks like this:

```
$ cat cash
```

Date	Amount	Balance	Description
840101	512		current balance
840101	–450		rent check
840101	1000		pay check
840115	–300		estimated tax payment
840115	1000		pay check
840115	–1000		living expenses
840120	–900		big purchase
840201	1000		pay check
840201	–450		rent check
840215	1000		pay check
840115	–1000		living expenses

cashflow needs two columns, one named *Amount* and the other *Balance.* (If you have to change these column names, you will have to edit the **cashflow** shell script.) The rest of the columns, or more columns, are optional. Have a line for each of your projected income and expense items. Income items are positive and expenses are negative. This is your flow of cash. The question is: does it go negative? Use the **cashflow** program to find out.

```
$ cashflow < cash
```

Date	Amount	Balance	Description
860101	512	512	current balance
860101	-450	62	rent check
860101	1000	1062	pay check
860115	-300	762	estimated tax payment
860115	1000	1762	pay check
860115	-1000	762	living expenses
860120	-900	-138	big purchase
860201	1000	862	pay check
860201	-450	412	rent check
860215	1000	1412	pay check
860115	-1000	412	living expenses

Oops! That *big purchase* is going to give us a negative balance in 860120. Now that you know, you can do something about it. One move is to put the big purchase off until the first of February.

```
$ cat cash
```

Date	Amount	Balance	Description
860101	512		current balance
860101	-450		rent check
860101	1000		pay check
860115	-300		estimated tax payment
860115	1000		pay check
860115	-1000		living expenses
860201	1000		pay check
860201	-900		big purchase
860201	-450		rent check
860215	1000		pay check
860115	-1000		living expenses

Now let's see if that works:

```
$ cashflow < cash
```

Date	Amount	Balance	Description
860101	512	512	current balance
860101	-450	62	rent check
860101	1000	1062	pay check
860115	-300	762	estimated tax payment
860115	1000	1762	pay check
860115	-1000	762	living expenses

860201	1000	1762	pay check
860201	-900	862	big purchase
860201	-450	412	rent check
860215	1000	1412	pay check
860115	-1000	412	living expenses

Ok. This will work. You can also try other options. Of course, if the purchase is */rdb software,* then buy it immediately, and put off the rent.

You can do all of this in the text editor, executing commands using the **vi** exclamation (!) shell feature. You also might want to write out to a *tmp* file and **mv** it back to cash so that your cash file is up to date. For example in **vi** you can type:

```
:!cashflow < cashtable > tmp ; mv tmp cashtable

:e!
```

The first line computes the *Balance* column, puts the result in a *tmp* file, and moves the *tmp* file to be the new *cashtable*. All of this is necessary because, in UNIX you cannot have one file as both input and output without wiping out the file. The second line, *:e!* pulls the new file into the **vi** editor and displays it on your screen.

Author

Rod Manis

Source

```
: %W% SCCS ID Information

: cashflow—computes the balance column of a cashflow table

USAGE = 'usage: cashflow < table
Amount must be column 2 and Balance must be column 3'
awk 'BEGIN { FS = " " ; OFS = "   "; }
      NR < 3 { print }
      NR > 2 { $3 = sprintf ("%7d", ($2 + prev)); prev = $3; print }'
```

Discussion

We use **awk** to compute the *balance* column ($3) from the *account* column ($2). The *BEGIN* line sets the field separator, *FS,* and the output field separator, *OFS,* to the tab character which separates our table.

NR is the number of the record. We simply print out the first two header lines of our table. For the rest of the table we add the Amount column ($2) to the previous balance. On the first row, the variable *prev* will be zero. Then we format the value into a seven-digit integer to fit the column and assign the value to the Balance column ($3). We save the Balance column for the next line and print out the current line.

Name

cpdir—copies one directory tree to another directory

Synopsis

cpdir   fromdirectory todirectory

Description

cpdir copies the directory tree, that is, all the directories and all of their files under the *fromdirectory,* to the *todirectory*.

    cpdir uses the **tar** command in a special way. **cpdir** conforms to the **cp** and **ln** commands format. In other words it copies from olddirectory to newdirectory; left to right. The first directory is the source and the second is the destination. The UNIX System III and higher **cpio** command can accomplish the same thing, but with a lot more options to get right.

Example

You might use this for backing up a large directory:

    $ cpdir /usr/rdb /usr/rdb.backup

Or to move a directory to a preferred place:

    $ cpdir /usr/he.left/goodstuff /usr/project/goodstuff

See Also

tar

Author

Rod Manis

Source

: %W% SCCS ID Information

```
: 'cpdir—copies a directory tree to another directory tree'

USAGE = 'usage: cpdir fromdirectory todirectory'
EUSAGE = 1

if test $# ! = 2
then
    echo $USAGE 1 > &2
    exit $EUSAGE
else
    cd $1; tar cf - . | ( cd $2 ; tar xf - )
fi
```

Discussion

This program uses special features of the **tar** command. After testing to make sure that we have exactly two arguments, we **cd** to the first directory. We use **tar** to put all of the files and subdirectories and their files into one file which we send through the pipe to the right. The c means create a file. The f means the next argument is the directory from which to take the files. The dot (.) stands for the current directory.

Now things get really tricky. On the right side of the pipe is a subshell in parentheses. In this subshell we **cd** to the second directory. This works because we are in a subshell. Then **tar** reads a file from the pipe on the right and breaks it out into files and directories and their files. The x means extract files from input. The − means take input from standard input, i.e., the pipe to the left.

Name

difference—outputs table of rows that are in only one table

Synopsis

difference   table1 table2

Description

difference produces a new table consisting of only the rows that are in one of the tables, but not in the other table. Think of it as the logical subtraction of the second table from the first. The two input tables must have the same columns. (Called ''union compatible.'')

 difference uses the UNIX **sort** and **uniq** commands. The rows have to be exactly identical including every space, tab, and nonprinting character.

Example

```
$ cat journal

Date      Amount   Account   Ref   Description
820107     14.00   meal      v     meal with jones
820113    101.62   car       v     car repairs
820114     81.80   insur     c     car insurance allstate
820114     93.00   car       c     car registration dmv
820119     81.72   vitamin   c     sundown vitamins
820121     20.83   meal      v     meal with john
820121   2500.00   keogh     c     keogh payment
820125     99.00   dues      v     dues to uni-ops unix conference

$ cat carexpense

Date      Amount   Account   Ref   Description
820113    101.62   car       v     car repairs
820114     81.80   insur     c     car insurance allstate
820114     93.00   car       c     car registration dmv

$ difference journal carexpense

Date      Amount   Account   Ref   Description
820107     14.00   meal      v     meal with jones
```

820119	81.72	vitamin	c	sundown vitamins
820121	20.83	meal	v	meal with john
820121	2500.00	keogh	c	keogh payment
820125	99.00	dues	v	dues to uni-ops unix conference

Author

Rod Manis

Source

```
: %W% SCCS ID Information

: 'difference produces table with rows in table1 that are not in
table2'

USAGE = 'usage: difference table1 table2'
EUSAGE = 1

if   test $# -ne 2
then
    echo $USAGE 1>&2
    exit $EUSAGE
fi

: first output the head of the first file
sed 2q $1

(tail +3 $1 ; tail +3 $2 ) | sort | uniq -u
```

Discussion

The **sed** command simply puts the first two headlines of the first file to the *standard-out*.

We get the bodies of each table with the **tail** +3 command. This means get the tail of the file starting with line three. In a subshell each **tail** sends its output through the pipe on the right of the subshell to **sort**. **sort** sees the two tables as one table, the first table followed by the second. It sorts them and passes them through the pipe to the *uniq -u* on the right.

The algorithm for this program depends upon a trick of *uniq -u*. Picture in your mind how the input table to *uniq -u* looks. Where there are matching lines there are two lines one after the other that are the same, that is, not unique. But lines that do not match are alone. *uniq -u* only sends to *standard-out* the lines that are unique, that are different from the two files. This then gives us a table of the unique or different lines in the two tables.

Name

domain—displays invalid values in a column

Synopsis

domain　domaintable [string . . .] [< one-column-table]

Description

domain displays all strings or all rows in the input table that do not match any column in the *domaintable*. This program is useful for validating that each item in a column is legitimate. First you build a file consisting of a list of all acceptable values. In relational theory these values are the **domain** of the column. To validate a column in a multicolumn table, simply project the column you wish.

　　The *domaintable* must be sorted because it will be searched by the **search** command using binary access method. **domain** is a shell script so if you wish to change its search method, you can edit it.

Example

You might have an order file for cars like this:

```
$ cat orders
```

Qty	Model	Colors	Options
1	sedan	black	3
1	sedan	green	1
1	sedan	farble	4
3	sedan	red	5
2	convert	white	1
1	sedan	purple	2
1	sedan	yellow	4
3	convert	blue	2

You would also need a file of possible car colors:

```
$ cat colors
```

Colors
black
blue

```
carmel
green
purple
red
silver
white
```

Now we can validate the *Color* column and see all unacceptable colors:

```
$ project Colors < orders | domain colors
```

```
Colors
farble
yellow
```

So, **domain** complains about *farble* and *yellow*. Neither is in our list. So you can call the orders file up in the text editor and edit it. Or add those colors to the approved list, if they are ok. In the **vi** editor, use the */pattern* command to find all of the patterns in the orders file. Or type something like:

```
:g/farble/s//purple/g
```

This **vi** editor command will find all instances of farble and change them to purple.

You can also validate strings.

```
$ domain colors red blue purple farble yellow green
farble
yellow
```

These command line strings should be quoted if they have any special characters in them. They are searched for by **grep.** If they contain a dollar sign ($), it should be protected with three backslashes. It will be scanned both by the shell and the **grep** command. It takes three backslashes to get one through.

Author

Rod Manis

Source

```
: %W% SCCS ID Information
```

```
:  'domain—searches the domain file for each field of input column
:    or string on the command line'
USAGE = 'usage: domain domaintable [string . . .] [< one-column-
table]'
EUSAGE = 1

EDOMAIN = 2

TMP = /tmp/$$domain
trap 'rm –f /tmp/$$*' 0 1 2 3 15

case "$#" in
0)
   echo $USAGE >&2
   exit $EUSAGE
   ;;
1)
   cat > $TMP
   search –mb $1 < $TMP >> $TMP
   sort $TMP | uniq –u
   ;;
2)
   if grep "∧$2$1" > /dev/null
   then
      exit 0
   else
      echo "$2"
      exit EDOMAIN
   fi
   ;;
*)
   FILE = $1
   shift
   for I
   do
      if grep "∧$I\$" $FILE > /dev/null
      then
         :
      else
         echo "$I"
         ERROR = true
      fi
   done
   if test –n "$ERROR"
   then
      exit EDOMAIN
   fi
```

```
        ;;
   esac
```

Discussion

We read each line of the input table and use **grep** to see if it is in the domain table. We use the up arrow (∧) and the dollar ($) in the **grep** search pattern to ensure that we are matching the whole line and not some substring.

We throw away all output to the null file. We don't want the output, we only want to test the status code return. If the grep fails, echo the line because it is not in the domain.

Name

intersect—outputs table of rows that are in both input tables

Synopsis

intersect   table1 table2

Description

intersect produces a new table consisting of only the rows that are in both of the input tables. Think of it as the logical AND of two tables. The two input tables must have the same number of columns. (Called "union compatible.")

   intersect is a simple shell script that uses the UNIX **sort** and **uniq** commands. Rows must match exactly to be considered the same.

Example

```
$ cat journal
```

Date	Amount	Account	Ref	Description
820107	14.00	meal	v	meal with jones
820113	101.62	car	v	car repairs
820114	81.80	insur	c	car insurance allstate
820114	93.00	car	c	car registration dmv
820119	81.72	vitamin	c	sundown vitamins
820121	20.83	meal	v	meal with john
820121	2500.00	keogh	c	keogh payment
820125	99.00	dues	v	dues to uni-ops unix conference

```
$ cat carexpense
```

Date	Amount	Account	Ref	Description
820113	101.62	car	v	car repairs
820114	81.80	insur	c	car insurance allstate
820114	93.00	car	c	car registration dmv

```
$ intersect journal carexpense
```

Date	Amount	Account	Ref	Description
820113	101.62	car	v	car repairs

| 820114 | 81.80 | insur | c | car insurance allstate |
| 820114 | 93.00 | car | c | car registration dmv |

Author

Rod Manis

Source

```
: %W% SCCS ID Information

: 'intersect—produces table with rows that are be in two input tables'

USAGE = 'usage: intersect table1 table2'
EUSAGE = 1

if test $# -ne 2
then
   echo $USAGE 1>&2
   exit $EUSAGE
fi

: first output the head for the first file

sed 2q $1

(tail +3 $1 ; tail +3 $2 ) | sort | uniq -d
```

Discussion

This is the same as **difference** except here we use the **uniq -d** option to list only those lines which are *not* unique. These are the lines that are in both tables. Or the intersection of the set of lines.

Name

label—for printing mailing labels from a mailing list

Synopsis

label   < list

Description

label will print mailing labels from a mailing list in list format. **label** is a shell script so it can be easily changed by the user to handle different lists and labels.

Example

If you had a file called *maillist* that looked like this:

```
$ cat maillist

Number      1
Name        Ronald McDonald
Company     McDonald's
Street      123 Mac Attack
City        Memphis
State       TENN
ZIP         30000
Phone       (111) 222-3333

Number      2
Name        Chiquita Banana
Company     United Brands
Street      Uno Avenida de la Reforma
City        San Jose
State       Costa Rica
IZIP        123456789
Phone       1234
```

You could generate mailing labels that would look like this:

```
$ label < maillist

Ronald McDonald
```

McDonald's
123 Mac Attack
Memphis, TENN 30000

Chiquita Banana
United Brands
Uno Avenida de la Reforma
San Jose, Costa Rica 123456789

Author

Rod Manis

Source

```
: %W% SCCS ID Information

: 'label—reads in a mailist and print mailing labels'

USAGE = 'usage: label < maillist'

while read COLUMNNAME INFO
do
  case $COLUMNNAME in
  Name )
    echo $INFO
    ;;
  M/S )
    MAILSTOP = $INFO
    if `test "$INFO"`
    then
      echo Mailstop: $INFO
    fi
    ;;
  Division )
    DIVISION = $INFO
    if `test "$INFO"`
    then
      echo Division: $INFO
    fi
    ;;
  Company )
    COMPANY = $INFO
    if `test "$INFO"`
```

```
            then
               echo $INFO
            fi
            ;;
        Street )
            echo $INFO
            ;;
        City )
            read State STATE
            read Zip ZIP
            echo $INFO, $STATE $ZIP
            if `test -z "$MAILSTOP"`
            then
               echo
            fi
            if `test -z "$DIVISION"`
            then
               echo
            fi
            if `test -z "$COMPANY"`
            then
               echo
            fi
            echo
            ;;
        esac
    done
```

Discussion

There are many ways to do this program with UNIX tools. You can use the macro capabilities of **nroff,** the word substitution powers of **m4,** the variable substitution abilities of the shell. One could also use **awk, lex,** etc.

This is not the best way to write a label program. It was one of the first shell programs that we wrote many years ago. We show it here because of its simplicity.

In the **while** loop we read each line of the input maillist. We then use a **case** statement to match the different fields we are looking for. We gather values and echo out the lines of the mailing label.

There is a trick at the bottom where we determine how many lines we printed and fill the rest with blank lines. The problem is that not all addresses have all of the lines. Yet when you print a mailing label, you must have the same number of lines, total, on each label. Otherwise, you will soon be printing on the perforations between the labels, and running on to the next label. If we did not fix the line printing, there would be blank lines. That would have been ok, but not as nice as what we have done here.

Name

letter—prints form letters from a mailing list

Synopsis

letter   letter.1 . . . < maillist

Description

letter will print form letters from a standard letter and a mailing list. **letter** is a shell script so it can be easily changed by the user to handle different lists and letters. Then you can modify it with a text editor to handle any special features of your mailing list and letters.

Example

If you have a file called *maillist* that looked like this:

```
$ cat maillist
```

```
Name        Ronald McDonald
Company     McDonald's
Street      123 Mac Attack
City        Memphis
State       TENN
ZIP         30000
Phone       (111) 222-3333

Name        Chiquita Banana
Company     United Brands
Street      Uno Avenida de la Reforma
City        San Jose
State       Costa Rica
ZIP         123456789
Phone       1234
```

And two parts of your letter in two separate files, called *letter.1* and *letter.2:*

```
$ cat letter.1
```

We have a new product that we want to sell to everyone at

```
$ cat letter.2
```

Please have everyone send us an order. We will be very grateful.

Sincerely,

Mr. Marketing
Makeapile, Inc.

You could generate letters that would look like this:

```
$ letter letter.1 letter.2 < maillist
```

Ronald McDonald
McDonald's
123 Mac Attack
Memphis, TENN 30000

Dear Ronald McDonald:

We have a new product that we want to sell to everyone at
McDonald's. Please have everyone send us an order. We will be
very grateful.

Sincerely,

Mr. Marketing
Makeapile, Inc.

< There are spaces here to skip down to the bottom of the letter. They are
removed here to save space. >

Chiquita Banana
United Brands
Uno Avenida de la Reforma
San Jose, Costa Rica 123456789

Dear Chiquita Banana:

We have a new product that we want to sell to everyone at United
Brands. Please have everyone send us an order. We will be very
grateful.

Sincerely,

Mr. Marketing
Makeapile, Inc.

< There are spaces here to skip down to the bottom of the letter. They are removed here to save space. >

This sample letter program prints out the mailing name and address and a Dear Name. It then cats *letter.1,* **echoes** the company name and finally cats *letter.2.* It writes all of its output to a temporary file *TMP* and then **nroff's** the *TMP* file to the *standard-out.* The **nroff** program causes the file to be reformatted (left and right justified) for each company name length.

By studying the letter shell script, and one of the UNIX shell's documentations, **(sh** or **csh),** you can do very fancy and complex form letters.

Author

Rod Manis

Source

```
: %W% SCCS ID Information

: 'letter—will write a letter from a form letter and a mailing list
:   letter picks up letter1 letter2 etc from the argument list'

USAGE = 'usage: letter letter1 letter2 . . . < maillist'

TMP = /tmp/$$letter
trap 'rm –f /tmp/$$*' 0 1 2 3 15

while read COLUMNNAME INFO
do
  case $COLUMNNAME in
  Name )
    name = $INFO
    echo > $TMP
    echo .nf ≫ $TMP
    echo $INFO ≫ $TMP
    ;;
  Company )
    COMPANY = $INFO
    echo $INFO ≫ $TMP
    ;;
  Street )
    echo $INFO ≫ $TMP
    ;;
  City )
```

```
            read State STATE
            read Zip ZIP
            echo $INFO, $STATE $ZIP ≫ $TMP
            echo ≫ $TMP
            echo ≫ $TMP
            echo Dear $name: ≫ $TMP
            echo .fi ≫ $TMP
            echo ≫ $TMP
            cat $1 ≫ $TMP
            echo $COMPANY. ≫ $TMP
            cat $2 ≫ $TMP
            echo ≫ $TMP
            echo ≫ $TMP
            nroff $TMP
            ;;
        esac
    done
```

Discussion

This is also a very early shell program that can be greatly improved. This program has to know too much about the letter it writes and the mailing list it reads. But let's look at it.

The big **while** loop reads each line of the input mail list and uses a **case** statement to match the different fields we want. We output a mail label, then part of the letter, then more fields, then more letter, etc. All goes into a temporary file, including some **nroff** commands. Finally, **nroff** is called to format the letter and send it to standard-out. The user can direct the output to the line printer. All of this is more like a programmed letter, than a general-purpose form letter program. We should be able to write the letter in one file, with variables inserted. Then our **letter** program should substitute the variables for the fields in each mail list record for us. See if you can write such a program.

Name

lock—locks a record of field of a file

Synopsis

lock   filename process id from to [indexfrom indexto]

Description

lock locks a record or file by writing a row into a common lock file. */tmp/Lfilename* contains one line for each locked record or field with and the process id of the process (program) that locked it, begin (from) and end (to) of the bytes to be locked. Also the index begin and end bytes to be locked, if they are to be updated. When a process attempts to lock a string of bytes that is already locked, **lock** returns an error condition.

Example

Let us use **lock** on the *inventory* table:

```
$ cat inventory
```

Item	Amount	Cost	Value	Description
1	3	50	150	rubber gloves
2	100	5	500	test tubes
3	5	80	400	clamps
4	23	19	437	plates
5	99	24	2376	cleaning cloth
6	89	147	13083	bunsen burners
7	5	175	875	scales

First we use **seek** (**/rdb** command) to locate the record and return the offset and size.

```
$ LOCATION = `echo 5 | seek –mb inventory Item`
$ echo $LOCATION
207 245 0 8
```

This means that the record is 207 bytes into the file and that it is 38 bytes long ending at byte 245.

Now we can call **lock** to lock the record:

```
$ lock inventory $$ $LOCATION
```

Note that we use the *$LOCATION* shell variable to supply the two values, offset and size. We also use the automatic shell variable double dollar *($$)* to put the process id on the command line.

Let's see what the lock file looks like:

```
$ cat /tmp/Linventory
207 245 0 8
```

See **unlock** for the unlocking routine.

Author

Rod Manis

Source

```
: %W% SCCS ID Information

: 'lock—locks an area, usually a record, of a file'

USAGE = 'usage: lock filename pid from to indexfrom indexto'
EUSAGE = 1

LOCKSET = 0
ELOCKED = 2

umask 000

case "$#" in
6)
   LOCKROW = "$2  $3  $4  $5  $6"
   LOCKFILE = /tmp/L$1
   TMP = /tmp/$$lock

   if test -s $LOCKFILE
   then
     echo "$LOCKROW" ≫ $LOCKFILE
     exec 0< $LOCKFILE
     while read PID FROM TO XFROM XTO
     do
       FILEROW = "PID  FROM  TO  XFROM  XTO"
       if test "$LOCKROW" = "$FILEROW"
```

```
            then
              exit $LOCKSET
            elif test "$3" -ge "$FROM" -a "$3" -le "$TO" -o "$4" -ge \
          "$FROM" -a "$4" -le "$TO"
             then
                sed "/$LOCKROW/d" < $LOCKFILE > $TMP
                mv $TMP $LOCKFILE
                exit $ELOCKED
             fi
          done

          # own lock gone means lock file updated with sed mv
          exit $ELOCKED

        else
          echo "$LOCKROW" > $LOCKFILE
          exit $LOCKSET
        fi
        ;;
    *)
        echo $USAGE 1>&2
        exit $EUSAGE
        ;;
    esac
```

Discussion

A case statement is used to make sure we have all of our required arguments. We check to see if there is a lock file already. If not, we write out
our lock, creating the lock file in the process.

If a lock file exists, we append our lock line to it. Then we read through
the lock file to see if any other lock exists. The long test checks for overlap
of two lock areas. This allows us to lock a single byte, up to the whole file.

If we find a lock on our area, we backout our lock line and report that
the file is already locked. If we find our lock line, we return successful lock.

If we fall out of the loop without finding our lock line, the file must have
been changed on us, so we report that the record is already locked. This
handles the rare case that someone else moves a lock file back over us.

A second user will append their lock line after us, find ours first and back
off.

Name

menu—root menu with some UNIX commands

Synopsis

menu

Description

menu displays a table of commands which you can execute by simply typing a number or name. Menus are useful for inexperienced users. They can be set up by more experienced users very easily. menu is a shell script that simply echoes the menu table of choices, then waits for the user to type in a number or name. Then menu uses a shell case statement to execute a command or series of commands for each choice.

Example

```
$ menu
                              menu
Number        Name        For
1             exit        exit menu and go to UNIX
2             Menu        goto the local menu (Menu)
3             sh          get unix shell
4             vi          edit a file
5             mail        read mail
6             send        send mail to someone
7             cal         see your calendar
8             who         see who is on the system
9             ls          list the files in this directory
10            cat         display a file on the screen

Please enter a number or name for the action you wish or DEL to
exit:
```

The underline at the bottom is the cursor. menu is waiting for you to type your choice of number or name. Numbers are quicker to type, but names are more mnemonic and help you learn how to do things at the shell level.

Setting Up Your Own Menus

You can nicely automate your operations with menus. If you have naive users, who might have trouble learning or remembering the UNIX or /rdb commands, you can set up menus for them. Also, when you have an operation in which a few commands are repeatedly executed, they can put them into a menu for simple choice.

You can put your menus in the directories in which they will be used or in your *$HOME/bin* or other bin directories.

To start, go to the directory of your choice and copy the */rdb* menu to your directory:

```
$ cp /rdb/bin/menu Menu
```

or

```
$ cp /rdb/demo/Menu .
```

You may have a different path to your **/rdb** directory. Type

```
$ path menu /usr/rdb/bin
```

We suggest the convention of using the name Menu with the capital M so that it will appear at the top of your list of files when you do an **ls** command. Therefore it won't get so easily lost among the other files in the directory. You can then name submenus: *Menu.other* where other is something that suggests the kinds of commands the menu covers.

Now edit the Menu command. If you use vi, type:

```
$ vi Menu
```

Menu has two basic parts:

Part one is the menu table, which is simply the menu text to be *echo* ed at to the screen:

```
echo " $0
Number     Name      For
1          exit      exit menu and go to UNIX
2          Menu      goto the local menu (Menu)
3          sh        get unix shell
4          vi        edit a file
5          mail      read mail
...

Please enter a number or name for the action you wish or DEL to
exit:
"
```

The **echo** command will simply send to the screen everything between the first double quote and the last double quote including the *Please enter . . .* line. The *$0* on the first line will be replaced by the name of the current menu. Double quotes are used so that the *$0* will be expanded by the shell. If you use a single quote, *$0* will not be expanded. But if you use a *$* anywhere else between the double quotes, be sure to put a backslash character before it.

The second part of Menu is a large **case** statement that you can edit to do what you want.

Here is a sample:

```
read ANSWER COMMENT

case $ANSWER in

1|exit)    exit 0 ;;
2|Menu)    Menu ;; # edit to other local menus like Menu.other
3|sh)      sh ;;
4|vi)      echo 'Which file or files do you wish to edit'
           read ANSWER COMMENT
           vi $ANSWER $COMMENT
           ;;
5|mail)    mail ;;
6|send)    echo 'Please enter login name of person to send mail
           to'
           read ANSWER COMMENT
           echo 'Type your letter, and end by typing CNTL-d'
           mail $ANSWER
           ;;
7|cal)     (cd ; calendar) ;;
8|who)     who ;;
9|ls)      ls ;;
10|cat)    echo 'Please enter the name of the file you wish to
           see'
           read ANSWER COMMENT
           cat $ANSWER
           ;;
*)         echo 'Sorry, but that number or name is not recognized.'

           ;;
esac
```

The **read** command waits for the user to enter his or her choice. The first word they type is assigned to the *ANSWER* shell variable. If they type any other words, they will be assigned to *COMMENT,* which might be used in your commands.

Next is the **case** statement that looks at the *$ANSWER* to decide which command to execute. Note that the number and name are separated by a vertical bar character | to mean *or:*

```
1|exit)   exit 0 ;;
```

This line will be selected if the user types either 1 or **exit.** The **exit** command is then executed. The double semicolons (;;) are required to show the end of the commands for this case. You can type in any command or series of commands that you could type at your terminal or in a shell script after each case choice. The **esac** at the bottom is **case** spelled backward and is required to end the whole **case** statement.

The **)* will catch any pattern that does not match earlier patterns. In this case a message is displayed. The sharp # symbol starts a comment. The shell will ignore the rest of the line after the sharp symbol. So you can add comments, which we recommend.

You have great power to do things as a result of the user selecting a choice. Of course you will need to match the name and number in your menu table with the patterns in the case statement. It is easy to edit one, and forget to edit the other.

Portability

menu uses a shell variable called *CLEAR*. Different UNIX systems have different ways of clearing the screen.

```
CLEAR = `tput clear`      # UNIX System V, Release 2
CLEAR = `clear`           # Berkeley UNIX
```

You will have to figure out how to do this on your system. You should put the proper assignment for your terminal in your *.profile* file in your home directory. Using the shell variable to clear the screen is much faster than executing a command each time.

Author

Rod Manis

Source

```
: %W% SCCS ID Information

`menu is the root of your personal menus`
```

```
        ANSWER = ""

        while true
        do
          if test "$ANSWER" = ""
          then
          echo "$CLEAR
        Number      Name      For UNIX MENU
        1           exit      leave menu or return to higher menu
        2           Menu      goto another local menu (if any)
        3           sh        get unix shell
        4           vi        edit a file
        5           mail      read mail
        6           send      send mail to someone
        7           cal       see your calendar
        8           who       see who is on the system
        9           ls        list the files in this directory
        10          cat       display a file on the screen
        11          rdb       display rdb commands

        Please enter a number or name for the action you wish or DEL to
        exit:
        "

            read ANSWER COMMENT
            fi

            case $ANSWER in

            1|exit)     exit 0 ;;
            2|Menu)     Menu ;;
            3|sh)       sh ;;
            4|vi)
                        echo 'Which file or files do you wish to edit'
                        read ANSWER COMMENT
                        vi $ANSWER $COMMENT
                        ;;
            5|mail)     mail ;;
            6|send)
                        echo 'Please enter login name of person to send mail
                        to'
                        read ANSWER COMMENT
                        echo 'Type your letter, and end by typing Ctrl-d'
                        mail $ANSWER
                        ;;
            7|cal)      (cd ; calendar) ;;
            8|who)      who ;;
```

```
    9|ls)      ls ;;
   10|cat)

              echo 'Please enter the name of the file you wish to
              see'
              read ANSWER COMMENT
              cat $ANSWER
              ;;
   11|rdb)    menu.rdb ;;
    *)        echo 'Sorry, but that number or name is not
              recognized.' ;;
   esac

   echo '
Hit the Return key when you are ready to see the menu again.'
   read ANSWER
done
```

Discussion

This program is discussed above because it is intended that the user get a copy of this shell script and edit it for any menu desired.

Beware of the *$CLEAR*. It must be set to whatever will clear your terminal's screen. For UNIX System V, Release 2, **tput** will let you do various screen actions from the *terminfo* file, which is the new *termcap* file. **tput clear** will clear your screen. On Berkeley UNIX there is a **clear** command. If you have **vi,** you will have */etc/termcap* which will have the string for clearing your terminal's screen listed after *cl =* .

Name

paste—outputs two or more tables side by side

Synopsis

paste   table1 table2 [. . .]

Description

paste displays the tables named side by side. There is a command, in UNIX system III and higher, with the same name and function, but most other UNIX systems do not have it. So it is provided here.

paste simply uses the UNIX **pr** command to list the tables side by side:

```
$ pr -m -t -s table1 table2 [...]
```

in case you didn't know you could do this function with **pr**.

paste differs from the UNIX **join** in that **join** looks for matching values in key columns and only puts out rows where a match is found. **paste** does not care what it is pasting together. You can get some interesting garbage with **paste**.

You can also do a kind of visual **diff** in which you can see, perhaps, an old and new file, lined up side by side. You could do this with two list files.

Example

If you had taken a table and projected it into two tables, you could put them back together with paste.

```
$ project Item# Value < inventory > tmp1
$ cat tmp1
```

Item	Value
1	150
2	500
3	400
4	437
5	2376
6	13083
7	875

and

```
$ project Cost Amount Description < inventory > tmp2
$ cat tmp2
```

Cost	Amount	Description
50	3	rubber gloves
5	100	test tubes
80	5	clamps
19	23	plates
24	99	cleaning cloth
147	89	bunsen burners
175	5	scales

Now, perhaps after some work, you could put them back together, now in a different order, with paste.

```
$ paste tmp1 tmp2
```

Item	Value	Cost	Amount	Description
1	150	50	3	rubber gloves
2	500	5	100	test tubes
3	400	80	5	clamps
4	437	19	23	plates
5	2376	24	99	cleaning cloth
6	13083	147	89	bunsen burners
7	875	175	5	scales

This is not an efficient way to do projects, which could all be done with one project instead of two. But it is a good way to put tables together if **join** is inappropriate. If you had wanted to use **join** here, you should **project** the *Item* column in both tables.

Author

Rod Manis

Source

: %W% SCCS ID Information

: 'paste outputs the named files side by side'

USAGE = 'usage: paste table1 table2 [. . .]'

```
EUSAGE = 1

if test "$#" -lt 2
then
   echo $USAGE 1>&2
   exit $EUSAGE
fi

pr -m -t -s $*
```

Discussion

This simply uses options to the **pr** print command to print two or more files side by side. Some early UNIX **pr** commands did not have this ability. So this will not work on them.

Name

path—finds the full path of a command: */usr/rdb/bin/path*

Synopsis

path   [command . . .]

Description

path will find the path to a command if it is in one of the directories in your *PATH*. A path means two things in UNIX. (1) It means the lists of directories that one must go through to find a file or program. (2) It means a list of directories *$PATH* to be searched by the shell to find an executable program that matches the command typed in.

The **path** program will look through the directories in your *$PATH* (2) to find the path(1) of the command. If **path** cannot find the command or if the command is not executable, **path** returns nothing.

Example

If you type:

```
$ path project
/usr/rdb/bin
```

and get this result, then project was in /usr/rdb/bin.

```
$ path awk
/usr/bin
```

Author

Rod Manis

Source

```
: %W% SCCS Information

: 'path returns the path to an executable command'
```

```
USAGE = 'usage: path command'
EOK = 0
EUSAGE = 1
ENOFIND = 2

: test for a command in our argument list

if test "$#" -lt 1
then
   echo $USAGE 1>&2
   exit $EUSAGE
fi

: parse the PATH variable into words

COMMAND = $1
OLDIFS = $IFS
IFS = :
set $PATH
IFS = $OLDIFS

: look for the command in the path directories

for DIR in $*
do
   if test -r $DIR/$COMMAND
   then
      echo $DIR
      exit $EOK
   fi
done

exit $NOFIND
```

Discussion

This program walks through the **PATH** directories looking for the first file that matches the command you give it. To do this, it parses the **PATH** string on the colon field separator. Then uses a **for** loop to walk through the directories. If it finds the command in a directory, it **echoes** out the directory and exits successfully. If it falls out of that loop, then it was unsuccessful, and exits with a nonzero status code.

Name

reportwriter—sample program to produce standard reports

Synopsis

reportwriter

Description

reportwriter is a shell program that produces a sample standard report. It uses **splittable** to divide the table into page sized tables. It shows several tricks for using UNIX shell programming tools to put together reports.

Example

Here is what the sample produces (with middle of each page replaced with . . .):

```
$ reportwriter

      Prices of Computers that ran UNIX(TM) in 1983
        From Urban Software of New York City
      Report Date: 9 Feb 1985

        Price   Company                              City
                Advanced Micro Devices               Santa Clara
                Alcyon Corporation                   San Diego
                American Telephone & Telegraph
                BASIS Microcomputer GmbH             D-4400 Muenster
                Corvus Systems                       San Jose
                David Computers Inc.                 Kitchener
                Digital Computers Ltd.               Tokyo 102
                Heurikon Corp.                       Madison
          . . .
                Western Digital                      Irvine
                Western Electric Corp.
          4.2   Venturcom/IBM PC                     Cambridge
          . . .
         13.9   Victory Computer Systems, Inc.       San Jose

        Page 1
      (formfeed)
```

254

Prices of Computers that ran UNIX(TM) in 1983
From Urban Software of New York City
Report Date: 9 Feb 1985

Price	Company	City
14.0	Dynabyte Business Computers	Milipitas
14.0	Plessey Peripheral Systems	Irvine
14.0	Televideo Systems, Inc.	Sunnyvale
14.5	ALTOS Computer Systems	San Jose
50.0	Digital Equipment Corporation	Maynard
70.0	Valid Logic Systems, Inc.	Sunnyvale
. . .		
150.0	Sperry Univac	Blue Bell
200.0	Gould Inc.	Fort Lauderdale
350.0	Amdahl Corporation	Sunnyvale
1838.8		

Page 2
(formfeed)

Author

Rod Manis

Source

```
: %W% SCCS Information
: reportwriter is a sample shell script to write standard reports
: it uses splittable to break up the table and adds headers and footers
: simply copy this file to your directory and edit for each report
: be sure to rename your copy and make executable: chmod + x yourreport
USAGE = 'usage: reportwriter'

TABLE = report$$

: you can edit this number to fit your page between header and footer
NUMBER = -50
: the next two lines get todays date
set `date`

DATE = "$3 $2 $6"
: edit the next line to start on a different page number
PAGE = 1
: preprocess the data in the table
```

```
total -l Price < unitprice > $TABLE
: split table into page size tables
splittable $NUMBER $TABLE
: loop printing each page from header, splittable and footer
for I in $TABLE[a-z][a-z]
do
echo "
   Prices of Computers that ran UNIX(TM) in 1983
      From Urban Software of New York City
         Report Date: $DATE

"
cat   $I
echo "

      Page $PAGE

"
PAGE = `expr $PAGE + 1`
done

: be sure to remove the split tables
rm $TABLE $TABLE[a-z][a-z]
```

Discussion

This shell program is to be copied and edited for each big report you want to write. Since you are in a shell program, you can do all the tricks. It is described above, because it is intended to be copied and modified by the user or developer.

There are a number of tricks. The basic idea is that the table to be printed is split into page-size tables and output a page at a time along with header and footer info.

You can also modify it in many ways. Do totals and subtotals with **awk,** etc.

Name

rmcore—removes all core files to free up space on the disk

Synopsis

rmcore

Description

rmcore searches for files named *core* in the current directory, and all directories below. When it finds a file named *core,* **rmcore** removes it.

Run this first when disk space gets small. **rmcore** starts at the directory you are in and goes down the file tree. If you are super user, you can issue this command at */ (the root)* and clean the whole system.

rmcore uses the UNIX **find** command.

Example

```
$ rmcore
./core
```

Author

Rod Manis

Source

```
: %W% SCCS Information

: rmcore will remove all files named core starting in the current
:    directory and proceeding down the directory tree

find . -name core -print -a -exec rm {} \;
```

Discussion

This program simply uses the UNIX **find** command to find all *core* files and executes an **rm** command to remove them.

find is a very useful command with a horrible syntax. It took us a long time to figure it out. There was no example in the UNIX documentation. One of the authors remembers the early days at Bell Labs when he had a colleague write down a **find** command line. But even that did not work.

This is an example of how to use it. The dot (.) means the current directory. **find** starts at this directory and descends to all of the subdirectories. The *-name core* tells **find** to look for files named *core*. When it finds them the *-exec* option tells it to execute the following command. The **rm** command removes the core file. The {} stands for the filename that was matched. Since curly braces are metacharacter to the shell, they are quoted for protection. Finally, the semicolon (;) is quoted with the backslash because it is meant to be passed on to the **find** command and not to the current shell that is scanning the line.

Name

splittable—divides table in smaller tables

Synopsis

splittable   [-n] table

Description

splittable will take in a table and break it into several smaller tables with headlines on the top. *n* (in -n) is the number of rows for each smaller table (not counting the two headlines). This command is most useful for report writing.

    splittable uses the UNIX **split** command, so read its manual page for details. Both create filenames ending with aa, ab . . . zz. This gives 676 possible files (26 squared).

Example

Here is an example using a very short table:

```
$ cat inventory
```

Item#	Amount	Cost	Value	Description
1	3	50	150	rubber gloves
2	100	5	500	test tubes
3	5	80	400	clamps
4	23	19	437	plates
5	99	24	2376	cleaning cloth
6	89	147	13083	bunsen burners
7	5	175	875	scales

```
$ splittable –4 inventory
```

Since inventory only has 7 lines we are using the *-n* option set to 4 to get at most 4 lines in each split table.

```
$ ls inventory*
inventory
inventoryaa
inventoryab
```

The **ls** command above shows us that we now have two new files ending in *aa* and *ab* as a result of the **splittable** command.

```
$ cat inventoryaa
```

Item#	Amount	Cost	Value	Description
1	3	50	150	rubber gloves
2	100	5	500	test tubes
3	5	80	400	clamps
4	23	19	437	plates

```
$ cat inventoryab
```

Item#	Amount	Cost	Value	Description
5	99	24	2376	cleaning cloth
6	89	147	13083	bunsen burners
7	5	175	875	scales

Author

Rod Manis

Source

```
: %W% SCCS Information

: splittable—takes a table and breaks it into many tables putting
:    the header on each

USAGE = 'usage: splittable [–n] table'
EUSAGE = 1

HEAD = /tmp/$$splith
ROWS = /tmp/$$splitr

trap 'rm –f /tmp/$$*' 0 1 2 3 15

case "$#" in
2)   NUMBER = $1
     TABLE = $2
     ;;
1)   NUMBER = 50
     TABLE = $1
     ;;
```

```
0)   echo $USAGE 1>&2
     exit $EUSAGE
     ;;
esac

sed 2q $TABLE > $HEAD
tail +3 $TABLE > $ROWS
split $NUMBER $ROWS $TABLE

for I in $TABLE[a–z][a–z]
do
  cat $HEAD $I > $ROWS
  mv $ROWS $I
done
```

Discussion

This program uses the UNIX **split** program to split a table into page-size tables with heads on each one.

The **case** statement is used to handle each of the possible numbers of arguments this program can have. Then we put the head of the table into one file and the body into another. We call **split** to split the body into page-size files.

Finally we walk through all the little files with the **for** statement and write the headlines onto it. When we are through with this there are lots of little tables ready for **reportwriter** or whatever.

Name

substitute—replaces old string with new string in files

Synopsis

substitute oldstring newstring file . . .

Description

substitute will replace *oldstring* with *newstring* in all files listed. Since it uses **sed,** be sure to backslash (\ ) protect all **sed** special characters: * ∧ $ and \ itself.

Example

```
$ cat inventory
```

Item#	Amount	Cost	Value	Description
1	3	50	150	rubber gloves
2	100	5	500	test tubes
3	5	80	400	clamps
4	23	19	437	plates
5	99	24	2376	cleaning cloth
6	89	147	13083	bunsen burners
7	5	175	875	scales

```
$ substitute 'rubber' 'latex' file
```

```
$ cat journal
```

Item#	Amount	Cost	Value	Description
1	3	50	150	latex gloves
2	100	5	500	test tubes
3	5	80	400	clamps
4	23	19	437	plates
5	99	24	2376	cleaning cloth
6	89	147	13083	bunsen burners
7	5	175	875	scales

Note that row one has changed.

Technical

substitute uses:

$ sed 's/oldstring/newstring/g' file . . .

Author

Rod Manis

Source

%W% SCCS Information

: substitute oldstring for newstring using sed in each file

```
USAGE = 'usage: substitute oldstring newstring file . . .'
EUSAGE = 1

if test "$#" –lt 3
then
   echo $USAGE 1>&2
   exit $EUSAGE
fi

TMP = /tmp/$$substitute

FROM = $1
shift
TO = $1
shift

for I in $*
do
   echo $I
   sed "s/$FROM/$TO/g" < $I > $TMP
   mv $TMP $I
done
```

Discussion

This program uses **sed** to make string substitutions to a lot of files in place. You can edit all of the files in a directory with this. It picks up the first argument as the old string and the second argument as the new string. It shifts the position parameters each time, because we want only the list of files left when we get to the *for* statement.

We walk through each file, making the substitution into a temporary file and writing the temporary file back to the original file. We also **echo** out the name of the file we are processing, so that you can see how things are going.

Name

tabletom4—converts table format to m4 define file format

Synopsis

tabletom4   < table > definefile

Description

tabletom4 will convert a two column table into a file of define statements that can be input to the **m4** macro processor. Define macros are in the form: *define(old,new)*. **m4** can do many things including word for word substitution. It can be used for language translation (in a stiff, inflexible way) and for other conversions of databases.

The definefile produced is required by the **translate** command. Only words that have a corresponding translation in the second column will be put in the define file. In this way you can use the file before you have all of the translations.

Example

Suppose we have a simple translation table:

```
$ cat ed.t

English    Deutch
I          Ich
love       liebe
you        dich
widgit

$ tabletom4 < ed.t > ed
$ cat ed
define(I,Ich)
define(love,liebe)
define(you,dich)
```

Note that widgit did not get converted because it did not have a translation in the table.

This ed file can now be used by **m4** or **translate.**

```
$ cat text
I love you.

$ m4 ed text
Ich liebe dich.
```

See Also

translate

Author

Rod Manis

Source

```
: %W% SCCS Information

: tabletom4—takes an /rdb table and makes an m4 file

USAGE = 'usage: tabletom4 table . . . > m4file'

for FILE
do
   sed   "1,2d
     /    $/d
     s/    /,/g
     s/∧/define(/
     s/\ $/)/"   $FILE
done
```

Discussion

This program uses the **sed** command to edit a table into a form that can be input into **m4**. The **for** command loops through each table on the command line. The first line of **sed** deletes the two headlines. The second line turns all of the tabs into commas. Finally, the line is grabbed and has *define(* put in front and a closing parenthesis at the back.

Name

tabletosed—converts table format to **sed** file format

Synopsis

tabletosed   < table > sedfile

Description

tabletosed will convert a two column table into a file of **sed** statements that can be input to the **sed** stream editor. **sed** macros are in the form:

s/old/new/g

sed can do many things including word-for-word substitution. The *sedfile* produced is used by the **translate** command. It can be used for language translation (in a stiff, inflexible way) and for other conversions of data-bases.

Example

Suppose we have a simple translation table:

```
$ cat ed.t

English    Deutch
I          Ich
love       liebe
you        dich
widgit

$ tabletosed < ed.t > ed.sed.1
$ cat sed.1
s/I/Ich/g
s/love/liebe/g
s/you/dich/g
```

We can now use the *ed.sed.1* file with **sed** or **translate.**

```
$ cat text
I love you.

$ sed –f ed.sed.1 text
Ich liebe dich.
```

It can also be used for form letters, etc.

See Also

translate

Author

Rod Manis

Source

```
: %W% SCCS Information

: tabletosed takes an /rdb table and makes an m4 sed file
: Note that first column must be single word for m4
: Note also that the second column must have a string to be used

USAGE = 'usage: tabletosed < table > sedfile'

OLDIFS = $IFS
IFS = '   '

: delete headline
: delete rows without a string in the second column
: delete rows with spaces in first column
: convert tabs to slash
: put the newlines into sed format

sed   '1,2d
  /   $/d
  /∧.* .*   /d
  s:   :/:
  s:.*:s/&/g:'
```

Discussion

See the source code comments for each of the **sed** actions.
Note we use colons (:) as separators because the slash is in the string.

Name

termput—gets terminal capability from */etc/termcap* file

Synopsis

termput   capability

Description

termput is used by a shell program to get control of the terminal screen.
You can do reverse video, blinking, etc. Whatever capabilities your terminal has can be defined in the */etc/termcap* file. Hopefully it is set up right
for you. A two-letter capability code is followed by a string of characters
that, when sent to the terminal screen, will turn on or off that capability.

termput searches the */etc/termcap* file for a terminal capability. **termput**
is like the UNIX System V, Release 2 **tput** command, except **termput** uses
the */etc/termcap* file so that it is compatible with all UNIX systems that
have **vi**. **tput** uses the *terminfo* system which is not portable to other UNIX
systems. The termcap idea was invented by Bill Joy when he wrote the **vi**
text editor. It enables the editor to work with the hundreds of different
computer terminals. Each terminal's capabilities are entered into the */etc/*
termcap file that comes with almost all UNIX systems today.

Capabilities

The capabilities are two-letter codes that are defined in your UNIX manual
under *termcap*. Here are some examples:

cl	clear the terminal screen
cm	cursor movement—see below
so	start standout mode like reverse video
se	end standout mode

Cursor movement is more complicated. The row and column you want must
be edited into the cursor movement command string. **cm** just gives you the
format of the cursor movement string. See the **cursor** command for details.

Example

Here we convert several characters.

```
$ termput cl               (clear screen)
$ termput se               (reverse video)
$ termput so               (normal video)

$
```

Setup

For screen handling, it is much faster to set up shell variables with the capability strings and to use them in your shell programs than to execute **termput** each time. To set up these shell variables put them in your *.profile* in your *$HOME* directory.

```
AE = `termput ae`          # end alternate character set—graphics

AS = `termput as`          # start alternate character set—graphics

CLEAR = `termput cl`       # use in here files

# ECLEAR="-n $CLEAR"       # use in echo commands—other UNIX

CURSOR = `termput cm`      # cursor movement—for the cursor command

MB = `termput mb`          # start blinking mode
ME = `termput me`          # turn off all attributes
SE = `termput se`          # end standout mode
SO = `termput so`          # start standout mode
UE = `termput ue`          # end underline mode
US = `termput us`          # start underline mode
```

export CLEAR CURSOR AE AS MB ME SE SO SE UE US

Once this is set up, you can put the shell variable in your shell program. If you want a message to stand out, you can use the *$SO* and *$SE* pair.

```
$ echo "${SO} LOGOFF NOW ${SE}"
```

LOGOFF NOW

See Also

clear, cursor, screen.

Author

Rod Manis

Source

```
: %W% SCCS Information

: 'termput—put terminal strings from /etc/tercap file'
: '   like tput in System V, Release 2, but portable'

USAGE = 'usage: termput feature'
EUSAGE = 1

if test "$#" –lt 1
then
   echo $USAGE 1>&2
   exit $EUSAGE
fi

# /etc/termcap example
# cpc|pc|PC|IBMpc:
#   :al = \ El:cd = \ E[J:ce = \ E[K:cl = \ E[0;0H \ E[2J:\
#   :cm = \ E[%2;%2H:co#80:dl = \ EL:\
#   :if = /usr/lib/tabset/std:\
#   :li#25:nd = \ E[C:\
#   :ku = \ E[A:kl = \ E[D:kr = \ E[C:kd = \ E[B:kh = \ E[H:\
#   :k0 = \ ED:k1 = \ E;:k2 = \ E<:k3 = \ E =:k4 = \ E>:k5 = \ E?:\
#   :k6 = \ E@:k7 = \ EA:k8 = \ EB:k9 = \ EC:\
#   :pt:sr = \ EM:se = \ E[m:so = \ E[7m:\
#   :sf = \ ED:up = \ E[A:us = \ E[4m:

sed    "1,/$TERM|/d
     /:\ $/q" < /etc/termcap |
grep ":$1 =" |
sed    "s/.*:$1 = //
     s/:.*//
     s/ \ \ \ \ E/∧[/g"
```

Discussion

sed is used to find the terminal entry. It deletes all lines from the first of the */etc/termcap* file to the terminal entry. It uses the pipe symbol (|) to try to make the terminal entry unique. **sed** then skips down to the end of the entry and quits so that only the entry goes through the pipe to **grep. grep** finds only the line with the feature in it. The last **sed** first removes the leading and trailing line, and then converts the backslash-E (\ E) to a real escape character. Note the four backslashes. The shell takes two away and **sed** needs two, because backslash is a meta character for **sed** and **ed** also.

Name

translate—word for word substitution using translation files

Synopsis

translate   language < text > translatedtext

Description

translate will do word for word replacement in an input file. It uses both **m4** for which it needs a *definefile* that can be produced by **tabletom4,** and **sed** for which it needs **sed** files that can be produced by **tabletosed.**

The *definefile* must be named: *language* and the preprocess sedfile: *language.sed.1* and the postprocess *sedfile: language.sed.2*

Define statements that can be input to the **m4** macroprocessor are define macros in the form: *define(old,new)*. It can be used for language translation (in a stiff, inflexible way) and for other conversions of databases. You can do a large language translation, if you are willing to type in a dictionary.

I translated this manual and the tutorial into German using this system. I used **word** to find all of the words and was surprised to discover that there are only a little more than 2000 different words. I must know more, I just did not use them all. Then I typed in the German words for a dictionary which took about 30 hours. Ugh! I then converted the table to defines with **tabletom4.** I handled a few sticky problems with the pre and post **sed** processors on, then used **translate** to do the word for word substitution. It was not good German; some sentences made no sense; but a lot was ok.

Example

Suppose we have a simple translation table:

```
$ cat ed.t

English    Deutch
I          Ich
love       liebe
you        dich
widgit

$ translate < ed.t > ed
$ cat ed
```

```
define(I,Ich)
define(love,liebe)
define(you,dich)
```

Note that widgit did not get converted because it did not have a translation in the table. This *ed* file (English to Deutch) can now be used with **translate.**

```
$ cat text
I love you.

$ translate ed text
Ich liebe dich.
```

This program was also used in a biomedical expert system.

The idea is to convert each word into its value after looking them up in a table. This is something lisp does a lot of.

Var	Value
age	42
weight	80

It can also be used for form letters, etc.

See Also

tabletom4, tabletosed, word

Author

Rod Manis

Source

```
: %W% SCCS Information

: translate converts from one language to another

USAGE = 'usage: translate langtolang < textfile'
EUSAGE = 1

TMP = /tmp/$$translate
TMP1 = /tmp/$$1translate
```

```
trap 'rm -f /tmp/$$*' 0 1 2 3 15

if test "$#" -lt 1
then
   echo $USAGE 1<&2
   exit $EUSAGE
fi

LANGUAGE = $1
shift
: preprocess if a sed.1 file

if test -r "$LANGUAGE.sed.1"
then
   sed -f $LANGUAGE.sed.1 > $TMP
else
   cat > $TMP

fi
: use m4 for word for word substitution

if test -r "$LANGUAGE"
then
   m4 $LANGUAGE $TMP > $TMP1
else
   mv $TMP $TMP1
fi
: postprocess if a sed.2 file

if test -r "$LANGUAGE.sed.2"
then
   sed -f $LANGUAGE.sed.2 $TMP1
else
   cat $TMP1
fi
```

Discussion

This program does a word-for-word translation with the **m4** macroprocessor programs. With a file of *define* statements it searches for the first word and replaces it with the second word. It passes the file through a preprocessing **sed** and afterward through a postprocessing **sed**.

The program tests for the existence of its command file. If the command file is not there, it just cats the file through. The *-f* option to **sed** means that the instructions are in the file whose name follows.

Name

union—appends tables together

Synopsis

union   tableorlist . . . [-] [< tableorlist]

Description

union produces a new table or list consisting of all the rows in the first input table or list followed by the rows of the second and so on. Think of it as the *concatenation* of the two tables or lists. The input tables or lists must have the same number of columns. (Called *union* compatible.) It is best that the columns have the same name and the same type of data.

The—tells where in the list of files the standard input is to go. This gives you the freedom to use union in a pipe and to put the input file anywhere in the output.

Example

```
$ cat journal
```

Date	Amount	Account	Ref	Description
820107	14.00	meal	v	meal with jones
820119	81.72	vitamin	c	sundown vitamins
820121	20.83	meal	v	meal with scott
820121	2500.00	keogh	c	keogh payment
820125	99.00	dues	v	dues to uni–ops unix conference

```
$ cat carexpense
```

Date	Amount	Account	Ref	Description
820113	101.62	car	v	car repairs
820114	81.80	insur	c	car insurance allstate
820114	93.00	car	c	car registration dmv

```
$ union journal carexpense
```

Date	Amount	Account	Ref	Description
820107	14.00	meal	v	meal with jones
820119	81.72	vitamin	c	sundown vitamins

820121	20.83	meal	v	meal with scott
820121	2500.00	keogh	c	keogh payment
820125	99.00	dues	v	dues to uni–ops unix conference
820113	101.62	car	v	car repairs
820114	81.80	insur	c	car insurance allstate
820114	93.00	car	c	car registration dmv

A more complicated example would be:

    $ union - carexpense < journal

which would have the same output as above, but could be used in a pipe.

Author

Rod Manis

Source

```
: %W% SCCS Information

: 'union—concatenates two or more tables or lists'

USAGE = 'usage: union tableorlist ... [ - < tableorlist ]'
EUSAGE = 1

if test "$#" –lt 1
then
   echo $USAGE 1>&2
   exit $EUSAGE
fi

cat $1
shift

for FILE in $*
do
   if test "$FILE" = "-"
   then
     sed 1,2d
   else
     sed 1,2d < $FILE
   fi
done
```

Discussion

The trick to this **union** program is that the first file is cat'ed through as is, but all the subsequent tables have to be decapitated before being passsed through.

A test is made to see if there is at least one argument. Then it is cat'ed to standard-out. The second argument is shifted down to the first and the remaining arguments are walked through with a **for** loop.

There is a test to see if a table is named - which means the standard-input. If there is one, a **sed** command without an input file is used, in which case it reads from standard-input. The standard-input of a child process inherits the standard-input of its parent.

Name

unlock—unlocks a record or field of a file

Synopsis

unlock   tableorlist process id from to indexfrom indexto

Description

unlock unlocks a record or file by removing a row from a common unlock file. */tmp/Lfilename* contains one line for each locked record or field with the process id of the process (program) that locked it, the begin (from) and end (to) of the the bytes to be locked, and the index begin and end bytes.

Example

Let us use **unlock** on the *inventory* table:

```
$ cat inventory
```

Item	Amount	Cost	Value	Description
1	3	50	150	rubber gloves
2	100	5	500	test tubes
3	5	80	400	clamps
4	23	19	437	plates
5	99	24	2376	cleaning cloth
6	89	147	13083	bunsen burners
7	5	175	875	scales

First we use **seek** to locate the record and return the offset and size.

```
$ LOCATION = `echo 5 | seek -mb inventory Item`
$ echo $LOCATION
207 245 0 8
```

This means that the record is 207 bytes into the file and that it is 38 bytes long.

Now we can call **unlock** to unlock the record:

```
$ unlock inventory $$ $LOCATION
```

Note that we use the *$LOCATION* shell variable to supply the two values, offset and size. We also use the automatic shell variable double dollar ($$) to put the process id on the command line.

Let's see what the lock file looks like:

```
$ cat /tmp/Linventory
cat: cannot open /tmp/Linventory
```

unlock will remove the whole file if the last lock line has been removed.

See **lock** for locking examples.

Author

Rod Manis

Source

```
: %W% SCCS ID Information

: unlock—removes lock on area, usually a record, of a file

USAGE = 'usage: unlock filename process id from to indexfrom indexto'
EUSAGE = 1

UNLOCKED = 0
ENOREAD = 2

case "$#" in
6)
   LOCKFILE = /tmp/L$1
   TMP = /tmp/$$unlock
   LOCKROW = "$2   $3   $4   $5   $6"

   if test ! -r $LOCKFILE
   then
      exit ENOREAD
   fi

   sed "/$LOCKROW/d" < $LOCKFILE > $TMP
   if test -s $TMP
   then
```

```
            mv $TMP $LOCKFILE
        else
            rm $LOCKFILE $TMP
        fi
        exit $UNLOCKED
        ;;
    *)
        echo $USAGE 1>&2
        exit $EUSAGE
        ;;
    esac
```

Discussion

We check for the required number of arguments. We delete our lock line from the lock file, and if it was the last lock, remove the lock file.

Name

> **vilock**—locks a table before vi and unlocks afterwards

Synopsis

> **vilock** tableorlist

Description

> **vilock** keeps others from editing a file while you are. **vilock** will change the name of the table to LOCKtable. *LOCK* is a temporary file. Then it will execute **vi** *LOCKtable*. When you finish your editing, **vilock** will move **mv** *LOCKtable* back to its original name. If anyone else trys to edit the table while you have it in **vilock,** they will get a message that it is locked or missing.
>
> Anyone can see the LOCKtable while you are in the editor.

Options

> Sorry, you lose the **vi** options for now.

Example

> $ vilock inventory

> Will put you in the editor, with a file called LOCKinventory. When you finally finish with the file and get out of the editor, **vilock** will **mv** *LOCK-inventory* back to inventory. If you list your directory again, you will now see the inventory file.

Author

> Rod Manis

Source

> : %W% SCCS ID Information

```
: vilock locks a file by moving it to another name. It then calls
: vi so you can edit it. When you return from vi, it moves the
: file back to its old name. If anyone trys to vilock it while
: you have it, they will get a message: file locked.

USAGE = 'usage: vilock file . . .'
EUSAGE = 1

LOCKED = "$1 is locked"
ELOCKED = 2

NOFIND = "$1 is unreadable, not in the directory, or nonexistent."
ENOFIND = 3

if test "$#" -lt 1
then
   echo $USAGE 1>&2
   exit $EUSAGE
fi

TMP = /tmp/$$$1

if test -f "$1" -a -r "$1"
then
   mv $1 $TMP
   trap "mv $TMP $1" 0 1 2 3 15
   vi $TMP
elif ls /tmp/[0-9]*$1 # 2> /dev/null 1>/dev/null
then
   echo $LOCKED
   exit $ELOCKED
else
   echo $NOFIND
   exit $ENOFIND
fi
```

Discussion

This program simply moves the file to be edited to the temporary directory,
calls **vi** and then moves the file back when **vi** exits.

Note the **trap** statement after the **mv** command. We want to be sure that
the file is there before we set the trap to move it back. After **vi** the program
exits, and **trap** catches the exit signals and moves the file back.

If the file cannot be found, we test to see if it is in the temporary directory. If so, we say that it is locked, if not the other message is given. **ls** is
used to see if the file is there. Both its normal and error output are thrown
away and **elif** tests its status code.

Name

word—converts text file to list of unique words

Synopsis

word   < text > table

Description

word will input any text file and produce a long list of unique words. It can be used for language translation (in a stiff, inflexible way) and for other conversions of databases by using the **translate** command.

Example

Let's find the words in the description paragraph above: I have saved it in a file called words.

```
$ word < words
It
a
and
any
bases
be
by
can
command
conversions
data
file
for
in
(. . .)
words
```

See Also

translate

Author

Rod Manis

Source

: %W% SCCS Information

: word—outputs a sorted list of each word in a text file

USAGE = 'usage: word < text > wordlist'

```
tr –cs '[A–Z][a–z]'  '[\012*]' |
sort |
uniq
```

Discussion

This program creates the word list with only three UNIX programs in a pipe, written down the page. The **tr** command translates the characters in the first string to the characters in the second string. To save us from having to type a long string we are using a lot of tricks. The -c options says to complement the first string. In other words, the string is every character *other* than the ones listed. The first string is two ranges, one uppercase and the other lowercase. The second string is the carriage return character, here represented in octal. The star (*) means to pad out the string to as many characters as are needed to match the number of characters in the first string.

In English, we are asking **tr** to turn all nonletter characters into newlines. So any characters betweens words, like spaces, commas, etc., become newlines. This turns the text into a long list.

The -s option says to suppress more than one repeated substitution character. This keeps us from have lots of blank lines in our list.

sort simply sorts the list which puts all of the repetitions of each work together. **uniq** throws away all but one of each word. This leaves us with a nice sorted list of each word in the text file.

Name

yourprog—one line description of yourprog goes here

Synopsis

yourprog   syntax goes here

Description

Description of your program goes here.

Options

List and describe all of the options (-o flags) here.

Example

Please show examples of yourprog here.

Section

If you need subsections, you can use .SS

See Also

List other related programs here.

Author

Your Name

Source

Include the source if you wish. Here we include a sample program that shows standard features. You can copy and edit it for your own programs.

```
: %W% SCCS Information

: yourprog—a description of the command
: any futher comments about the command
: this is a sample program for you to copy and modify
: edit the line below to represent the syntax of your program

USAGE = "usage: yourprog -o arg . . . [ oparg . . . ]< filein > fileout"

: the above is standard, below is optional
: if you have abnormal exit status codes, define them here
: error—bad syntax or usage

EUSAGE = 1

: error—other error messages and return codes with increasing numbers

MOTHER = 'Error: other error message.'
EOTHER = 2

: if you are going to use temporary files, include a line for each

TMP = /usr/tmp/$$yourprog
TMP1 = /usr/tmp/$$1yourprog

: be sure to trap interrupts and remove the temporary files

trap "rm -f /usr/tmp/$$*" 0 1 2 3 15

: if you have required options, you can test for them here
: be sure to send error messages to standard error

if test "$#" -lt 1
then
   echo $USAGE 1>&2
   exit $EUSAGE
fi

: here is a crude sample of argument parsing

for ARG in $*
do
   case $ARG in
   -a)   OPTIONA = true ;;
   -o)   OPTIONO = true ;;
   *)    OPARG = "$OPARG $ARG" ;;
```

```
    esac
done

: finally the program code simply echoes the name of this program

echo yourprog
```

Discussion

Discuss the source, the algorithms and special tricks you used.

This is just a sample program showing the standards we recommend. Each section is discussed in the comments.

Index

Bibliography

BENTLEY, JON. "Programming Pearls: A Spelling Checker." *Communications of the ACM* (May, 1985). *(The UNIX spell program.)*

BOLSKY, M. I. *The C Programmer's Handbook.* Prentice-Hall, Inc., 1985. *(AT&T Bell Labs C reference book.)*

BOURNE, STEVEN R. "The UNIX Time-Sharing System: The UNIX Shell." *Bell System Technical Journal* (July–August, 1978), Vol. 57, No. 6, pp. 1971–1990. *(Description of UNIX shell by its author.)*

DOLOTTA, T. A., AND JOHN R. MASHEY. "An Introduction to the Programmer's Workbench." *IEEE Proceeding of the Second International Conference on Software Engineering* (13–15 October, 1976). *(Introduces UNIX tools idea for large software development projects.)*

—, "Using a Command Language as the Primary Programming Tool." *Proceedings of the IFIP TC 2.7 Working Conference on Command Languages* (10–14 September, 1979). *(Argues for, and shows how to use, shell programming for software development.)*

FELDMAN, S. I. "Make: A Program for Maintaining Computer Programs." *Software Practice and Experience* (April, 1979), Vol. 9, No. 4, pp. 255–65. *(Describes the UNIX make program for controlling execution of complex software systems.)*

FERRIN, THOMAS, AND ROBERT LANGRIDGE. "Interactive Computer Graphics with the UNIX Time-Sharing System." *Computer Graphics (ACM)* (4 February, 1980), Vol. 13, No. 4, pp. 320–331. *(Describes the University of California, San Francisco, Medical Center biomedical computer graphics system that the authors developed and which is the leader in the field.)*

FOURTANIER, J. L. "Operating Systems in Shared Time: The UNIX Phenomenon" *Automation and Inf. Ind. (France)* (June–July, 1980), No. 88, pp. 37–41. *(Discusses history and reasons for spread of UNIX.)*

HARBISON, SAMUEL P., AND GUY L. STEELE, JR. *A C Reference Manual.* Prentice-Hall, Inc., 1984. *(Advanced C by authors who have ported C to several environments.)*

JOHNSON, S. C. "Language Development Tools on the UNIX System." *Computer* (August, 1980), Vol. 13, No. 8, pp. 16–24. *(Discusses **lex** and **yacc** for compiler writing.)*

—, AND M. E. LESK. "UNIX Time-Sharing System: Language Development Tools." *Bell System Technical Journal* (July–August, 1978), Vol. 57, No. 6, Part 2, pp. 2155–2175. *(Discusses **lex** and **yacc** for compiler writing and other applications.)*

KERNIGHAN, BRIAN W. "PIC–A Language for Typesetting Graphics." *IEEE Proceeding of the Second International Conference on Software Engineering* (8–10 June, 1981). *(Describes pic program for typesetting diagrams.)*

—, AND DENNIS RITCHIE. *The C Programming Language.* Prentice-Hall, Inc., 1984. *(Still the essential C book. Good tutorial and the official C manual.)*

—, AND JOHN MASHEY. "The UNIX Programming Environment." *Computer (IEEE)* (April, 1981), pp. 12–24. *(Describes UNIX tools approach.)*

—, AND ROB PIKE. *The UNIX Programming Environment.* Prentice-Hall, Inc., 1984. *(Must reading. Chapters on shell programming, **lex**, **yacc**, and text formatting.)*

KEVORKIAN, D. E. "System V Interface Definition." *AT&T,* 1985. *(AT&T UNIX System standard. Covers mostly system calls with page on command syntax.)*

KORN, DAVID E. "Introduction to KSH." *Usenix Proceedings* (Summer, 1983). *(The developer's description of the New Korn shell.)*

EL LOZY, MOHAMED. *Editing in a UNIX Environment: The vi/ex Editor.* Prentice-Hall, Inc., 1985. *(Complete description of the **vi** text editor.)*

LUDERER, G. W. R., J. F. MARANZANO, AND B. A. TAGUE. "The UNIX Operating System as a Base for Applications." *Bell System Technical Journal* (July–August, 1978), Vol. 57, No. 6, pp. 2201–7. *(Whole issue devoted to UNIX.)*

MASHEY, JOHN. "Using a Command Language as a High-Level Programming Language." *IEEE Proceeding of the Second International Conference on Software Engineering* (13–15 October, 1976). *(Introduces UNIX shell for programming development.)*

—, AND D. W. SMITH. "Documentation Tools and Techniques." *IEEE Proceeding of the Second International Conference on Software Engineering* (13–15 October, 1976). *(Describes early editor and formatting programs (**ed**, **nroff**, and **troff**).)*

MILLER, R. "UNIX: A Portable Operating System." *Operating Systems Review* (July, 1978), Vol. 12, No. 3, pp. 32–37. *(Describes first port of UNIX from PDP-11 to Interdata 7/32 (now Perkin-Elmer).)*

PERLMAN, GARY. "Data Analysis Programs for the UNIX Operating System." *Behavior Research Methods and Instrumentation* (October, 1980), Vol. 12, No. 5, pp. 554–558. *(Statistical programs that can be piped together with UNIX commands.)*

RITCHIE, DENNIS M. "The Evolution of the UNIX Time-Sharing System." *Language Design and Programming Methodology, Proceedings of a Symposium*

(10–11 September, 1979). *(Early history of UNIX by one of its principal developers.)*

—. "The UNIX Time-Sharing System: A Retrospective." *Bell System Technical Journal* (July–August, 1978), Vol. 57, No. 6, pp. 1947–69. *(Strengths and weaknesses of UNIX.)*

—, AND KENNETH THOMPSON. "The UNIX Time-Sharing System." *Communications of the ACM* (July, 1974), Vol. 17, No. 7, pp. 365–375. *(The first article describing UNIX by its authors.)*

—. "The UNIX Time-Sharing System." *Bell System Technical Journal* (July–August, 1978), Vol. 57, No. 6, pp. 1905–1929. *(Description of UNIX by its principal developers.)*

ROOME, W. D. "Programmer's Workbench: New Tools for Software Development." *Bell Labs Record* (January, 1979), Vol. 57, No. 1, pp. 19–25. *(Describes the UNIX software development and text processing system.)*

STONEBRAKER, M. "Retrospection on a Database System." *ACM Transactions on Database Systems* (June, 1980), Vol. 5, No. 2, pp. 225–240. *(Mistakes in developing the Ingress relational database system on UNIX.)*

THOMPSON, KENNETH. "UNIX Time-Sharing System: UNIX Implementation." *Bell System Technical Journal* (July–August, 1978), Vol. 57, No. 6, pp. 1931–1946. *(The developer of UNIX describes how it works.)*

—, AND DENNIS RITCHIE. "Turing Award Lecture." *Communications of the ACM.* *(Top computer award to Thompson and Ritchie for developing UNIX.)*

THOMPSON, T. J. "Designer's Workbench: Providing a Production Environment." *Bell System Technical Journal* (November, 1980), Vol. 59, No. 9, pp. 1811–1825. *(Describes UNIX designers workbench which uses shell programs.)*

WAIDHOFER, GORDON W., AND MICHAEL SWEENEY. "4.2BSD–Berkeley's Answer to the UNIX System." *UNIX/World* (February, 1985), pp. 36–37, 39–42. *(Differences between UNIX systems.)*

WALKER, B. J., R. A. KEMMERER, AND G. J. POPEK. "Specification and Verification of the UCLA UNIX Security Kernel." *Communications of the ACM* (February, 1980), Vol. 23, No. 2, pp. 118–131. *(Work on secure operating system specified and verified.)*

WITTEN, IAN H., AND BOB BRAMWELL. "A System for Interactive Viewing of Structured Documents." *Communications of the ACM* (March, 1985), pp. 280–288. *(Program for viewing UNIX troff text.)*

WOODWARD, J. P. L., AND G. A. NIBALDI. "A Kernel-Based Secure UNIX Design." *MITRE Corporation Technical Report F2254H4* (May, 1979). *(Prototype for secure operating system based on UNIX.)*

MORE
FROM
SAMS

☐ Advanced UNIX™—A Programmer's Guide *Stephen Prata, The Waite Group*

This advanced guidebook shows how to use simple and complex commands, including the Bourne Shell, shell scripts, loops, and system calls; how to create UNIX graphics; how to allocate and structure data in memory; and how to maximize the C-UNIX interface and the C Library.
ISBN: 0-672-22403-8, $21.95

☐ UNIX™ Primer Plus

Mitchell Waite, Donald Martin, and Stephen Prata, The Waite Group
This primer presents UNIX in a clear, simple, and easy-to-understand style. This classic is fully illustrated, and includes two handy removable summary cards to keep near your computer for quick reference.
ISBN: 0-672-22028-8, $19.95

☐ UNIX™ SYSTEM V Primer

Mitchell Waite, Donald Martin, and Stephen Prata, The Waite Group
Waite at his best! This *UNIX V Primer* differs from most UNIX books in several ways. The entire powerful family of EX editors is included, of which V is a subset. Shell scripts and shell programming are covered in detail, as is the SED stream editor. UNIX filters, text cut and past functions, and the text formatting utilities of NTOFF and TROFF are thoroughly explained. Complex forms of FIND and AWK are also covered. Includes hands-on examples, easily referenced "Command" summaries, a complete glossary of UNIX buzzwords, and three tear-out reference cards.
ISBN: 0-672-22404-6, $19.95

☐ C Primer Plus

Mitchell Waite, Stephen Prata, and Donald Martin, The Waite Group
It's Waite at his best. Provides a clear and complete introduction to the C programming language. Interfacing C with assembly language is included, as well as many sample programs usable with any standard C compiler.
ISBN: 0-672-22090-3, $22.95

☐ Data Communications, Networks, and Systems *Thomas C. Bartee, Editor-in-Chief*

A comprehensive overview of state-of-the-art communications systems, how they operate, and what new options are open to system users, written by experts in each given technology. Learn the advantages and disadvantages of local area networks; how modems, multiplexers, and concentrators operate; the characteristics of fiber optics and coaxial cables; and the forces shaping the structure and regulation of common carrier operations.
ISBN: 0-672-22235-3, $39.95

☐ Programmer's Guide to Asynchronous Communications *Joe Campbell*

For intermediate and advanced programmers this book provides the history and technical details of asynchronous serial communications. Upon this foundation Campbell builds the specifics for the technical programmer, with an emphasis on popular UARTS and pseudo assembly language code.
ISBN: 0-672-22450-X, $21.95

☐ Computer Dictionary (4th Edition)

Charles J. Sippl
This updated and expanded version of one of SAMS' most popular references is two books in one — a "browsing" dictionary of basic computer terms and a handbook of computer-related topics, including fiber optics, sensors and vision systems, computer-aided design, engineering, and manufacturing. Clarifies micro, mini, and mainframe terminology. Contains over 12,000 terms and definitions with scores of illustrations and photographs. The 1,000 new entries in this edition focus on the RAF classifications: robotics, artificial intelligence, and factory automation.
ISBN: 0-672-22205-1, $24.95

☐ Printer Connections Bible

Kim G. House and Jeff Marble, The Waite Group
At last, a book that includes extensive diagrams specifying exact wiring, DIP-switch settings and external printer details; a Jump Table of assorted printer/computer combinations; instructions on how to make your own cables; and reviews of various printers and how they function.
ISBN: 0-672-22406-2, $16.95

☐ Modem Connections Bible

Carolyn Curtis and Daniel L. Majhor, The Waite Group
Describes modems, how they work, and how to hook 10 well-known modems to 9 name-brand microcomputers. A handy Jump Table shows where to find the connection diagram you need and applies the illustrations to 11 more computers and 7 additional modems. Also features an overview of communications software, a glossary of communications terms, an explanation of the RS-232C interface, and a section on troubleshooting.
ISBN: 0-672-22446-1, $16.95